Childhood and the Nation in Latin American Literature

American University Studies

Series XXII
Latin American Studies

Vol. 27

PETER LANG
New York • Washington, D.C./Baltimore • Boston • Bern
Frankfurt am Main • Berlin • Brussels • Vienna • Oxford

Richard L. Browning

Childhood and the Nation in Latin American Literature

Allende, Reinaldo Arenas, Bosch, Bryce Echenique, Cortázar, Manuel Galván, Federico Gamboa, S. Ocampo, Peri Rossi, Salarrué

PETER LANG
New York • Washington, D.C./Baltimore • Boston • Bern
Frankfurt am Main • Berlin • Brussels • Vienna • Oxford

Library of Congress Cataloging-in-Publication Data

Browning, Richard L.
Childhood and the nation in Latin American literature: Allende, Reinaldo
Arenas, Bosch, Bryce Echenique, Cortázar, Manuel Galván, Federico
Gamboa, S. Ocampo, Peri Rossi, Salarrué / Richard L. Browning.
p. cm. — (American university studies. Series XXII,
Latin American studies; vol. 27)
Includes bibliographical references.
1. Spanish American fiction—20th century—History and criticism.
2. Childhood in literature. 3. State, The, in literature. I. Title. II. Series.
PQ7082.N7 B67   863.009'352054—dc21   99-051780
ISBN 0-8204-4259-3
ISSN 0895-0490

Die Deutsche Bibliothek-CIP-Einheitsaufnahme

Browning, Richard L.:
Childhood and the nation in Latin American literature: Allende, Reinaldo
Arenas, Bosch, Bryce Echenique, Cortázar, Manuel Galván, Federico
Gamboa, S. Ocampo, Peri Rossi, Salarrué / Richard L. Browning.
–New York; Washington, D.C./Baltimore; Boston; Bern;
Frankfurt am Main; Berlin; Brussels; Vienna; Oxford: Lang.
(American university studies: Ser. 22, Latin American studies; Vol. 27)
ISBN 0-8204-4259-3

The paper in this book meets the guidelines for permanence and durability
of the Committee on Production Guidelines for Book Longevity
of the Council of Library Resources.

Printed in the United States of America

To Ray

The researching and writing of this work has been both a professional exercise and a personally fulfilling undertaking. I wish to thank those who have lent me their moral and professional support and guidance: Elena Rodríguez, Laura Boland, Mark Griffin, Tola Mosadomi, Joyce Naylon, John J. Kearns, Dipo Mosadomi, Mark and April Nosacka, Richard E. Greenleaf, Maureen Shea, Gertrude M. Yeager; my friends and colleagues from the University of South Alabama, Isabel Brown, Caryl Lloyd, Federico Pérez Pineda, Bernie Quinn, Larry Scherer and Terri Wilbanks; my first mentor, Ray Verzasconi, who continues to guide me; and Nicasio Urbina, who teaches by example the professionalism, dedication, love for literature, and respect for our students which we should all strive to emulate in our academic life. I would also like to thank the *Journal of Interdisciplinary Literary Studies* for permission to reprint my article "El Niño Excluido: Relaciones Familiares en *Cuentos de Barro* de Salarrué," 4.1-2 (1992): 71-88.

CONTENTS

INTRODUCTION

> We haven't all had the good
> fortune to be ladies, we ha-
> ven't all been generals or
> poets, or statesmen, but
> when the toast works down
> to the babies, we all stand
> on common ground.
> —Mark Twain[1]

In his seminal work, "The Anthropology of Fiction," Wolfgang Iser asks why it is that human beings need fiction. His answer, in simple terms, is that humans require fiction for its boundary-crossing, limits-enhancing qualities; it is fiction that allows us to question ourselves, our systems, our cultural contexts of all kinds, and to play at re-creating them. Literature always points to the possibility of the existence of other realities, as literature is not per-fectly mimetic, thus "if what is, is not everything, then what is must be changeable" (282). He asks, "Why have we created this mode of staging and why has it accompanied us throughout our history? The answer must cer-tainly be the desire, not to repeat what is, but to gain access to what we oth-erwise cannot have" (282). The doubling, the mirror which reveals what is not there as well, "allows us to see ourselves as that within which we are en-tangled, and in this respect literature is a decisive means of shaping cultural reality" (283). It is for an analogous reason that authors have utilized children, child-like characters and childhood in their re-examinations of self and society; for Western civilization has highly valued, particularly since the age of romanticism, the child's insouciant regard for the boundaries society diligently seeks to impose on the youngest of us, and the child's creative use of language and relative lack of corruption which allow him or her to see—and judge—the world in a non-adult fashion. The child has been seen, then, not only as the future of the nation, as the potential adult who would carry on the modes of behavior and thought of the previous generations, but also as the embodiment of the potential for change. Such a view of childhood is inherently contradictory, however, as both conservative and progressive forces may focus on the child as they seek stability or change, respectively.

Jean Franco has noted that in Latin America, until the counter-insurgency movements of the 1960's and beyond, the child was one of a protected class of citizens, along with priests, women and nuns, a sector of society which enjoyed a degree of immunity, "in theory if not in practice," from the ravages of political, economic and ethnic warfare ("Killing" 416). In that same essay, Franco emphasizes the role of the family, particularly of the maternal force, in the teaching of resistance as part of the socialization process. Inherent in the perception of the family "as a refuge, a place for turning one's back on the world" ("Killing" 415), is the idea that the individual will learn within the domestic sphere to rebel against societal pressures. We may study the family, then, as a place where the individual acts out his or her reactions to society's demands (Lomnitz and Pérez-Lizaur 9–10).

This domestic duality is not unlike the many dialectical relationships, or choices, that have been blamed for the entrapment of the Latin American in search of a definition of his or her identity. Numerous critics have commented on that dialectic, and the way in which being forced into choosing between two extremes has led to an acceptance of rebellion and violence in the region (Murray; G. Martin 8–9, 11–12). Violence leads to trauma, of course, both individual and societal, and to the idea, theorized by psychoanalysis, that the traumas of childhood affect one's adult life. At the societal level, this trauma has been part of the debate about Latin American cultural and national identity, but it also reaches back to St. Augustine who pointed out that "adult traits can be traced back to one's earliest years" (Sommerville 56). In the nineteenth century it was thought that difficult childhood experiences would make for an adult more able to handle the stresses of life.

The child encompasses both sides of a dialectic: On the one hand, they are creative, hypersensitive, innocent, a work in progress, holders of immense secrets, somehow closer to the spiritual realm; and on the other hand, they are physically and intellectually incomplete, ignorant of Western knowledge, more susceptible to diseases, dependent, able to communicate at a much reduced level, and capable of great cruelty. The child embodies as well a key cultural duality, as illegitimacy in Latin America becomes "one of the supreme forms of social injustice" in both the psychological and symbolic spheres (G. Martin 15). The illegitimacy of the *mestizo* child, product of the rape of the conquest, is important at individual and social levels:

> ...illegitimacy, then, product of an unending dialectic of violation and vengeance, has remained a central theme of Latin American culture: the social and racial illegitimacy of the governed—and hence of the whole half-breed culture—has for most of its history been matched by the political and moral illegitimacy of their governors. The violence was there at the beginning and no myths can disguise it. (G. Martin 16)

We see the dystopia versus utopia juxtaposition so prevalent in Latin American civilization (see Murray 29-30) as analogous to the child versus adult dichotomy, where childhood is often seen as a paradise lost, and a place to which some adults will attempt a return in search of a greater understanding of their personal and/or national identity. When we imbue childhood with the qualities of romanticism or some utopia, there "remains a space, or dislocation, between the entity and the meaning it has been given, ... something remains dislocated from them [the meanings], and eludes the eye" (Steedman 18). We explore here some of these often ambivalent qualities which are assigned to childhood in Latin American literature, and how authors explore and exploit that ambivalence in their contributions to the construction of national identities. Indeed, at times the authors equate artists, and themselves, to children as both may pose a threat to the reigning social order, while at other times the artist serves as the teacher-father figure for the nation's children.

The representation of children and childhood in Latin American literature and diaries before the second half of the twentieth century is relatively infrequent compared to that seen in North American and European letters. The romantics' pragmatic side in Latin America (e.g., Rodríguez Alcalá; Kuteischikova; Pena 12-13, 77-78, 528), we believe, limited nineteenth-century exploration of the qualities of childhood, a task which attracted numerous participants in Europe. The romantics in Latin America were immediately thrust into the work of creating an orderly nation, of constructing a national identity, and for them liberty was less individual and more related to social duty than in Europe (Pena 91-93). Positivism and realism followed closely on the heels of romanticism in Latin America, as well, and they did not facilitate anything more than a scientific examination of children and the developmental or evolutionary processes. We see a contrast, for example, in the attitudes toward childhood of Sarmiento and Martí in nineteenth-century Latin America; where Sarmiento saw the young child as a barbarian in need of education, Martí saw them as repositories of hope, as a refuge and as a "symbol of personal and public salvation" (Insanally 35–36). Lloyd notes a similar pragmatism in the conservative forces of nineteenth-century France where "any desire for intellectual freedom was anathema, and what was to be trained was not the imagination but a respect for conformity" (218). The romantics, on the other hand, saw rationalist thought and its concurrent educational institutions as "an imprisonment of the mind" (Lloyd 218). Thus children and childhood, infrequently found in nineteenth-century Latin American literature, even in the memoirs or autobiographies of the great thinkers and statesmen (Carrilla 117–18), may have been too slippery an issue for these writers, too chaotic a proposition; they looked to science as the holder of ultimate truth, rather than to the mystical, ambivalent child. The child, especially the child's presence in the street, and his or her ability to push linguistic and social boundaries, represents rebellion and a lack of order or control, all of which would make the child a difficult protagonist for nineteenth-century writers, except in the guise of a *pícaro*[2] or an 'objective' witness. The message of so many of the *bola* novels (realistic tales of rebellion) in Mexico, for example, was anti-insurgency, in spite of the revelation of social problems in the novels; children, as well, would have been problematic personages to explore, representing as they do the insurgency and unpredictability of the younger generation. In addition, taking into account the concern regarding illegitimacy, childhood may also have been too private a topic, the exposure of which would violate that interior patio garden and the immunity of the home described by Franco ("Killing" 418–19). The "common ground" of childhood may also have been too leveling a proposition, as writing about universally "innocent" children would require the admission of equality among the children of various races and social classes.

The romantic image of the child, nevertheless, does permeate the culture, as we shall see in our analysis of works from the nineteenth and twentieth centuries. Steedman notes how childhood became the focus of scientific, educational and spiritual attention in the nineteenth century in Europe and North America, and how, similar to Mark Twain's epigraph, "The idea of the child was the figure that provided the largest number of people living in the recent past of Western societies with the means for thinking about and creating a self: something grasped and understood: a shape moving in the body ... something inside: an interiority" (20). For the romantics, in particular, the child and the artist represented the possibility of avoiding "fixity," and of living fully "all concepts that are mastered" (Plotz 64, 73–74). Such a life would require freedom from censorship or corruption, however. In the climate of the romantic versus rationalist debates, the very scientific concepts that were being explored through the study of the child could potentially "fix" and "censor" the creative essence of childhood. One principle on which both sides of such arguments could agree, as Steedman notes, was the value of the child as a being whose qualities force adults to look inward. That inward gaze may seek the spiritual or scientific origins of human kind—of life itself— and its development, or the clues to the development of the individual or the national identity. The literary works explored here all turn their gaze toward childhood in some way and, in a sense, this work takes part in the same pre-occupation with childhood that we identify in the authors.

We will examine the ways in which childhood is exploited and explored in a number of Latin American literary works as the authors turn to childhood to explicate the fine line between fixity and freedom in modern society. We will return repeatedly to the ways in which authors connect the nation to the child, or to some idea of childhood. They do this at times on a rhetorical level, equating the child's potentiality with that of the nation, or drawing an analogy between the parent-child relationship, and the nation and its constituents. At times childhood is used for its supposed hidden secrets regarding the origin of humankind, but in the national analogy the desired origins are those of the nation. The child, or childhood, like so much literature in general for a good deal of Latin America's post-colonial existence, serves a practical, or utilitarian purpose.

More recently, a protagonist's recapitulation of his or her childhood, or an author's exploration of the characters' childhoods, is meant to parallel a re-examination of the nation's current situation, or that of a particular marginalized sector of society. Rosemary Lloyd concludes that there is, in nineteenth-century French literature, a direct relationship between the level of alienation in a fast-changing society, and the presence of children in that society's literary works. The images of the foundling, the orphan and the abandoned child became progressively more common in this climate of modernization (138–39, 241). Scholars of Hispanic letters have similarly discovered a connection between the topic of childhood and the individual's alienation (Godoy Gallardo 9–10, 19–20; Insanally 36–37). We would add the influence of Revolutionary rhetoric in the twentieth century as well, where the left seeks to take its place as the new, more progressive father of the child of the revolution (see the quotation of President Calles which begins our Chapter Two); right wing, often military regimes make similar claims. Carlos Monsiváis notes the surge in importance of a yearning for utopia in Latin American culture after the Mexican and Soviet revolutions (386–87). The child would embody or represent one side of the utopia-dystopia dichotomy, with progressive regimes clamoring for indoctrination of the children into the ways of the revolution, and conservatives nostalgically seeing in children a past, orderly utopia.

No matter what the political orientation of an author's exploration or exploitation of childhood, however, the danger in the ambiguity of that "dislocation" between the assigned values and the actual entity—the child—is clear throughout our study, and has implications for a nation's identity. We draw an analogy here to Homi Bhabha's description of the ambivalence inherent in the idea of the nation:

> [It is an] ambivalence that haunts the idea of the nation, the language of those who write of it and the lives of those who live it. It is an ambivalence that emerges from a growing awareness that, despite the certainty with which historians speak of the 'origins' of nation as a sign of the 'modernity' of society, the cultural temporality of the nation inscribes a much more transitional social reality (1).

We examine here the ways in which authors fall victim to the duality of the child figure, or the ways in which they exploit that ambivalence as they attempt to reassess, or even change, their national reality. We find that, just as New World Indians are homogenized in post-colonial Latin American narrative (Chanady 35–37), their diversity ignored in the name of literary expedience in the worst case, and the uncovering of their marginalization in the best case, the child is also dehumanized throughout most of the works examined here. The child's romantic qualities are exploited or explored, but there is little humanity, precious little agency, left in the child that is presented. This appears to be acceptable precisely because of Twain's remark noted above: We all have been children, we share that common history; it is a leveling experience on which to base "foundational" literature. But that point of view ignores the dislocation between the entity and the qualities bestowed upon it, between the many realities of childhood (influenced by one's race, class, gender and individuality) and the dualities with which the child is imbued.

Our work inserts itself into the criticism of the discourse of national identity, indeed of Latin American identity, which for so long has fascinated scholars. In addition, it contributes to the little-studied history of childhood in Latin America. Although the works treated here could easily be re-read to glean from them the history of the everyday lives of children, that is not our goal. It is the history of childhood which interests us here, though both approaches—the history of childhood and the history of children—using literature as the primary source, could be categorized under the rubric of Literary Anthropology.

As Joseph Hawes and N. Ray Hiner delineate in the introduction to their 1991 anthology on research methods and resources in the history of children and childhood, there has been a tremendous surge in interest in the topic over the last three decades. They attribute this in large part to the growing attention paid to 'inarticulate' groups in general, and to the youth movements of the 1960's. We would add the increased attention, since the middle of this century, paid to the history of the family as well, much of it driven by feminist criticism, which has naturally led to studies of the family's component parts. The study of children and childhood results in a body of work that is inherently highly interdisciplinary, according to Hawes and Hiner. They also note: "Historians now understand that children in the past were central to the reproduction of class and the transmission of culture, important elements in the maintenance of political stability, and a significant source of labor for their families and communities" (2). The tremendous variety of resources cited in the chapters of their anthology, as the editors themselves remark, implies the potential expansiveness of the topic.

The most influential book of this recent period of heightened interest, not necessarily for the validity of the conclusions it draws, but more so for the debates and criticisms it has sparked, is Philippe Aries' *L'Enfant et la Vie Familiale Sous L'ancien Régime* (1960) (*Centuries of Childhood: A Social History of Family Life*) (trans. Bellingham). Aries' contention, based primarily on the analysis of artwork and diaries, was that childhood was an invention, that medieval cultures did not possess a concept of childhood. Aries is rather nostalgic for the pre-modern period when children were not segregated into schools and treated like a separate class of citizen; but others, such as Lloyd de Mause, are not as positive about the cozy existence of the pre-modern child (Hawes and Hiner 3–4). De Mause's characterization of progressively better treatment for children throughout the history of Western society itself comes under attack from scholars such as Linda Pollock, who tend to see more continuity in the treatment and consideration of children over time. Hugh Cunningham writes of just how important it was for the nation's self-image in nineteenth-century Great Britain to see itself as a civilization which treated children well, not like slaves (61–63, 133–34). Dickens' use of child redeemers was, in a sense, meant to show the high degree of 'civilization' of the British citizen who was capable of being touched by the plight of the suffering child (H. Cunningham 138). Rosemary Lloyd points out in her study that the responses to the theme of childhood abounded in nineteenth-century literary works: "It almost seems that each generation of adults, in order to recover its own experience of childhood, needs the goading conviction that previous generations failed to comprehend the meaning of youth" (1). The point is that in Western Europe and North America in the last three decades we have seen a plethora of studies on the history of childhood and children from a wide range of disciplines (we would direct the reader to the introductions and bibliographies of Hugh Cunningham, Pollock, Lloyd and

Steedman in particular for their exhaustiveness), and the studies have reached
a self-reflexive level as they examine in great detail historians' own interest
in childhood. While many of these historical studies, such as those by Cunningham and Steedman, have utilized literature as just one of many sources,
others, such as Rosemary Lloyd's 1992 book, have concentrated on literature
itself.

Many of the literary studies explore the role of childhood in the shaping
of national and cultural identity. Andrew B. Wachtel, in *The Battle for
Childhood: Creation of a Russian Myth* (1990), while focusing a great deal on
genre formation, traces as well the "relationship between literature and the
broader social system in order to explain the increasingly strong ideological
and cultural importance of conceptions of childhood" in the period he studies
(2). He notes the mythologization process whereby mid-nineteenth-century
works of "pseudoautobiography" became icons for Russian childhood in general, and also became models for recalling the past. Those conceptions were
challenged in the twentieth century, creating a counter myth (202–3). Rosemary Lloyd's *The Land of Lost Content: Children and Childhood in Nineteenth-Century French Literature* (1992) examines the ways in which children
and childhood are presented in several genres, and concludes, as we have
noted above, that the presence of children in literature is directly related to the
level of alienation of the individual in a rapidly modernizing society (138–39,
241). She also explores the two-way relationship between writers and children as the former take advantage of the technical and thematic possibilities
available in autobiography and other genres where childhood is centered. The
exploration of childhood brings attention to it, and to very real children, but
it also gives the author the means to innovate (242). In her 1991 study, *Metaphors of Identity: The Treatment of Childhood in Selected Québécois Novels*,
Roseanna Lewis Dufault describes three main categories of the exploration or
use of childhood: Novels of social criticism which use the innocent child as
an observer and victim of society's failings (included here is the *pícaro*); novels which exhibit the "roots phenomenon" in which there is a cathartic return
to ethnic and cultural roots in an effort to valorize differences between anglo
and francophone Canada; and fictionalized autobiographies in which the narrator presents a wistful "paradise lost" image of childhood (78). In *La Infancia en la Narrativa Española de Posguerra, 1939–1978* (1979), Eduardo Godoy Gallardo focuses on the trauma of the Spanish Civil War and the experience of exile as stimuli which encouraged authors to re-create an earlier
world. In that re-creation, writers utilize the dichotomies of happy versus
unhappy childhood, paradise versus inferno, with the war responsible for unhappiness, and the pre-war period the site of happiness. Carolyn Steedman's
1995 study, *Strange Dislocations: Childhood and the Idea of Human Interior-*

ity, 1780–1930, follows the presence of the Mignon character in European literature, particularly in drama. Through an interpretation of the discourses of scientists, social reformers, historians, and literary figures, she explains the importance of childhood in all of these discourses, and thus the rational for the ubiquitousness of the child-acrobat named Mignon. There are many more literary studies, of course, far too numerous to list here, and the topic's popularity continues.

While we have seen an abundance of studies on family and childhood in Europe and North America over the last several decades, Latin Americanist scholars have only just begun to address these issues in their work. Many of these studies, in addition, focus on gender so that only secondarily do we gain an understanding of the history of childhood and children in general. In several of the articles in anthologies such as those edited by Asunción Lavrin, *Sexuality and Marriage in Colonial Latin America* (1989), and Elizabeth Jelin, *Family, Household and Gender Relations in Latin America* (1991), children and concepts of childhood do come to the fore. It would be highly fruitful to re-examine the resources used in such work on gender and the family in Latin America to see what they would yield with regard to childhood. There are articles and book chapters from a variety of disciplines that focus on children in history. Josefina Muriel offers an apologist's look at the Spanish crown's and the Catholic Church's policies toward the protection of abandoned and orphaned children. Carmen Castañeda examines eighteenth- and nineteenth-century court cases of sexually violated girls, a study that offers some limited insight into public and private treatment of this topic. One of her conclusions is that in the families in which these violations occurred, the parents did not care properly for or protect their children, leaving them with drunkards, sending them out alone on errands, placing them as laborers with other families. She sees this practice as an expression of the lack of value of the child to these mostly lower-class families (110). Cristina Ruíz Martínez and Kathleen A. Myers make use of the writings of members of religious orders, giving us an idea of the daily life of the child within the family, but also of the stereotype of the saintly child to which nuns and monks attempted to conform their autobiographies. Studies of children's genres, such as those of children's literature (Alga Marina Elizagaray; Carmen Bravo-Villasante), of comic books (Cornelia Butler Flor), and of television (M. Antonieta Rebeil Corella), as well as the general interest in "popular" or "mass" culture to which children are so heavily exposed, are contributing to a growing body of scholarship focusing on childhood.[3]

As Lavrin notes in her chapter on Mexico in the Hawes and Hiner anthology, the history of childhood has generally been assimilated to the histories of education and welfare, thus childhood and children are buried under institutional approaches to history (421). Unlike Elizabeth Kuznesof, who attempts to write the history of childhood in Brazil in her chapter in Hawes and Hiner, Lavrin admits the difficulty of doing so at this point and concentrates instead on guiding the reader to potential sources related to education, health, legal status and treatment, labor, psychology, religion and other topics. As the editors point out in their introduction: "Anyone who approaches this literature [of the last thirty years] with an obsessive need for obvious coherence and unimpeachable conclusions will be greatly disappointed. It would be extremely presumptuous for anyone to claim mastery of this enormous literature" (Hawes and Hiner 2). Lavrin's many suggestions make obvious the tremendous interdisciplinary potential of the study of children and childhood, and include the analysis of literature and art (434), with the former being our focus here.

We have chosen literary works as our primary source in this study for two basic reasons. First, as we see in Chapter Four, writers and children are perceived in similar modes resulting in a marginalization based not on race, gender or class, but on the potentially disruptive effects of their creativity; it is for their ability to deconstruct societal norms that they are marginalized. We attempt here a deconstruction of that perception of the artist and child in which we show how it is based on an ensnaring dialectic, as we have noted above. Second, literature is a reasonable place to investigate individuals' reactions to society's expectations and dictates. Literary anthropologists have engaged in this kind of criticism, seeking to analyze the symbolic behavior of the characters that an author might use to describe his or her society (Aldridge 44; Erickson 123). A work of fiction that displays such observations can be used as an archive of the social strategies and values of a community (Stewart 101):

> The artist who uses words as his medium, no less than the artist who works with paints or in wood or stone, acts as a creature of his culture; his responses are always relative to its formal patterns, and his values reflect its underlying values. (Herskovits 419)

We examine here the strategic use of and value placed upon children in the works of the authors studied.

In the field of Latin American literary criticism, there has been relatively little attention paid to children and childhood, though certainly more than we see in the field of history. Most of this work is based in psychoanalysis and in feminist readings of patriarchy. Children may appear, then, as indicators of the psychoses of adult characters; or, the critic might explore the children in their Oedipal and Electra relationships; often it is the introduction of the child to the "world of the name of the father" which is centered. Such readings are especially common in the criticism of the Boom authors and of women authors, which reflects the timing of the advent of psychoanalytical and feminist criticism—and simply of their influence on society in general—and of the conscious utilization by authors of psychoanalytical constructs in their work. Save in an exemplary study such as that by Marina Gálvez Acero, however, there is little in such criticism to be gleaned about the meaning of childhood in general in the Latin American context. Psychoanalytical and structuralist approaches dominate *Escribir la Infancia* (Pasternac, et al), a 1996 anthology that treats contemporary women authors from Mexico; the work also emphasizes autobiographical writing by the authors covered. Several of the articles touch on some of the themes we treat here, such as the relationship between childhood and exile, and childhood and the artist. At the other end of the scale of theorization, if you will, we find articles such as those in the 1978 anthology edited by J. Cruz Mendizabal, which resulted from a conference at Indiana University of Pennsylvania. The convening of the conference was stimulated by the United Nations' declaration of the year of the child. These articles on children in Hispanic literature are for the most part descriptive and superficial.

One area that has received relatively more attention in Latin American literature is that of the idea of the child as narrator and witness. Many of these studies, again, also focus on gender, such as Irene Matthews' 1993 book chapter entitled "Daughtering in War: Two 'Case Studies' from Mexico and Guatemala," an excellent work of psychoanalytical criticism which illuminates the effects of twentieth-century warfare on children, women, and the mother-daughter relationship in Latin America. Related to Matthews' work are articles such as those by Linda Britt (1988) and Barbara Bockus Aponte (1982–83) which explore the use of the 'innocent' yet unreliable child narrator, thus complicating the reading of the text. These children may be there to "enliven" the text (Britt 128), but their perspective is "idioreliable," that is, "totally true to their own view of things but unrelated to a 'reality' perceived by others. Such viewpoints serve as transparent lenses only for the children's realities" (Britt 129). We will argue in Chapter Four that this perception of the child itself falls into the trap of perceiving the child within a dialectic of good-evil, complete-incomplete, part of reality-disengaged from reality.

The Bildungsroman novel, once again, especially that of the female protagonist, has also come under some scrutiny in recent years. As Gabriela Mora points out, this genre also includes the anti-Bildungsroman, a parody of the classic tale of development ("Bildungsroman" 72). For Mora, this type of novel reveals the individual's reactions to her emergence into the adult world, into the oppression of adult institutions, though in Goethe's classic model, that emergence ended happily ("Bildungsroman" 71–72). There are numerous examples of the genre in Hispanic letters, including a few, such as *Enriquillo* (1882) and *El Palacio de las Blanquísimas Mofetas* (1975) (*The Palace of the Very White Skunks*) which we examine in this work.

In Chapter One, we analyze *Enriquillo* by the Dominican Manuel de Jesús Galván, and *Suprema Ley* (1896) (*Supreme Law*) by Federico Gamboa, a Mexican. Both authors severely limit the participation of women in the works studied here, eclipsing the importance of motherhood and biological fathers in favor of an emphasis on fraternal relationships and surrogate parents. Biological parents are fungible in these works, as we would expect from two authors imbued with positivism; however, the romantic image of the child also permeates these novels. In *Enriquillo*, the childhoods of the protagonist and his consort mirror the beginnings of the Dominican nation, thus childhood is used for its connection to origins. The couple also is left forever young, infantilized, and dependent upon Father Las Casas as well, thus perpetuating the Dominican people's subordination to Spanish culture. Gamboa's work takes place during a crisis of the *petit-bourgeois* in Mexico. Here the nihilism and gradual decay of the protagonist father are contrasted with the "natural socialism" of the children. The young are seen as potential redeemers of the decadent adults, as well, a common theme in late-nineteenth-century European literature. In this chapter, then, we read a broad range of romantic qualities of the child and the ways in which these two positivist authors exploit them in their examinations of the nation's condition, in the Gamboa work, or its origins in Galvan's.

Chapter Two examines the more or less explicit battle for the allegiance of the child that rages between parents and the state in a number of works from the 1930's to the 1990's: Salarrué's *Cuentos de Barro* (1933) (*Stories of Clay*), El Salvador; Julio Cortázar's *Rayuela* (1963) (*Hopscotch*), Argentina; Reinaldo Arenas' *El Palacio de las Blanquísimas Mofetas*, Cuba; Cristina Peri Rossi's short story collection *La Rebelión de los Niños* (1980) (*The Rebellion of the Children*), Uruguay; Alfredo Bryce Echenique's *La Vida Exagerada de Martín Romaña* (1985) (*The Exaggerated Life of Martín Romaña*), Peru; and Isabel Allende's short story "De Barro Estamos Hechos" ("We Are Made of Clay") from the collection *Cuentos de Eva Luna* (1990) (*Stories of Eva Luna*), Chile. The examination of these works is based on the premise that the state utilizes familial rhetoric in presenting itself as the replacement for the family (especially for the father) in a modern world. This brings the state into conflict with parents, as the former sees the latter as replaceable. The second premise concerns the state's great preoccupation with gaining the allegiance of children. Regimes are concerned with their own survival, thus they need to capture the minds of the next generation, and they are well aware that the family may be a training ground for resistance to the state, just as it may, on the other hand, be a reinforcement of the patriarchal state's structure and values.

The third chapter is an exploration of the child as representative of the marginalized sectors of society in the short stories of Salarrué, noted above, the Dominican Juan Bosch, from several collections spanning four decades, and the Argentine Silvina Ocampo's *La Furia y Otros Cuentos* (1959) (*The Fury and Other Stories*). These authors utilize children to represent the effects of racism, industrialization and urbanization, migration, sexism and civil war on the people living at the margins of society. At times, such as in many of Bosch's tales, they appeal to the reader through the use of the emotive power of the suffering child, of the youth whose potential is extinguished by the powerful, yet foreign, changes occurring in society. Ocampo's title story, in our reading, points to the way in which children learn of their racial inheritance and then realize the arbitrary limits that this entails. For this child the creative exuberance of childhood is all the more bittersweet as she very early in life becomes aware of its ephemeral quality. She reacts against her new-found knowledge with acts which are seen as cruel by the rest of society, but which would then fit into the dialectical construction of the image of the child as embodying innocence and evil. The final story from the collection lays out what we might call a thesis on the child as a member of the underclasses, and also as an imaginary being whose life is at the service of the adults who choose to recall their childhoods. In our reading, then, while Juan Bosch and Salarrué exploit the bestowed qualities of childhood, Silvina Ocampo explores and deconstructs them.

Our final chapter re-examines the above-mentioned works by Julio Cortázar, Cristina Peri Rossi, Reinaldo Arenas and Alfredo Bryce Echenique. We focus in this chapter, however, on ways in which these authors equate the romantic qualities of childhood and the child with literary and other artistic projects, as well as with the artist. While in *Rayuela* the myth of the child as medium for the artist persists, the other authors, in our reading, reach the conclusion that childhood, though perhaps desirable for its creative potential, is a vulnerable, dangerous state. While the artist is linked to the child through their respective creative dispositions, we also see a connection made between the artist and the child as persecuted members of society; they are endangered and pursued precisely because of the boundary-crossing creativity, and its concurrent threat to the established order, which they represent.

We treat a relatively large number of authors in this work whose critical traditions do not usually include the theme of childhood. Galván's novel has generally been analyzed in its capacity as a historical, realist and *indigenista* novel (Piña). Doris Sommer has examined the erasure of race in the work and its function in the creation of a modern Dominican national identity

(*Foundational*). We will examine how childhood is important in the writing of Galván's foundational text: We read an infantilization of the protagonist and his wife, an emphasis on the fungibility of biological parents, the use of childhood as a source of new beginnings, and a disregard for real children, except for the two young lovers.

Federico Gamboa is most recognized for *Santa* (1903), his work on the life of a prostitute. His writing, like that of many of his contemporaries, has traces of naturalism, romanticism, realism and modernism. He is particularly noted for his attempts to point out social ills in his work (Brushwood, *Mexico* 154–55; Woolsey 294–97; Lay 52). We focus on the children in *Suprema Ley* in order to demonstrate just how the author utilizes the child as a potential redeemer of the adult male gone astray. Parents are also replaceable in this work, as they are in *Enriquillo*, reflecting the author's positivist education.

Salarrué has received little attention outside of Central America. That criticism has tended to be impressionistic with little theoretical foundation, focusing on his "humane" treatment of Indians, his use of regional language, the surreal or fantastic, and the role of nature in his literature. In her 1977 doctoral dissertation, Sherry Young Cherry attempts to explain Salarrué's unifying vision of reality and fantasy (most criticism on Salarrué at least mentions this distinction in his work) through his theosophic beliefs. Most of her work, however, is descriptive and superficial. Rafael Lara Martínez's 1990 book on myth and history explores these elements in Salarrué, demonstrating how the author's work optimistically seeks to unify not only ethnic and political sectors of Salvadoran society, but also those who favor violence as a solution with those morally opposed (Salarrué included) to such an alternative. Our interpretation of the short stories in *Cuentos de Barro* examines just how the author equates children with the marginalized Izalco Indians, and marginalized sectors in general, and how the state attempts to act as a surrogate parent as it seeks to control those sectors. In our reading we do not see the striving for unification that Lara Martínez sees in other Salarrué works, though we do share Cherry's observation that Salarrué's "leitmotiv of poverty and suffering constitutes an indirect criticism of social injustice" (69).

Juan Bosch's numerous short stories have been examined at length for the resonance within them of the author's political leanings, for their regionalist qualities, and for the author's short-story writing technique. Margarita Fernández Olmos' 1982 book analyzes a number of Bosch's stories in an attempt to delineate themes such as resistance, exile, and the societal effects of modernization and civil war. A common topic of debate regarding Bosch's work concerns his place in Dominican literary history; in particular, his influence (or lack thereof) on writers of post-Trujillo Dominican Republic (Barradas). Children appear only briefly in this criticism as noted victims of socio-political upheaval. As in much of Salarrué's work, character development in Juan Bosch is often subordinated to the exploration of a particular theme whose significance is often driven home with an ironic ending; these are works, writes Fernández Olmos, where author and narrator separate, and where the former's solidarity with the reality presented is revealed with a distant, reserved emotion (162). We expand on this perception of Bosch's work, and Salarrué's as well, noting the marginalized condition of the child as outlined in Roger Sawyer's book, *Children Enslaved* (1988).

The criticism surrounding Silvina Ocampo's work has generally focused on the fantastic elements of her short stories (Lockert; Klingenberg, "Twisted"). Wherever children are concerned, it is usually to outline the shock value of her frequent utilization of child narrators, or to note, within a psychoanalytical tradition, the good-evil dichotomy in the children (Balderston; Klingenberg, "Mad"; Araújo). Blas Matamoro, in his 1975 book *Oligarquía y Literatura*, dedicates a chapter to Ocampo. Matamoro begins to move the criticism toward a socio-political consideration of the representation of marginalized sectors in general in Ocampo's work, and Klingenberg (*Infiel*) makes reference to the possibility of solidarity between members of distinct sub-divisions of those sectors (41, 65). In our reading of "La Furia," we explore Silvina Ocampo's use of childhood as a time when a person begins to recognize the arbitrary limits (according to race, class or gender) which society places upon him or her. In this light, the cruelties and 'evil' of childhood are seen as a reaction to those limitations rather than as inherent qualities of childhood. When considered alongside, for example, Peri Rossi's stories, it is clear, as well, that the 'cruel' reactions of children mirror the atrocities of the adults' political and domestic regimes. We also analyze the final tale of the collection *La Furia* for its presentation of a world where the workers are children. The children in "La Raza Inextinguible" are enslaved by actual labor, and by their role as psychological and historical builders of the future, the future, that is, of the adults in the story.

The critical tradition covering the work of Julio Cortázar is immense; critics have well-documented the innovations of his 1963 novel *Rayuela*. As it relates to our exploration of the role of childhood in the novel, the works which are most instructive are those such as Rodger Cunningham's, in which he intends "to show that *Rayuela*'s protagonist, Horacio Oliveira, is beset by systematic confusions as to the nature of both the 'reason' he rejects and the non-rational he embraces. I hold that these confusions contribute to thwarting his quest for wholeness" (93). Here we attempt to center not only the child Rocamadour (and other appearances of children and childhood) in our reading of the novel, but also Oliveira's incessant search for the metaphoric bridge to the kibbutz of desire. As the novel ends with the protagonist in a child-like position, *incomunicado*, staring down at a hopscotch game, he at once reaches childhood and insanity. We show in our reading just how dependent this search is upon the romantic ideal of the child, how the child as a blind clairvoyant, a bridge for the intellectual, serves a similar purpose as that of the infantilized Indian of the nineteenth century, and, of course, of the child of nineteenth-century romantic literature. Cortázar himself notes that the romantic writer is an author for whom a *certain* (his emphasis) reality exists, and whose mission is to find it; over Rimbaud's footprints, he adds, there is no other way to find that "suprareality" than the restitution of, or the re-encounter with, innocence (qtd. in Ferré, *Cortázar* 22). In Chapter Two we discuss the further paradox of the intellectual in *Rayuela* who attempts to free himself from the bourgeois family and the responsibilities of parenthood. As Jean Franco makes clear, however, the family against which Cortázar writes, no longer exists in the form that he criticizes; the qualities which seem to make his writing innovative are the very qualities favored in bourgeois society ("Crisis"). Thus, we find Cortázar's innovative work hamstrung by romantic ideals.

Much of the analysis of the work of Reinaldo Arenas treats the themes of exile and homosexuality, some of it couched in theory and rooted to his texts, but much of it stimulated by the author's biography. A number of works treat the theme of the carnivalesque and the fantastic in Arenas; and some critics, such as Perla Rozencvaig, analyze the use of the child narrator. The topic of the author's role in society, his or her reaction to the socio-political situation, is also relatively common, once again perhaps driven in large part by his biography. Roberto Valero, among other themes, treats the lack of paternal authority in Arenas's work, and the subsequent overburdening of women with familial responsibilities. We extrapolate on the role of the writer in society by focusing on the protagonist of *El Palacio de las Blanquísimas Mofetas*. He is not only a severely repressed and oppressed individual, he also attempts to empathize with the other members of his family; in particular, he re-lives their childhoods in order to investigate the traumas which have led to their present unhappiness. In so doing he also examines the socio-economic situation of the nation. Childhood is important, therefore, as a site of memory for citizens in general, and for the artist. The novel also expresses the opinion that the romantic ideal of childhood is a myth, a cruel hoax.

Much of the criticism around Cristina Peri Rossi's work as well deals with exile, due to her personal experience, but also due to the prevalence of the theme in her work. As such, the struggle between citizens, particularly the intelligentsia, and the state comes to the fore. Criticism of the work *El Libro de mis Primos* (1969) (*The Book of my Cousins*) often treats the narrative innovations in the novel, as well as the author's criticisms of the bourgeois family. Our reading of her 1980 collection *La Rebelión de los Niños* finds the author further exploring familial relationships, but also severely criticizing the state's appropriation of familial rhetoric in its attempts to control dissent in society. The state focuses upon children specifically because of their creative potential, their ability to push the limits set for them; and it focuses on families because it understands that resistance may be taught within families. Thus, while Peri Rossi acknowledges the oppressive nature that the bourgeois family can have, she also sees its potential as a refuge of resistance. This perspective on her work adds to our understanding of the state's familial rhetoric, and also of the paradox which the author faces as he or she struggles for freedom from society's dictates at the same time that he or she recognizes the importance that the very heart of society—the family— can have in his or her development as an artist.

The protagonist in Alfredo Bryce Echenique's 1985 novel *La Vida Exagerada de Martín Romaña* struggles with the same paradox. Much of the criticism of this Peruvian's work has focused on his humor and on his young protagonists' sly critique of middle-class and elite Peruvian society. In the novel treated here, we read a recognition, as with Peri Rossi, of the importance of the family as a refuge for the child who experiments with resistance. The protagonist, Martín, admits his family's faults, but expresses love for them in any case. We further the exploration of the protagonist's child-like qualities and relate them to his life as an artist. He avoids the trap of *Rayuela*'s Oliveira, who becomes *incomunicado* at the moment of finding his infantile, and supposedly liberating state, but Martín does not avoid the paradox of the adult artist who strives to keep alive his child-like qualities in a world where the child lives a vulnerable, dangerous life, a world in which he is misunderstood, misinterpreted, and in which he suffers painful consequences for having been misinterpreted.

The majority of the criticism of the work of Isabel Allende, the last writer treated here, focuses on aspects of gender within patriarchal Latin American society. Some, including Gabriela Mora, have criticized Allende for allowing stereotypical clichés to be a part of the ideologies of even her more progressive characters ("Novelas" 56–58), while others have emphasized her tendency to invert and blend stereotypes in an effort to break cycles of violence and to encourage reconciliation (Handelsman; Helsper; Shields). In our examination of the child in her 1990 story "De Barro Estamos Hechos," it is clear that Allende is searching for a way of uniting opposite poles of political, ethnic and social class sectors in Latin American society. In this tale, she utilizes a child as the focal point of a recapitulation of one man's individual history, as well as the history of his marginalized people. In our reading, the author is calling for a cathartic testimony, which might lead to greater comprehension among those disparate sectors. As with the first work considered here, Galván's *Enriquillo*, the child is the site of a new beginning, or at least a reconsideration of a people's history; but here, rather than racial erasures, there is an acceptance of past suffering, and a plea for the protection of the child.

All of these works have in common the themes of exile, marginalization and alienation; but they also share the centering in the child, or in the society's commitment to the child, of hope for a reconciliation of the dialectic that has so plagued Latin American identity. It is, perhaps, presumptuous of authors and artists to align themselves with children as they do in our reading of their creativity in the following chapters. We must ask whether it is just another exploitation of the duality of the child. However, we believe it is a valid alignment, as both share the task in Western society of uncovering society's weaknesses, its contradictions and its cruelties. Wolfang Iser notes that literary anthropology puts literature back at the center of our study, rather than the literary theories and frameworks; it makes literature an instrument of exploration (264). He warns that as such "Literature is never self-sufficient, so it could hardly bear its own origin within itself," but rather is what it is as a result of its function, and it is always tied to the "singularity" of its historical moment (264–65). And what is the function of fiction? Iser responds with an answer that could just as well apply to our reading of childhood in these selected works from Latin American literature: "Fictions are inventions enabling humankind to extend itself—a state of affairs which can be studied from various angles" (265). Childhood, like authorship, is often a dangerous proposition in the works studied here: "We may perhaps conceive the fictive as a means of overstepping the given, which is bound to cause a transformation of what is" (Iser 268). It is precisely fear of—and hope for—that "transformation of what is" which attracts both artists and their censors to children and childhood, and it is what attracts us to the study of these texts.

NOTES

[1] *Mark Twain Speaking*, Ed. Paul Fatout, Iowa City: U of Iowa P, 1976, p. 131.

[2] In reading picaresque works, however, the reader is always conscious of the presence of the adult who is recounting the tale. There is an awareness of the filter through which the *pícaro* speaks, of the often pedantic goals of that filtering agent, and also of the reminiscent quality of the narrative.

[3]See Thomas Niehaus' bibliography for many contemporary studies from Latin America which treat problems associated with childhood in the region.

CHAPTER ONE

(Re-)Writing National Origins and Nation (Re-)Building:
Positivism and Childhood in Manuel de J. Galván
and Federico Gamboa

In the last third of the nineteenth century, replete with positivism and incessant debates concerning education, particularly the education of females,
Latin America's elites and its emerging middle classes looked for ways to
justify their hegemony. The endemic political chaos of the period limited opportunities to publish works critical of political regimes, and at the same time
spurred various writers to produce works which pleaded for and metaphorized
national unity. These works of "national foundation" intended to unite various sectors of social or racial hierarchies: Countryside and city, *hacendados*
and the middle class, liberals and conservatives, *mestizos* and whites, etc. (see
Sommer, *Foundational* 233-35, 251). These fictions, like those of other post-
colonial regions, made use of convenient political or racial erasures in order
to eliminate a painful memory from the nation's past, and thus unite that nation (Renan 11-12).

In this chapter we shall see that the erasures made in Manuel de J. Galván's *Enriquillo* (1882) and Federico Gamboa's *Suprema Ley* (1896) (*Suprema Law*) are of the woman's role in the education and socialization of chil-

dren—in *Enriquillo*, even reproduction is eliminated—in favor of tutorial relationships between men and boys or younger men. The nineteenth-century emphasis on the woman's role as the tempering influence on males, or as the redeemer of a male gone astray—and, metaphorically, of the nation—is given over to children or infantilized, child-like figures. Both of the novels are, in a sense, projects in the education of young protagonists. They reflect in their plots the nineteenth-century shift away from the family and toward figured relatives or institutions, as moral educators of the next generation. Both authors were positivists and involved in debates regarding the education of the nation's youth. We shall see in the following analysis of two of their literary works, just how childhood is central to both authors, to their concern for unity in the often chaotic late-nineteenth century.

In the 1800's, as critics of European literature and historians have made clear in recent years in their analyses of childhood, the child became central in a number of scientific, sociological and literary projects, ranging from studies of evolution, to the writing of national histories, to reformers' critiques of slavery, education and modern labor (see our Introduction; Steedman; Lloyd; and H. Cunningham). It is only natural that the figure of the child, so romanticized by authors earlier in the century, should be central to the 'scientific' writing against romanticism. While we find far fewer children in nineteenth-century Latin American literature than in European works, the presence of the spontaneous, innocent romantic child can be found, as it is written against, captured and educated for the future of the new Latin American nations. Childhood is central to the nineteenth-century concern for order in at least three ways: First, uneducated, unemployed children roaming the streets make adults uncomfortable, they are an outward sign of a lack of control; second, the stages of childhood and the education of the child parallel those of the positivists' perception of the evolution of societies, thus child development mirrors that of the society; third, the control of one's progeny (and women) is central to the maintenance of a male's and a family's prestige in a modernizing Latin America. Before analyzing the two works noted above, it is essential to give a brief overview of the positivist ideas that became so prevalent in nineteenth-century Latin America.

The Comtean positivist philosophy that came to Latin America in the mid-19th century from France expressed a belief in the family unit as the base upon which a society must build its future; it was to be the place where people would learn to subordinate their personal desires to more social or altruistic goals. The roles of mother, father and children were clearly spelled out and the progression of the individual from an egocentric being to a social being was diagrammed: The mother was said to be morally superior and thus played the major role in that social education, an education carried out within her primary sphere of influence, the home; the father was to occupy himself with the supposedly more mentally rigorous tasks of the public sphere, while taking part in the education of his children and allowing his wife to be a guiding moral influence on him and his progeny; the children, the future of society, meanwhile, were to obey their parents without question and learn from them how to become the altruistic social beings desired under positivist philosophy.

Comte placed a great deal of importance on the family in his positivist philosophy. Society is not, or at least should not be composed of individuals: "The true social unit is certainly the family—reduced, if necessary, to the elementary couple that forms its basis" (Lenzer 267). It is within the family that the individual first learns to subordinate self-love to social feelings, where he or she will be given the education which will enable the individual to pass through the three successive states of morality which correspond to the three principal stages of human life: The personal, the domestic, and the social (Lenzer 338).[1] The goal is for the individual to learn altruism in the home and then to carry that feeling outside of the home where he and his family cooperate with other families and with society in general. Division of labor and cooperation within the home prepare one for such relationships between families and eventually lead to a stable society: "When a regular division of employments has spread through any society, the social state begins to acquire a consistency and stability that place it out of danger from particular divergences" (Lenzer 272). Each family fulfills a social function, more or less indispensable to the whole society. An individual then is educated, diversifies and eventually is employed in a function most suited to him or her: "Even the most vicious and imperfect (short of monstrosity), may be finally made use of for the general good" (Lenzer 272). Implicit in this philosophy is the idea that one's potential is buried somewhere within, but that it can be realized with proper socialization and education.

These special functions or employments within the family are assigned according to gender and generation; indeed, the family is "instituted" by the subordination of the sexes, and then is maintained by the subordination of the younger generations: That is, the sexual union comes first, and then the raising of progeny maintains the marriage. Equality of the sexes is impossible, according to Comte, since "each sex has special and permanent functions that it must fulfill in the natural economy of the human family, and that concur in a common end by different ways..." (Lenzer 268). Women, says Comte, are not fit for rigorous mental activity, but are far superior to men in their sympathetic or social life. Men allow their personal instincts to overrule such social feelings, so the woman's role is to modify the male's "affective life," making him a more social and sympathetic creature (Lenzer 269).

Children within the family are in a naturally subordinate position, while the parents find themselves with authority over children. Children display "respectful spontaneous obedience" to their parents, at first due to necessity and later out of gratitude. Parents are devoted to their progeny, a devotion rarely seen in a superior party, writes Comte. We see in the Comtean family "absolute authority united to entire devotedness" (Lenzer 269).[2] Comte does address the potential abuse of power by parents, those who control the means of providing for the material needs of family members. In positivism this potential for "the despotism of material force" must be controlled by moral force, and it is the woman's role to provide that moral force. The woman's "highest and most distinctive sphere of work," therefore, is the family (Lenzer 376).

Positivism has been a great preoccupation of Latin America's historiography, and of Mexico's in particular: On the one hand because of the association of the philosophy with the *científicos* against whom, for many, the Revolution was fought; and on the other hand because most of the bureaucrats and leaders who emerged from the Revolution had been educated under a positivist system. Thus historians like Leopoldo Zea have devoted considerable energy to criticism of the positivists and to studying the philosophy's influence on the course of Mexican culture and history. According to Zea, the "moral force" with which the female was to imbue the Mexican male must have been absent or went unheeded in Porfirian Mexico as positivism resulted in men who were "submissive" and "indifferent" (Zea 34), rather than the altruistic, social-minded men described by Comte. Like any philosophy, positivism had to be interpreted within and adjusted to the national reality. Positivist thought during the late-nineteenth century in Latin America became mixed up with Darwin's theories on evolution and natural selection, with the middle class and elites usurping positivist philosophy to justify their own pursuit of economic progress and the further exclusion of the lower classes and castes from such progress. Latin American positivist thought was marked, then, by its heterodoxy (Jaksic 60). In Mexico, positivism was used under similar circumstances as those under which it was used in France following the French Revolution: The Mexican bourgeoisie had attained power and needed an order which would allow them to maintain that power, to defend themselves from the military on the right and the liberals on the left. Education—formal education—was the arm with which the bourgeoisie would persuade the other sectors of its right to a privileged status within Mexican society. However, positivists had to identify their sector's interests with the national interest in order to defend themselves from liberal attacks; they found themselves using the old conservative arguments to maintain power (Zea 50–53, 102). The basic Comtean concern with the family appears in Mexico, for example, to have given way to an emphasis on economic progress and flexibility.[3] Meanwhile, the generation educated under positivism found itself rebuffed in its attempts to contribute to the cultural life of the nation, leading to its discontent and eventual alienation from the positivist philosophy (Zea 34).

Under the guise of providing a scientific education to the nation's youth, the venue of the moral education that would lead to altruistic and sympathetic behavior was shifted, although perhaps not entirely, from the home to the state-run school. Morality was of direct public interest, and so its teaching should not be left up to individuals, but rather should be the task of a social organism (Zea 116–17). The professed desire for altruism meant that society's needs should be put ahead of the individual's, with society given the right to violate the individual's rights for the good of the community. In the Mexican case, the individual had to abandon any philosophy that could not withstand a "scientific" test, that is any that could not be proved through demonstration. The Mexican bourgeoisie could not accept any idea that did not support the order that it had created, so its own self-serving order eventually came to replace the ideal positivist order (Zea 135–44). Indeed, throughout Latin America positivists, later in the century, and even the romantics of early in the century, were preoccupied with maintaining order; and, education—a positivist education later in the century—was seen as a key to harnessing the nation's youth and securing order and progress (Rodríguez-Alcalá; Jaksic 64). Education had also become increasingly important to the emerging middle classes as they recognized it as the most significant inheritance that they could leave their children; children born without great lands or titles to inherit.

By institutionalizing the goal of moral education, the burden for that task should have been removed significantly from the woman, as would a great deal of the blame for the failings of the males who were under her sphere of influence. Gamboa's novel seems to emphasize the importance of individual initiative, and perhaps fate, and not female influence in modifying the male's behavior. Gamboa does take an interest, in much of his work, in the condition of the woman in Porfirian society; but, he does so, according to Lay, to prove that the prostitute or "fallen woman" was thus not because of social conditions or limitations placed upon her ability to work, but rather because of "atavism, fatal determinism" or, simply, her "carnal appetite" (Lay 54). Similarly, Galván, in his attempt to rehabilitate the Spanish for the Dominican reader, places all excesses and injustices in the laps of "bad" individuals, rather than faulting the colonial enterprise and colonial relationships (Piña 60–61, 142). Gamboa and Galván were education reformers, and their "moral" and "scientific" education had political goals. Galván in particular sought to provide the "proper" education for Dominican women, but in the Dominican

Republic, elites such as Galván were most concerned with order and stability, and education was meant to help achieve social peace. He was an annexionist during his early political life as the landowners struggled with the emerging middle classes for power, but later became an opponent of annexation while at the same time privileging Spanish culture in his writing, as he occupied numerous governmental posts (Piña 22–27).

The realist, naturalist and, in the case of *Enriquillo*, historical novels of the nineteenth century lend themselves especially well to our study since their authors were trying to provide an accurate portrait of life during their time (Ramos Escandón 120), while also serving a pedantic purpose (Grass, *López-Portillo* 6; Warner 107–8). Gamboa described his own writing as "medio velando con el manto diáfano de la fantasía, la fuerte desnudez de la verdad" (Hooker 110). He continues with a plea for a kind of realism and truth in art: "La condición esencial del arte legítimo es la verdad...la que nos horroriza porque sale a contar en las letras de molde lo que se ha visto dentro de nosotros, la que se torna en acusador de nuestros vicios y de nuestros defectos..." (Gamboa, *Impresiones* 267) ("The essence of legitimate art is truth...truth which horrifies us because there emerges from the written word that which we have seen within ourselves, truth which becomes our accuser, signaling our vices and our defects"). Galván's novel too, basing itself primarily on the writings of Bartolomé de las Casas, makes a claim to historical accuracy, which, interestingly enough, has been accepted by many historians. Piña notes that the dialectic between history and fiction in Enriquillo is so perfect that many historians and critics have, quite often, been unable to distinguish when they are dealing with history, such as that narrated by Las Casas or Fernández de Oviedo, and when they are dealing with fiction. (Piña 40). Piña goes on to note that much of the "daily life" portrayed in the novel is that of the Spanish colonists or of Hispanized Indians, not of the indigenous people who supposedly are the main focus of the novel. Thus, the historical 'accuracy' of the novel, that is, its cultural realism, limits itself to Hispanic culture, excluding for the most part the indigenous cultures.

The following discussion will enhance our understanding of the Mexican interpretation of positivism, in Gamboa's case, while also providing another view of the Mexican family during the *Porfiriato*. It will be shown that (1) in this Gamboa work there is a marked romantic emphasis on children, rather than on the woman, as the potential redeemers—or modifiers—of the male head of household gone astray; (2) that males and females together are responsible for managing the household and educating the children; and (3) that Gamboa, like many positivists, emphasizes the individual's responsibility for his own faults and weaknesses, thus avoiding direct criticism of the Porfirian power structure and its effects on society. First, however, we will examine the Galván work, showing the ways in which the author eliminates practically all children from the novel, with the exception of the protagonist and his wife, while at the same time infantilizing the young-adult Enriquillo and placing him in a position of perpetual tutelage. While in both novels there remains in the children a touch of the innocence of the romantic child, the authors have veritably drained from this image the spontaneity and creativity associated with that child. The children become much more functional and purposeful than in the romantic ideal. In like fashion, their parents are functionally fungible, easily replaced by a network of male friends and a moral guide, Las Casas, in Enriquillo's case, and an artist-teacher in *Suprema Ley*. We will show in the end that Galván and Gamboa privilege the male teacher—and, by extension, themselves as writers—as the new fathers of their respective nations.

In Manuel de J. Galván's *Enriquillo* (1882), the reader observes the growth and development of the protagonist and his wife, Mencía, who become, in a sense, the founding parents of the Dominican nation. The trouble is, they never have any children in the novel (nor does any other couple), nor do they ever escape their own position as the pupils of Father Las Casas. Even the title of the work, a diminutive name, keeps the protagonist in perpetual tutelage. We see in these two characters a clear deterministic belief that children are born with an inherent greatness, or lack thereof. All that is needed is the proper tutor to nurture the child's predetermined qualities. This parallels the nineteenth-century emphasis on the search for beginnings, a search based on a rejection of "superstition" and religion, and on the belief that the trained scientist, using the appropriate scientific methods will uncover the sought-after source of life; the well-equipped historian can uncover the "truth," the beginnings of nationhood; the child, with the proper education, appropriate to his or her sex, class, or ethnicity will be able to fully realize his or her potential, to reach back into the past—a past that they carry within them—and fulfill their internal mandate (Steedman 5, 12, 15). Carolyn Steedman notes that the child and childhood became important at the same time that the modern idea of history did, an idea which "suggests that by a painstaking dredging through the detritus left behind—the documents and other traces—it might be possible to conjure the past before our eyes, 'in its own terms'" (12). This results, in much nineteenth-century thinking, in a kind of determinism, of course, which denies the existence of a meritocracy in the nation, and reinforces social determinism. These points will be explored later in this chapter.

A major project of *Enriquillo*, according to Sommer, is the racial erasure that it makes as it eliminates Africans from the Dominican nation's history, emphasizing instead the country's indigenous and Spanish heritages, with the former subordinated to the latter. This erasure serves to differentiate the Dominican Republic from its neighbor, Haiti. Nineteenth-century trends in scientific thought regarding development and growth, and the rise of anthropometry—the measuring of that development—solidified belief in the existence of ideal types of all species. Children were central to these scientific trends as they could be studied for signs of development of certain qualities. Through their observation of childhood, observers could chart ideal growth and describe what they believed would be an ideal type for the species. It was also believed that in a child's development one could watch a sort of re-enactment of the stages of evolution of the entire human species (Steedman 74–75). This is analogous to re-writing Dominican national history using the stages of development of the young protagonist Enriquillo. The novel ends with the still young Enriquillo married and victorious, supposedly with a long future ahead of him. This appears to be the hope for the future of the Dominican nation as well. He represents an ideal type for the author and the nation as he is native to the Americas, yet highly Hispanized; he is also void of any African heritage, and he is malleable in the hands of the morally superior Las Casas.

This novel, like others examined by Sommer in *Foundational Fictions*, portrays a crisis in the new nation—in this case, in its colonial past—or in the nation's future in sexual terms, where a romantic heterosexual union is a metaphor for a united nation. It is, for example, a progressive nation in *Martín Rivas* (1867), or a pure and conservative one in *Cumandá* (1879). In these nations, "public" men would lead the *padre patria* and women would accept their roles as guardians of the home and reproducers of the nation; the woman's tasks (daughter or mother) would be carried out within the domestic sphere. In addition, the land that would be tamed by men is represented in feminine terms: The woman-land then, is something fixed, immobile in spatial and historical terms, while the male roams through city and country in his conquests, negotiations and struggles for his national ideal. The woman in such teluric novels represents the unchangeable, while the male, in the outside world, is capable of change (Franco, "Beyond"; Chatterjee); the task of this woman is to preserve the nation's traditional mores, and provide the country with the future generations of individuals who will occupy their designated places within a hierarchy. That hierarchy is usually presented in familial terms, with a fecund—sometimes benevolent, often oppressive—patriarch to be found at the top, whether in the present or in the nation's memory. The critical attention paid to that family and its functions and meanings in Latin America has been relatively plentiful in recent years, but little attention has been paid to the children or the concept of childhood within that family (see our Introduction).

Enriquillo, however, does not follow the models of these fictions in at least three ways. First, it does not assign to women certain roles that other "foundational fictions" designate as female. Second, the novel is void of a fecund patriarch. Third, the 'noble savages', the indigenous couple with Spanish protectors and a creole education, are not allowed to grow up, but are instead infantilized—they are perpetual children. The result is that an entire people is infantilized to the historical parents from Spain and the early colony, to Queen Isabel and Las Casas. Enriquillo and Mencía are not so much the parents of the new nation, as they are the nation, the spiritual children of Spaniards, and the biological children of the island. This contributes to the sense of timelessness in the novel. The nation is forever young, forever Spanish. As Dominicans identify with this couple, they identify with their indigenous and Spanish heritages, and deny the African. They also situate themselves as perpetual children to their Spanish parents, just as Enriquillo and Mencía, denied the narrative opportunity to procreate, remain forever child-like. Piña notes that Galván appears to intend to present in *Enriquillo* the origins of the Dominican people. The protagonist is the prototype Dominican: He is native to the island, but he possesses Spanish culture and, at the same time, struggles for freedom from the very people who have imbued him with their culture (49).⁴

This status as perpetual children, however, is not only indicative of a dependent state; the child also represents liberty and creativity for the nation's people. Lloyd notes a nineteenth-century propensity among French writers, such as Hugo, to identify the child with the proletariat. She sees in this identification a "freedom from the shackles of a conventional usage of language [that] allows both the child and the populace a vision of existence that has a freshness and energy inaccessible to the cultured, except by an effort of imaginative recovery of the state of childhood. For the historian, therefore, the child acts as spokesman for the uneducated" (234). The child as rebel, then, became a symbol of freshness, of newness and imaginativeness, though they are not usually seen as political beings (Lloyd 234–36). Plotz calls this newness the "limitless potentiality" and "perfectibility" of the romantic hero desired by romanticism (64–66). Enriquillo is seen as just such a perfectible youth; he was a kind of Nat Turner, a Spanish experiment that would prove that the Indians were capable of being "civilized" (Piña 48). Nineteenth-century anthropologists (and reformers) saw "savagery" in children (of the poor), and childishness in "savages" (H. Cunningham 123–25; see Steedman 82–83). The child and the noble savage are both beings whose inner potential can be brought out by, as in *Enriquillo*, the colonizing tutors; however, determinism binds the savage to a less than perfect outcome, leaving him more child-like in the end than the Spanish child, for we are always conscious of his inability to achieve the perfect "type." Galván's Enriquillo retains his pupil status at the end of the novel, remaining somewhat less than a mature adult hero.

The use of such heroes sets up a permanent need for mentors or tutors. In Galván's infantilizing narrative, we see how Enriquillo's freshness or rebelliousness is kept in check by the more politically aware and wiser Las Casas; and, of course, by Galván's presentation of Enriquillo as patient and submissive—his rebellion, for example, does not take place until his protector is out of the region, and he is supremely patient as he takes grievances before the authorities. Real parents are not needed in the late nineteenth-century positivist version of this child-hero's life, as the learned male, in the form of a father figure or within a fraternal relationship, will take the parents' place. Parents are not needed when the teachers, the scientists, the (male) moral leaders of the nation will produce the next generation.

Indeed, one could argue that Galván, in the end, is the father of them all, for he has charged himself with writing this infantilizing history of the foundation of the Dominican nation. Galván is following the model of the magisterial voice and father-tutor of patriarchal literature described by Gelpí in his work on Puerto Rican literature (2, 24). Childhood is central to this writing process, once again, as romantic writers often developed the self by laying down a history and placing themselves or some symbolic protagonist in that chronology. "The child within was always both immanent—ready to be drawn on in various ways—and, at the same time, always representative of a lost realm, lost in the individual past, and in the past of the culture" (Steedman 10). In our reading, Enriquillo is the "immanent" child of Dominican history and culture, and Galván is the ultimate magisterial voice who acts as his teacher and biographer.

Enriquillo is not born into a traditional family, however. Galván has produced, instead of true familial relationships, a foundation of fraternal relationships—some of them sanguineal, most of them fictive—and of perpetual tutelage for the protagonist. Sommer notes that in Gómez de Avellaneda's novel _Sab_, there never appears a "legitimate" or "effective" father, and that there are not any mothers save Sab's. Sommer conjectures that love and romance replace power as a coercive force in order to eliminate the violence of nation-building negotiations (_Foundational_ 119, 125). Our thesis regarding this period agrees with Sommer to a certain point; however, in _Enriquillo_ the author has erased the patriarchal family, in addition to the racial heritage noted by Sommer, as well as the female's active roles within the domestic sphere, in order to replace them with fraternal relationships and, with regard to the pairing of Enriquillo and Mencía, a sterile marriage that operates more in a spirit of comradeship and duty than love and romance. The political vacuum created by the diminishment of royal power in the far-off colony is not filled, we believe, by romance, as Sommer asserts, but by the aforementioned fraternal relationships.

The basing of a national history on such brotherly machinations reflects well Renan's assertion that such struggles are "comforting" to the young nation; fights between brothers who then go on to build together are a sign of a maturing nation, and one which is no longer under attack from outsiders. Brotherhood has a unifying quality as well, as Anderson says:

> Finally, it [the nation] is imagined as a *community* [Anderson's emphasis], because, regardless of the actual inequality and exploitation that may prevail in each, the nation is always conceived as a deep, horizontal comradeship. Ultimately it is this fraternity that makes it possible, over the past two centuries, for so many people, not so much to kill, as willingly to die for such limited imaginings. (7)

The kinds of fraternal negotiating we see in *Enriquillo* may suggest a nonviolent way out of national disagreements, much as Sommer suggests in her book is done through romance, yet the ultimate goal, we believe, is most likely to prepare for a unified defense of the nation, to form fraternities which will fight to the death for the nation. Fraternal relationships, in addition, are more fluid and free of the responsibilities of a true parent-child relationship. As Mount suggests, they are "weaker." Thus implicit in them is the need for a "father" figure, and the child-like status of the "brothers."[5]

A key to the maintenance of these fraternal relations, as Smart notes with respect to the literature of Quebec, and Franco with regard to nineteenth- and twentieth-century Latin American literature, is the suppression of the female voice and elimination of her maternal roles, those of reproducer and socializer of children. Franco notes a second phase of this process in authors from the middle of the twentieth century as they "feminize" their male protagonists' values. These characters, facing the failure of violence and the political and social chaos of a period of "modernization," usurp positive feminine values in order to criticize machismo. They have taken from the female, through their monstrous images of maternity and childbirth, for example, credit for such values. Thus, these men have reaffirmed their authority as male authors (Franco, "Beyond" 508–11). Smart notes something similar in the teluric literature of Quebec: Many of these works begin with the (often slow) "assassination" of the mother. Her analysis shows that even in the so-called domestic sphere, a woman's power and control are superficial, tenuous, and easily and regularly supplanted by husbands and fathers (94–95, 101, 265). In our reading of *Enriquillo*, Galván works just such a usurpation in the colonial setting of his novel.

While determinism is evident in the development of both Mencía and Enriquillo, it is only the latter's growth that is meticulously detailed in the novel; and, his is a growth which continues into his adult years. That is, it is the male who carries into adulthood this potential for development that is associated with the child. It is his 'history', that is worth seeking out, his potential that is worth realizing. This bi-cultural man who would be the father of the Dominican nation is a child, as his name implies. While re-writing the racial heritage of the vast majority of Dominicans, eliminating the African component, Galván also infantilizes those very Dominicans, maintaining them in a state of perpetual tutelage.

Galván participates in a long tradition of artists, ascetics, philosophers and religious—including Latin America's first novelist, José Joaquín de Lizardi—who see the family as a competitor for the faithfulness of its members. Ferdinand Mount, though he does not treat Latin America, traces the history of these "family-haters" from Plato to the contemporary period. Leaders of utopian movements—and we can consider here such characters of foundational fiction as participants in a type of utopian national vision—express their resentment for the egotistical nature of the family which competes with the utopian hierarchy (Mount 153–57). In the period and culture in which Galván wrote, however, one could not express such resentment directly. He resorts instead to a narrative that eliminates traditional families, sons and fathers, in favor of fraternal and filial relationships most of which are figured (or fictive). The fraternal rhetoric is used in such situations precisely because it is the most "diluted," emotionally, of all familial relations; it possesses that quality of equality which permits negotiation and cooperation; however, this relationship is also characterized by a lack of responsibility: A lack of responsibility between brothers who, as adults, compete for power, and who also are no longer the responsibility of their fathers (Mount 180).[6] Figured fathers and brothers take Enriquillo under their wings, then, infantilizing him, perpetuating his childhood.

We see numerous examples in *Enriquillo* of such "fraternal" relationships, friendships which flow and ebb as the young males move between groups of friends, testing alliances, looking for the most advantageous relationships. Indeed, it is the violation of such a fraternal trust between the protagonist and Andrés Valenzuela that, we believe, prompts Enriquillo to rebel. In chapter 23 of the third part of the novel, Francisco Valenzuela, who is on his deathbed, and who is the father of Andrés, exhorts his son to treat the young *cacique* "like a brother" (214). Don Francisco has been like a father to Enriquillo, and now he wants Andrés to obey his dying wish with regard to the liberty of the Indians who are part of his *encomienda*. Enriquillo repeatedly notes with regret that Andrés is not liberating the Indians, an act which would satisfy the wishes of his late father (229). Their brotherly relationship becomes something like that of Caine and Abel as Andrés constantly plans the demise of Enrique, the favored "son," as Andrés calls him. It is also important to note that the *cacique* is generous and lenient with transgressors, save one who is a "pretendido pariente" ("supposed relative") of Enriquillo. Enriquillo himself hangs this Indian, who has tried to betray the protagonist (278).

Enriquillo's emotional reactions with regard to insults hurled at his protector Don Francisco, the mistreatment of the Indians, and the attempted violation of his wife are curiously similar. He is angered, but soon calms himself and hopes for a just resolution. In the first two cases, he puts his faith in the efforts of Father Las Casas and in his belief in Andrés's good will (e.g., 222). Upon learning of the altercation between Mencía and Andrés, however, he realizes that he cannot rely upon Las Casas in this domestic matter, and begins in vain his own search for justice in the affair. Although Enriquillo says that he has set as a limit to his patience the respect due to his wife (250), the three petitions he takes before the justices are for the liberty of his friend Galindo, the denial of Valenzuela's control of Mencía's property, and the termination of the Indians' status as Andrés's *encomendados* (250): He does not demand Andrés's arrest for the attempted assault on his wife.

Later, although the authorities deny his petitions, Enriquillo does not immediately throw himself into a rebellion. As on other occasions, he considers the possibility, but whereas before he refuses to rebel due to his faith in Las Casas and Andrés, now he remains passive for some nebulous reason that seems to have something to do with Mencía (though this does not seem to be a recognition of any tempering influence of Mencía on Enriquillo as she has not tried to influence his decision regarding a rebellion). He simply states that if it were not for her, he would not have been able to tolerate the injustices and tyrannies which he has suffered, and he would not be free:

Si no fuera por ti, Mencía, amor mío—continuó con exaltación el cacique—; ya todas las tiranías y las infamias hubieran acabado para mí: yo alzaría la frente del libre con justa altivez, y nadie pudiera jactarse ... de que tu esposo el cacique Enriquillo no es sino un miserable siervo. (253)

After the attempt against his wife's purity, Galván's Enriquillo focuses on his status as a servile Indian, not as a spouse whose honor, which supposedly lies in the sexual purity of his wife, has been violated. In addition, during the rebellion, there is no mention of this incident as a cause of the uprising. They continue to emphasize the liberty of Enriquillo's Indians as an autonomous community that has suffered under the oppression of the Spaniards who have treated the Indians as private property: The words "slavery" and "slaves" are repeated often during this period. Enriquillo espouses his resolution to continue the struggle against the Indians' enslavement until the crown decrees their liberty, and that the decree must take effect throughout the colonies (279). Only Tamayo—not Enriquillo—the most bellicose of the leaders under Enriquillo's command, notes the violation of women in his recriminations against Andrés during a battle, saying that the latter should not continue his "evil ways," which include "dishonoring the poor women" (263). Enriquillo himself, however, is not driven into battle by the need to avenge his wife's supposed loss of honor.

It is important to note that Andrés, after this frightening incident when Tamayo threatens him, repents before Las Casas and becomes kinder to others, even managing Mencía's property more justly. Galván uses a curious and cruel sarcasm toward women at this point as he notes that he does not know whether Andrés was punished in the afterlife, or whether his marriage to the "scatterbrained" Elvira was sufficient penitence in this life (270). Andrés's punishment for having been greedy and having violated his fraternal loyalty, according to Galván, was to marry the "scatterbrained Elvira." As with nearly all of the married couples in this novel, the reader is left to wonder whether any children were conceived in the union. In this case, we know that Elvira was widowed soon after she was wed; thus, once again, the reproductive role of the woman is denied to her.

It seems Enriquillo is to be the only 'child' of this fictional world. In fact, there are almost no true parents in this novel, either, although there are many fictive or figured parent-child relationships: Las Casas, Don Francisco Valenzuela and Diego Colón are all father figures for Enriquillo, the orphan; the viceregal couple are like parents to Mencía; a young Franciscan is another student, or son, of Las Casas; and there are various examples of such relationships among the numerous *conquistadores* and colonists throughout the narrative. Enriquillo's orphanhood, however, serves the purpose of establishing his link to the nation. Like the Dominican nation of the nineteenth century, he is free from the direct control of 'parents' (the Spanish empire), yet not from the cultural heritage and memory that he has inherited from them. Also, his and the nation's earliest memories are scarred by the pain of separation; his from the loss of his parents, and the nation from the separation from the crown.

Rosemary Lloyd says that in nineteenth-century France, many writers search for or create a "first memory," and that many of these are painful (39–42). Pain and memory are thus linked. Also, as Steedman notes, "We are accustomed to children arriving from nowhere, out of the silences of a piece of fiction, or out of actual Aveyron forests, bearing the bodily and psychic marks of terrible harm done them" (163). In Galván's historical novel, then, the writing of Dominican history is linked to the painful childhood memories of Enriquillo; one could say that the writing of Dominican history begins with those childhood memories, written by Galván. Enriquillo, emerges out of the gardens—typically part of the refuge of the Latin home (Franco, "Killing" 418-19)—where he played with Mencía, later from the forest where he accompanied his uncle during a rebellion, and then from the monastery's gardens, bearing the psychic scars of his parents' deaths and of the slavery of his people. The author acknowledges the importance to the young *cacique* of the experiences with the uncle at such a "tender age" (19), and even notes the impact of his rigorous education on the boy's personality noting that the care with which the young Indian was educated must have made his unhappy condition even more painful during his days of greatest adversity (51).

Enriquillo's beginnings imbue him with the qualities of the hero as described by Joseph Campbell. First his people celebrate his birth, as he is destined to be a powerful *cacique* someday. He then faces the loss of his parents, though he miraculously survives the massacre of Jaragua as Father Las Casas is there to save him and Mencía. The child Enriquillo is sensitive, spontaneously affectionate and indebted to Las Casas for his survival (50–51). The boy is then educated by holy men in the Convento Vera Paz, a Franciscan school, as was the custom with the sons of *caciques*. Cristina Ruiz Martínez has outlined some of the qualities of the stereotypical "saintly child" which she has gleaned from the biographies of members of religious orders in colonial Latin America. We see that Enriquillo conforms to at least two of the major characteristics in that he is a "an extraordinary child" (51); he is highly intelligent and, from a very early age, is concerned for those less fortunate. He possesses a "privileged soul" reflecting his noble birth and inner potential. Father Remigio, the child's first teacher, answers the boy's incisive questions, depositing in his "privileged soul" the "seeds of honor and rectitude" (51), giving us the image of the noble Indian child as a fertile ground to be cultivated by the Spaniard.

This view of the child Enriquillo reflects well the nineteenth-century belief that by cultivating and understanding the child, one would understand better the society's culture and history. Anthropologists turned to the child when they were unable to find a living specimen of primitive humans. The child's linguistic development could be studied for evidence of the process of evolution. The growth of the child represented "a historical phenomenon, and the child of the species was used as working material for its investigation. A child psychology was partly constructed in the expectation that cultural and historical evidence enclosed within the child's body and mind could be retrieved and used" (Steedman 85). Thus there was the expectation of a sort of harvest during Enriquillo's subsequent development. In this view, however, that harvest was very much pre-determined: Enriquillo's greatness, his cultural heritage, his ability to be taught, his personality traits, were all present within him—they only had to be revealed and interpreted.

Although biological parents are largely absent from this novel, their image or myth persists. The ideal mothers are mythified here, for example, and are the deceased queens, Isabel of Castilla, representing the nation's Spanish heritage, and Anacaona, the famous widowed Indian queen. We also see Anacaona's daughter, Ana de Guevara (Higuemota), who is known for her kind heart, and whose "instinto maternal" is noted early in the novel as she cares for her daughter Mencía (11). Anacaona and Isabel are the last women to possess power within the patriarchy presented in the novel. Anacaona was the last to truly reign, a queen whose sphere of influence included all of the kingdom, including the chief (7); and Fernando, without Isabel, becomes cold and greedy:

> Muerta la egregia and magnánima reina Isabel, las Indias quedaron abandonadas muy temprano por la fría política de Fernando el Católico a la explotación y el lucro. Para aquel monarca egoísta los descubrimientos no tenían más valor que el de las ventajas materiales que pudieran producir a la corona.... (208)

After these women, all attempts by females to exercise power, including those of tempering the male personality and managing the domestic scene, will be supplanted by males. The *vireina*, for example, does not serve as a go-between for the young lovers in this novel, as Father Las Casas occupies this role, arranging their marriage, including the preparations for the wedding supper.

During the life of the young *cacique* Enriquillo, the usually female roles of being an "amable influencia" and a protector of the weak, have been occupied by the likes of Las Casas, Don Francisco and Don Diego. Las Casas is like a mother and father to the *cacique*, teaching him, and comforting him. This is a reflection, we believe, of the nineteenth-century change of venue of moral education from the home to the state-run school, as morality was recognized as being of direct public interest; although much lip-service was still paid to the socialization role of the mother in the home, there was increasing emphasis on her receiving her education in an institution as well. Nineteenth-century positivism, based on Comte, as we have noted above, claimed that women were not fit for rigorous mental activity, but were far superior to men in their sympathetic or social life. Men allow their personal instincts to overrule their altruism, so the woman's role is to "modify" the male's "affective life," making him a more social and sympathetic creature (Lenzer 269). Enriquillo, and by extension the Dominican people, are forever under Las Casas's tutelage; indeed they "need" to feel protected: "[Enriquillo] mismo necesitaba sentirse amparado y protegido por un ser verdaderamente fuerte, en quien la bondad hiciera veces de responsabilidad" (194). Las Casas takes over the moralizing or tempering role of the woman. Queen Isabel has faded to a specter of morality; she is the figured mother of the nation, not Mencía; but, of course, the queen is not active in the novel. Generally in the modern nation, females were reduced to "the role of reproducer of citizens" (Pratt, "Brotherhood" 51), but that task has been taken away from her in this very sterile novel. The moral and political domestic leaders of this new era, about whom Galván writes, are to be male. Strong female leaders belong to the past, not in the new nation being built by the likes of Galván.

Las Casas's bridging of genders in this novel places him in a role similar to that of a grandfather, according to Freudian logic. The grandfather is to possess the emotional and nurturing qualities of the mother, as well as the authoritative and worldly qualities of the father. This image of the grandfather, however, is a child's fantasy that has been created as the "compensatory lap" after the child has fallen off the parental lap (B. Martin 94). We interpret Galván's use of such a grandfatherly Las Casas as a child-like attempt to replace the lost royal parents, both the indigenous parents of Enriquillo and the Spanish royal parents of the colony. While Las Casas becomes the grandfather-patriarch in this scheme, a patriarch who can encompass the roles of both male and female, father and mother, Enriquillo, who is both son and grandson, himself plays such a role as he serves as a protector of and a sobering influence on the Indians under his command, and on his wife. Females are denied both of these roles within the novel, and there is no hint that they will become biological mothers or have such roles in the future.

In the lives of the Colones, María de Cuellar, who dies a virgin, and Mencía, among others, no progeny appear. Galván does not permit his characters to worry about the needs of the next generation of Dominicans (save when the adoptive parents take the time to raise Enriquillo and Mencía). Even the uprising headed by Enriquillo does not mention a struggle for the future of their children; in fact, the only children who appear during this period of the novel are the briefly mentioned student-virgins to whom Mencía teaches "religión, virtud, labores de mano y rudimentos literarios" (277). Perhaps Galván, knowing that the Indian race had practically died out, considered it too fictitious, or sad, to include such hope within the novel for a late-nineteenth-century audience. As Sommer notes, by leaving open the future of the Indians in the novel, the author invites all Dominicans to reclaim their Indian heritage and thus reject their African ancestors (*Foundational* 252).

Benedict Anderson expresses something similar in that the imagined generations to come, in any nation, are a source of nationalism (140–44). Also, if Mencía and Enriquillo do not have children, all Dominicans can feel as though they are the sons and daughters of this "first couple" of the Dominican nation. Of course, as we have noted above, a lack of children translates into a lack of conflict with regard to a woman's loyalty to her husband. Women remain faithful to their husbands—they do not have to intercede in father-son conflicts, or other intergenerational tussles; they do not have to make such difficult choices—while their husbands wander about the countryside testing various combinations of fraternal and paternal relationships in order to best meet their "public" goals, whether they are beneficent, as are Enriquillo's, or malevolent, such as those of the greedy Mojica. Additionally, as Mary Louise Pratt writes regarding the Republican period in Latin America, "the reproductive capacity, so indispensable to the brotherhood is a source of peril, notably in the capacity of those nonfinite, all-too-elastic female bodies to re- produce themselves outside the control of the fraternity" ("Brotherhood" 52). Thus in our reading, Galván avoids the sticky problem of the faithfulness of women to their husbands and fathers, and those of illegitimacy and incest, by simply sterilizing his characters. In this way he does not play the game of revealing at a novel's end the secrets of parentage, a game so common in the works of his contemporaries. Galván successfully excludes women from what Pratt calls the "horizontal brotherhood" ("Brotherhood" 52), and thereby limits the potential for conflict.

Patricia Smart has noted the slow "assassination" of the mother in nine- teenth-century Québécois novels (265), and in *Enriquillo* we see a killing off of motherhood and mother-child relationships, which causes women to fade further into the background of Dominican history. In her work on "demo- cratic patriarchy," Florencia Mallon describes how the gerontocracy of Mexi- can village life excluded women, and how the patriarchy persisted even as democracy invaded (literally) the villages. Democracy promised opportunities for women and youth, and the patriarchy persisted as it became the guarantor of equality and opportunity. The "good patriarch" of the village system con- tinued, and served to temper the individualism of liberalism (Mallon 5-7). Such a patriarchal discourse not only maintains control over women, but also over lower-class revolutionaries who, Mallon notes, emerge as perpetual adolescents (19-20). Applying this concept to the *cacique* Enriquillo, then, we see how his childlessness and perpetual tutelage serve to limit his power to a youthful energy that is not to be taken as a serious threat to the hierarchy.

One final note about the "first couple": Not only do they not have chil- dren (at least in Galván's novel, and this differs from other "foundational fic- tions" of Latin American nationhood), nor do we know for sure the extent to which Enriquillo's love is requited by Mencía. The young woman says clearly to her fiancé Enriquillo, and to her female friends, that she loves the *cacique* as she would a family member, and that she will marry him in order to satisfy her mother's will (176). The fact, mentioned by Mencía, that they grew up together—like siblings—during a number of years indicates a possible 'spiritual' violation of the incest taboo should the marriage ever be consummated. Enriquillo, upon confronting his wife's attitude about their romance, hopes that once she has been "initiated into the mysteries of matrimony," her "innocent and chaste love" will acquire a measure of "tenderness and passion" (177). We do not know, however, whether Mencía was ever "initiated" into those marital mysteries since the spouses sleep in separate chambers in their country home, and we are never notified of the production of progeny. It seems that Enriquillo wants a more romantic, passionate love from Mencía, whereas she is apparently happy to marry someone whom she loves as a brother in order to fulfill her mother's wishes. This brotherly matrimony contributes to the image of Enriquillo as not quite an adult.

Mencía's love for Enriquillo does change at some point, but it is not due to her becoming acquainted with the above-mentioned mysteries, but rather with her seeing Enriquillo return victorious from his first battle:

> …entonces el corazón de Mencía palpitó a impulsos de imponderable satisfacción y de legítimo orgullo…besó con santo entusiasmo su rostro varonil…corrieron sus cristalinas lágrimas…y sus labios, trémulos de grata emoción, murmuraron apenas esta frase expresiva: —Grande, libre, vengado…; ¡así te quiero! (277)

She loves him for his public deeds, not for some romantic, physical chemistry between two individuals.

This love for Mencía, which disturbs Enriquillo is contrasted with the love that he feels for his "zealous protector," Las Casas, who "is like a favorite star indicating the north of hope in the somber sky of his existence" (194). It is not Mencía, then, who serves as the hero's muse or "amable influencia," but rather Las Casas. In addition, the love that he feels for the priest is something much purer; a love which does not inspire the "shadows" and "anxieties" of romantic love:

> Pensaba ciertamente con embeleso en la hermosa doncella que le estaba prometida; pero sin saber por qué, una especie de vago presentimiento agravaba su tristeza al considerarse ya dueño de aquel tesoro de gracias. No así cuando el recuerdo querido de Las Casas se ofrecía a su mente: entonces su alma se abría sin reserva a la plácida emoción de un afecto blando y puro, libre de sombras, exento de inquietud. (194)

The narrator explains Enriquillo's concern about his love for Mencía noting that this relationship would bring with it great responsibility (194). We see here a clear preference on the part of the narrator for the supposedly more emotionally simple relationships between men. Heterosexual love carries with it "shadows" and "anxiety", whereas love between men leads to a sense of freedom and tranquility. (This appears to exclude romantic and/or physical love between men.) The female complicates love, almost as though it would be better if there were no heterosexual love, but only fraternal love. We should note again that even the romantic pairing of Mencía and Enriquillo is between "spiritual" siblings who have been raised together.

Mount suggests in his discussion of fraternal love that such relationships typically lack a spiritual communion, however, and that males seek such communion in romantic love. There is no evidence in this novel that Enriquillo finds some sort of spiritual communion in romantic love. In fact, the *cacique* does not respond in the narrative to Mencía's show of affection when he returns from battle. Life goes on as before, with the exception that Mencía seems to resign herself more easily to living with the "upsets" and "harshness" of their life (277). Mencía does not love Enriquillo as a spouse, then, but as Galván wants all readers of the novel to love him, as a defender of Indians—an indigenous Las Casas, we might say—and as the epitome of the combination of the best of the morals of both cultures, and of both sexes. He is a feminized and infantilized hero: Sensitive, tied to the land, self-denying, and faithful to a 'father' (see Galván, 50, for a list of Enriquillo's many qualities).

We have proposed here that throughout the novel fraternal and filial relationships, real and figured ones, are emphasized, and that it is the violation of these relationships between men that precipitates Enriquillo's rebellion. The woman in this narrative is denied the usual roles attributed to her in the nineteenth century: She is not associated with the land, as this relationship is reserved for the sensitive and poetic Enriquillo (244), or at times for the child-like Las Casas, nature being for him the "motivo de éxtasis"; nor is the woman a reproducer of the people, a role that is not attributed to anyone in this sterile novel; nor is she charged with tempering, either directly or through socialization, the violent or greedy tendencies of the male in order to make him more humanistic and benevolent, but rather other men serve these "feminine" roles. One of the erasures that Galván achieves, then, is that of the fertile patriarchal family. He replaces it with fraternal relationships and, as far as the Mencía-Enriquillo pair is concerned, a marriage that operates in a spirit of comradeship and that is characterized more by familial duty and sibling love than romance. The female in Enriquillo is converted into a summarily passive being: There is not even a childbirth here. Heterosexual sex, whether for lascivious motives as in the cases of Mojica and Andrés, or for reproductive reasons, seems to be a dangerous power in this novel. All of this contributes to the justification of the position of the male as "author" in a period in which the liberation and education of women was being so hotly debated. Under this nationalistic regime, the woman-mother finds herself in a domestic limbo, without any active role; her mythic image is all that remains of her meaning in this version of the patriarchy.

As we have noted above, the child of the nineteenth century's scientific focus was not only a site of growth and development, but also a harbinger of death. Well into the nineteenth century, child-rearing manuals talked of the death of a child while at the same time dispensing the usual child-care advice. The end of childhood signaled the beginning of the decline of the person (Steedman 64–76). The boundaries between the animate and the inanimate were marked by the way in which their shapes were depicted. Inanimate objects (crystals, for example) were angular in their development; indeed, death was shown as being rigid, angular and planar, "but in the child-care manuals, where each depiction of growth was also a chronicle of a death foretold, what the child embodies glides and flows, carrying what is implied in the child's beginning to its certain end" (Steedman 74).

Theories of evolution "described hope, by depicting children as the embodiments of the history that ostensibly implied death and extinction" (Steedman 83). We might speculate here that the perpetual tutelage of Enriquillo and Mencía, and the lack of other children in the novel might be related to a linking of the child and death, a linking of the child with the potential death, that is, of the new nation. Galván, in our reading, focuses on beginnings in this novel, he then arrests the development of the hero, resisting death and decay—"the implications of growth," as Steedman calls them: "History and childhood, as ways of thinking and ways of knowing, both strenuously attempted to delimit and resist the implications of growth, and both ways of thought pushed these questions to the interior" (95). The world "was turned inside, so that history itself might be dehistoricised, removed from the time that allowed growth and decay, so that they might be overcome, in the lost and—crucially—timeless place within" (95). The child in literature has the effect of prolonging our gaze, in a sense, of creating a feeling of timelessness as we search for beginnings and meanings. In *Enriquillo* that gaze rests upon a forever-young, indigenous disciple of Spanish culture, signifying the commencement of a period of growth and stability. It is a comforting history for the reader in search of a homeland.[7] For the Dominican reader, that home is located within a colonial relationship with Spanish culture, and it is void of African heritage.

In the next novel to be analyzed, rather than establishing a beginning for the nation's history, Federico Gamboa's contemporary image of the half-grown youth leads to a questioning of the Mexican nation's current state of development, a questioning which parallels as well the father's decline in the novel. In the end, the failed father's illness kills him, while another couple takes in his children; the biological father is fungible, easily replaced by a member of the national fraternity.

Gamboa, born in Mexico City in 1864, was the son of General Manuel Gamboa, a conservative who fought the North Americans in 1847 and then Benito Juárez in 1862. Federico Gamboa's mother, Lugarda Iglesias, the sister of politician José María Iglesias, died when the writer was just 11 years old (Hooker 7-8). Gamboa was educated in various private schools in the capital and at the Escuela Nacional Preparatoria. At the age of 16 he went to New York City for one year with his father where he learned English and enjoyed an active nightlife. After returning to Mexico he studied law for three years until his father died, at which time he left his studies. One of his three brothers, a lawyer, helped him obtain a position as a clerk in a penal court, a job Gamboa disliked, and one which figures prominently in *Suprema Ley*. The young Gamboa pursued a career in journalism, writing for *El Diario del Hogar* and *El Foro* (Monterde viii-ix). He left *El Diario del Hogar* when it began criticizing the Díaz regime. Gamboa continued writing and editing for other newspapers and magazines, finding particular success in his theater reviews. He eventually joined the diplomatic service in 1888 (Hooker 8).

Gamboa, an admirer of the dictator Porfirio Díaz, moving slowly and steadily through the diplomatic ranks, was stationed in many countries. He was eventually named a special envoy to Central America and later the under secretary of foreign relations. Gamboa was able to combine his diplomatic career with literature, turning out several theatrical pieces (some during his journalistic career), newspaper articles and eventually, in 1892, the first of his seven novels, *Apariencias* (Monterde x-xv; Hooker 8-10). He published his best known, and perhaps his best novel, *Santa*, in 1903 (Brushwood, *Mexico* 153). Gamboa's politics eventually led him into self-exile. He accepted the position of foreign secretary in 1913 during the Huerta regime and then the Catholic Party's presidential candidacy. After his loss in the elections he went to the U.S. and to Cuba, eventually returning to Mexico where he pursued a career as a part-time journalist and part-time professor. He was named director of the Academia Mexicana in 1923, a position he held until his death in 1939 (Monterde xi).

Gamboa is considered by some (erroneously, according to Brushwood) to be Mexico's only naturalist writer, but there are strong elements of romanticism as well as the more subtle influences of modernism in his works (Brushwood, *Mexico* 149-50). Perhaps most importantly, Gamboa was a positivist and supporter of Díaz who found himself, as many other writers of the period, trapped between a desire for social reform, which implied criticism of Díaz as well as potential social turmoil, and a recognition that the relative peace of the Díaz dictatorship gave him the means to write. Criticism, therefore, had to be of the individuals portrayed in the novels, and their real-life counterparts, with solutions based in individual changes in morality, and not in a change of national leadership (Brushwood, "La Novela" 374, 380–81). Authors of Gamboa's generation lived through a period of Mexican history which would not lead them to believe that revolution would bring about much needed changes (Brushwood, "La Novela" 402). In fact, most writers of the Porfiriato did not condone revolution, and many strongly criticized it (Grass 327). Brushwood does note that Gamboa, more than his contemporaries, equated some characters with the general conditions of the nation, thus writing novels "of questioning unrest" during the Porfiriato, leaving the reader with the sense that "the world is not turning as it should" (*Mexico* 154–55). Besides Gamboa's first-hand knowledge of the chaos of nineteenth-century Mexico, his positivism as well would have led him to seek order, thus we would not expect him to condone revolution. As a nineteenth-century realist and romantic he put his pen to the task of outlining the need for social reforms.

Federico Gamboa was especially critical of the social condition of child laborers, women and workers in general. He criticized the lack of social institutions that might help those children whose families were unable to support them adequately (Lay 52). This theme of criticizing a society that does not become concerned about an individual until he has run afoul of the law, is prevalent throughout Gamboa's work (Woolsey 294–97). It is in his portrayals of these impoverished individuals, and of social conditions in general, that Amado Lay feels Gamboa's work most accurately reflects the historical studies on the period (90–91). Gamboa's writings, however, can leave the reader confused as to the author's favored solutions for these social ills. He seems to concern himself either with social defects that are limited to very particular institutions or social groups, or with problems of excessive reach. As he vacillates between these extremes, the social criticism to which Gamboa seems to dedicate his novels does not apparently offer an intelligible philosophy for resolving those social maladies (Navarro 306). Or, as Prado González says, "Sus novelas son un amasijo de teorías e impulsos contradictorios," (72) due primarily to Gamboa's mix of conservative Catholicism, naturalism, romanticism and positivism. As Iván Jaksic notes, during the late nineteenth and early twentieth centuries, many reformers displayed a tremendous heterodoxy of positivist, religious and other doctrines in their striving to find peaceful solutions to social problems (61), which would explain Prado González's above-mentioned criticism.

For some authors, the changes in individual morality mentioned above were to be instigated in the home by the woman: "...there is a tendency to seek a strengthening of Mexican society in general through a strengthening of the family unit. This concept is typically expressed more or less symbolically through the redeeming powers of a woman's love" (Grass 327). In our analysis of *Suprema Ley*, Gamboa recognizes such redeeming powers in women; however, he emphasizes those of children, as do many nineteenth-century European writers such as Dickens. As we note in our Introduction, there was, in Great Britain, a sense of national pride involved in this use of the child, as the citizen could show his degree of civilization in his reaction to the suffering child (H. Cunningham 61–63, 133–34, 138). Love for and responsibility to children are a constant influence on several male characters in *Suprema Ley*, but in the protagonist's case, romantic love proves to be a stronger influence, leaving him eventually to die a lonely death.

Suprema Ley is ostensibly the story of the moral decline of Julio Ortegal, a lower middle-class penal court clerk who hates his job. The novel traces his fall from hard-working family man and low-level bureaucrat to an adulterous stagehand. He is married to Carmen Terno, her name suggesting tenderness, a marriage sought by Julio not out of love, but rather because he was orphaned in his early twenties and hoped to find someone to take care of him and to give him children. We see immediately in this novel, then, a preoccupation with the loss of childhood, a theme which recurs throughout the work. His attempts to recuperate that state, to locate a motherly influence in a purely sexual relationship, will lead to his death. We read in this novel a strong acknowledgment of the effects of childhood reality on the life cycle outcomes for the adult. Julio's orphanhood, and that of his own children, and the childhoods of other characters display various manifestations of this preoccupation with the importance of childhood.

While the Ortegal family grows each year, the father's salary does not, leaving the family progressively more impoverished. Julio becomes melancholy in this situation, even finding the work place, which he generally dislikes, to be a refuge at times from the economic strains of his household. He expresses repeatedly that he loves his children a great deal; as he begins his decline they are at first a source of energy and hope to him. He is an involved father, just as Comte would have him be, taking his children on Sunday outings, and making family plans and decisions jointly with his wife, in spite of the fact that his children required tremendous sacrifices of him, he lived for them, loving them all (235). It is thinking about his children that, in the beginning, keeps Ortegal from succumbing to the temptations and vices that afflict other employees in his office.

Eventually, however, a beautiful young woman enters his life. She is Clotilde, who has been jailed, accused of killing her lover. The court eventually determines that the lover committed suicide and Clotilde is freed, but not before Julio has secretly fallen in love with her. Her father, who has disowned her for running off with her fiancé, feels pity for his daughter and requests that Carmen and Julio accept a monthly stipend for caring for Clotilde. Her presence temporarily improves the financial state of the Ortegal home, but Julio ultimately seduces her, though she never seems to truly love him, and their affair destroys the family as it had existed up to that time (although it is later rehabilitated by an outsider, a situation described below).

Clotilde comes from a well-off family from Mazatlán, her father having worked hard for many years to build the family's modest fortune. Her childhood was idyllic, with her parents taking great pride in their daughter, and the father, when not away due to his work, taking an active part in her upbringing.[8] The father, with the mediation of his sister, Clotilde's aunt Carlota, eventually realizes that he has been too harsh in his treatment of his daughter and sends a letter to Mexico City with Carlota expressing his love for Clotilde and asking her to return home. Clotilde's mother plays only a small part in the father's change of heart; he is influenced by his love for his daughter and a recent illness that has made him more aware of his own mortality. Within the Ortegal family, as the affair between Julio and Clotilde progresses, he gradually abandons his involvement in managing the household and raising the children, though he does continue to send his salary home and to think about his children often. He is painfully aware of the damage he is doing by abandoning them, and yet his love for Clotilde is like an illness that he cannot overcome, not unlike the tuberculosis that is slowly killing him.

As Carmen and Julio grow further apart, Julito, the eldest child, grows closer to his mother. He reads romance novels to her at night as she knits. He eventually quits school to take pottery lessons and is soon offered a job by his pottery instructor, Eustaquio, an artist and professor. It is at this point that we see the father-son conflict prevalent in Mexican society which Boling notes in the 20th-century works of Carlos Fuentes: Carmen insists that Julito ask his father's permission to go to work; the young man resents his father's control over their lives and his virtual abandonment of the family. Such abandonment and resultant resentment clearly violate the Comtean idea of the perfect fit between filial piety and the benevolent dictator, and would seem to indicate that it is acceptable for a son to reject his father when the latter has not upheld his end of the father-son bargain described by Comte.

Eustaquio's role in the Ortegal family grows in significance at this point. We see in him another father driven to act by the love for a child, in this case his late son. Eustaquio, we find out, encouraged Julito in his work because of the young man's physical resemblance to the artist's dead son. When Julito becomes gravely ill, Eustaquio takes in the mother and the children. Julio by this time is living in a hotel, dividing his time between work and Clotilde, who lives in a house in a *colonia*. In the upper-middle class home of Eustaquio and his wife, which he has built up through his dedication to his art and teaching, the Ortegal family seems nearly to be in a state of bliss. The younger children quickly forget about their father, while Carmen and Julito secretly hope that Julio will reform and return to them. Eustaquio, by providing for the family and participating in the education of at least one of the children, is exhibiting the altruistic behavior that Comte saw as the goal of a social being's life. Gamboa, in this instance, seems to be encouraging the view that children from the various classes are alike and are entitled to—and need in order to survive—parental love and guidance. Eustaquio and his wife, Agnese, in turn are reinvigorated by the playful, musical presence of the children. We read in this situation a possible exchange of energies between the surrogate parents and the newly arrived children. The latter will likely serve as an inspiration for Eustaquio's work, while they will be provided for both materially and emotionally.

As the artist-teacher easily replaces Julio, we see that biological fathers are highly fungible in Gamboa's novel. While there is not the intense emphasis on fraternal relationships in this work that we have read in *Enriquillo*, we do see a horizontal move here from one set of biological parents to another, figured set. Just as Enriquillo exchanged surrogate parents a number of times, Julio's children find a new source of love and authority in non-relatives. It is significant that the fungible father is a cog in the wheels of the massive state bureaucracy; he is replaceable as a father just as he is replaceable as a clerk. Eustaquio, meanwhile, is an artist and teacher, and, we suspect, more unique than Julio. We have made above a connection between Galván and Las Casas as authorities with power over the writing of Dominican history, both members of the fraternal guild of nation builders. We read a similar relationship in *Suprema Ley* between the writer-educator Gamboa and the artist-educator Eustaquio. The author is establishing his brotherhood of creative teachers as the future fathers of the nation, as opposed to the bureaucrats and politicians in the novel who are mired in apathy and corruption. Such a view is no doubt a reflection of the nineteenth-century belief in education as a cure-all for social problems, but it is also a slight departure from the view held by many positivists who saw art as a childish waste of time.

In *Suprema Ley*, the artist Eustaquio is driven by love for his children, but there is little mention of the woman's role in his actions. This absence contradicts, to a certain extent, the character's own discourse in which he echoes positivist sentiment regarding the moral superiority of the female, including her greater capacity to love children. Taken with the rest of the novel in mind, there does seem to be a suggestion that man should follow woman's moral example with regard to loving children, but he is not necessarily to be "saved" or "redeemed" by her. When Carmen is lauded by the narrator as a Christian woman, "una santa" who, through her acts, compensates the rest of us for the cruel inconsistencies of the world (288), it is, ironically, for accepting the presence of Clotilde in her home, an act that leads to her home's dissolution. Julio Ortegal, rather than seeing salvation in woman, laments in an interior dialogue the fact that man is unable to maintain "el inofensivo socialismo" of childhood; life would be simpler and more natural if people were driven by a thirst for infinite love, "like that of childhood" (260). This attitude seems to support Comte's idea that within the family the child learns altruism, but that his social affections diminish the further he gets, figuratively, from the family, although the individual should always strive to display universal love (Lenzer 271–72). Children, then, can serve both as an example to a parent caught up in the temptations of modern life, as well as a redeeming object of parental love. Childhood is idealized here, representative of the premodern, proto-communist society which it became popular to associate with indigenous cultures in the Americas in the early twentieth century. Amaryll Chanady explains that such an idealization of Indians for the likes of Peruvian José Carlos Mariátegui, "serves the purpose of justifying an anticapitalist ideology" (40). In *Suprema Ley* such idealization serves as an alternative to the wretched life of the father, yet not necessarily to any grand political or economic systems. These "socialist" children are meant to influence the behavior of the parents, not necessarily to instigate a revolution.

Two cases of a father's acknowledgment of his children's moral influence over him are also found in two minor characters in the novel: Apolonio, a man convicted of murder and condemned to death; and a nameless neighborhood guard whom Julio meets near the end of the novel when he is wandering late one night. They are clearly meant to contrast with Julio's selfish indulgence in his love affair, and with his inability to gather the strength to resist the world's temptations for the sake of his children. The two fathers described below are, in a sense, more civilized than Julio by dint of their capacity for redemption at the mere thought of their own children.

Apolonio, whose execution Julio must witness as part of his job, is obsessed with escaping from his predicament, but at the same time thinks continuously of his little son. Apolonio's tale is related in the form of a dialogue with a priest. The condemned man saw his father only a few times, and his mother loved his stepfather more than Apolonio. His initial legal troubles stem from a fight with the stepfather—his mother testified against him in his trial for that crime. Apolonio was able to turn his life around through hard work, but a "revolution" intervened and he was conscripted. During the fighting he learned how to steal, rape and murder, and has been running afoul of the law ever since. When the priest tells him that he should think about his son's future, Apolonio pleads for his son not to follow in his footsteps (281). When the priest relates his own biography, it turns out that he was also an "abandoned" child. He tells Apolonio his life story in an attempt to encourage the condemned man to talk. The priest lived an idyllic country life in Spain until his parents pushed him to go to America to seek his fortune. He notes that when he boarded the ship for the New World he was an "abandoned child" (276). These two characters point up the narrator's belief in the need for parental guidance and the potential danger to society of the abandoned child, but also of the strong investment the individual makes in the child as the hope for a better future.

The second case, that of the guard in Clotilde's neighborhood, is perhaps the most explicitly stated expression of a father's responsibilities and of his ability to love his children. Julio is just winding up a long lament about his own situation, which has put the guard to sleep, when he asks the man whether he has any children. The guard responds that of course he has children, he's poor: "¿No ve usted que soy pobre? ¿Cómo no había de tener hijos?...tengo tres" (451). Julio asks whether he loves them and whether he would give them up for a woman. The guard responds that he loves the children more than he loves their mother, and that he could not give them up because they are not "animals"; in fact, he says, they are his only happiness (451). The guard's sentiments (and later the great show of affection between him and his children) demonstrate Comte's assertion that while it is romantic love that begins the marriage, it is love for one's progeny that maintains it. The guard's use of the comparison of children to animals could also signal Gamboa's acceptance of the concept of free will, and a rejection of the naturalist's acceptance of blind determinism, as well as his recognition of distinctions between man and animal (Lay 51).

It is significant to note, given the positivist emphasis on the woman as the spiritual redeemer of the male, that there is little reference made to the wives in any of the above-mentioned situations in which the author has emphasized the father-child relationship, although there is the implication that they have stood by their men and, in some cases, will live out their lives as faithful widows. Indeed, in Clotilde, by her insistence on keeping alive the memory of her dead lover, and in Carlota, who has lived nearly her entire life as the widow of a *novio*, we see Comtean and Catholic emphasis on the importance of the permanence of marriage. In addition, Carmen does not give up on her husband, on the possibility that he will reform himself and return to her and the children, until he is actually dead.

The minor character Alfredo Berón, in a monologue in the court where he is a prosecutor, seems to epitomize all that is fatalistic in naturalism and positivism with regard to family life. Berón says that children will turn out the way they were meant to turn out whether parents are present or not, and that bandits and prostitutes come from all classes of society; the only thing to be demanded of all parents, he argues, no matter their social class, is that they give their children a scientific education. Science, this lawyer argues, is "a thousand times more moralizing than money." Any man who says he puts up with his life for the love of his family, says Berón, is a liar and a coward (365). Thus, Berón at once is encouraging Ortegal to follow his heart and not worry about his family, and telling him that it is his duty to be sure they are given a scientific education. But since, as noted above, such moralizing education is now supposedly in the hands of the state, Ortegal would appear to be free to follow his egocentric impulses with Clotilde. Gamboa places that moralizing education specifically in the hands of an artist-teacher, thus he does not deny the need for secular education, but he does not place an emphasis on "science" in this work. While parents are fungible—fathers can be replaced—he is obviously pointing to a more humanistic and less scientific "father" than the positivist state.

As noted above, the late Porfiriato was a difficult time for Mexican novelists, as well as other intellectuals educated within the positivist philosophy: The same system that gave them a relatively peaceful environment in which to write also seemed not to have the solutions for their nation's social ills. Criticizing the system might be considered disloyal, so novelists for the most part criticized the way individuals behaved within the system. While we see in Federico Gamboa's *Suprema Ley*, a novelist struggling to reconcile the fatalism of his own naturalism, and that of Mexican positivism, with the positivist assertion that a scientific education and individual initiative will allow a person to realize his full potential for the betterment of society, we also believe he is dealing with the problem of the role of the artist in society.

Gamboa seems to be aware of the hypocrisy of the Mexican elite's positivism and to place hope for a progressive Mexico in the next generation, and in *cristianismo social*. While society's goal might be to produce altruistic individuals, it is love for the next generation—one's progeny—which should be the modifying influence in one's life, not necessarily the guiding morality of the woman. Indeed, although characters in the novel, most notably Eustaquio, laud the female's moral superiority, women are not assigned the task of influencing the grown male's character. Though they do still serve as educators within the home, this aspect of the woman's role is not a great focus of the novel. Rather, the emphasis is on the need for both parents to be involved in the moral education of the children. Hugh Cunningham sees a similar emphasis after the 1860's in Great Britain where childhood was both a "refuge for those wearied by life's struggles and a source of renewal which would enable the adult to carry on. In effect, that is, childhood was a substitute for religion" (151–52). In the often anti-religious perspective of the Latin American positivist, this kind of substitution, similar to that secularization of values which put moral education in the home earlier in the century (and in public schools later), seems reasonable in our reading. This emphasis on the socialism of children, on the state's responsibility for moral education, the fatalism expressed through Berón's monologue in particular and the fact of Clotilde's "fall" in spite of her exemplary upbringing, would all seem to ease considerably the pressure put on the woman to be the moral pillar of society. This would, in turn, relieve her somewhat of the burden of guilt when progeny do not fulfill their social obligations. The woman in this capacity, however, as Pratt notes, is reduced all the more to a mere reproducer of the citizenry ("Brotherhood" 51–52). Warner writes that the "supreme law" of the novel is purported to be romantic love, but that sexual desire is more powerful than the individual's moral code (108). We have tried to show here that while certain characters claim that romantic love is the "supreme law," the overall tenor of the novel is that love for one's progeny *should* be the *ley suprema* of one's life.

Our reading of both novels in this chapter points up the positivists' apparent vision of a family in which biological parents are fungible, easily replaced by Father Las Casas or certain right-thinking supporters of the Crown in Galván's novel, and by an artist-teacher in that of Gamboa. In *Enriquillo* we see that the family is in intense competition with the Crown's authorities for the loyalty of citizens. Galván eliminates the competition, in a sense, so that the major players may make the fraternal relationships necessary for the formation of a new political system. We see in this novel, then, a recognition of the family's strength, and a shift away from the family, in particular away from the maternal role. Jean Franco has noted that "the family has been a powerful rival to the state, somehow more real" ("Killing" 416). While the patriarchal family is deeply rooted in Latin society and has served to perpetuate the social order, and thus is due the feminist criticism it has attracted, "such criticism has perhaps underestimated the oppositional potentialities of these female territories whose importance as the *only* [Franco's italics] sanctuaries became obvious at the moment of their disappearance" ("Killing" 420). We can see from our reading of these two novels that the attack against these "immune spaces" was underway before the beginning of the twentieth century.

The component parts of the family in *Suprema Ley* are replaceable as well. The mother is as passive as she was in *Enriquillo*. The children in both works, the infantilized Indian and the progeny of the low-level bureaucrat, hold together the narratives as they represent the nation's hope for the future. While not the victim of the violent invasions of twentieth-century military regimes, in a sense the home in these two works had already lost its immunity to the ideological pressures of the positivist historians, writers and statesmen who depicted it. These writers attempt, however, to give a new home to these children of national foundation and national reassessment. Whereas in Steedman's study the child Mignon does not find a home—and that is the source of the perpetual nostalgia surrounding her (41–42)—Galván has located a domestic space for Enriquillo in Hispanic culture and the Dominican countryside, and Gamboa's children find shelter and love in the urban home of an artist-teacher. These domestic spaces are refuges for the nation's progeny, and are resources, in a sense, for the writing of the nation's origins, or new beginnings. Our next chapter makes a closer examination of such competition between the family and the state for the allegiance of children in several twentieth-century works.

NOTES

[1]As we shall see later, this idea is analogous to the description of the life cycle as stages. Childhood was one of three (usually) stages in such descriptions, with the end of it signaling the beginning of decay. Thus in biological thought and in social thought, the end of childhood or youth could signify the beginning of the end of a productive, growing body, whether that body was a living being or a community.

[2]The Mexican Miguel S. Macedo echoed Comte's philosophy regarding the role of women in society. He posited that in all relationships there is a superior and an inferior being. Macedo also notes the existence of superior-inferior relationships based on intelligence and "practical force." Among these he cites that the rich are superior to the poor because the former have the means to work for the public good, whereas the poor are concerned only with survival. No one should interfere with someone involved in such beneficent works, such interference would be a "lack of respect" due the superior (Zea 174–76).

[3]In an example from Mexico, Sylvia Arrom (1985) shows how this preference for economic flexibility was reflected in changes in the civil code which (1) recognized the importance of the woman's domestic educational tasks by giving widows more control over their children and their inheritance, (2) lowered the age at which a child could marry without pa-

rental consent and at which a single woman could take control of her personal financial affairs and leave home, and (3) eliminated the *décima*, which previously had required an equal division among the surviving children of any inheritance from a deceased parent.

[4]We will return to this theme later in this volume when we explore the relationships between authors, writing and childhood. This conflict between the debt one owes to ones precursors and one's struggle to be free of their conventions is a major theme of the critical work of Juan Gelpí, and also is a preoccupation of the protagonist of Julio Cortázar's *Rayuela*.

[5]Such brotherly negotiations and functions remind one of cell theory, which became well dispersed during the mid-nineteenth century. Cells came to be seen as individuals, building blocks, working harmoniously together to form the whole organism (Steedman 56–57). If we remember the organic societal models of this time period, we see how the fraternal relationship could be seen as a social parallel to cell theory.

[6]This has implications for the study of the political and military instability of nineteenth- and twentieth-century Latin America. We might view such struggles as fraternal fights for control after the loss of the colonial "father." These brotherly machinations, rather than seeming chaotic, may feel "comforting," as noted above, and natural.

[7]Franco Moretti makes this point regarding European literature, noting that the Bildungsroman is a "'comfort of civilisation' because of the way in which it uses historical explanation to make the world a homeland—a place to be at home in—for its characters and its readers" (Steedman 78).

[8]It is perhaps significant that she is an only child, whereas Julio and his wife have several children.

CHAPTER TWO

Confused Allegiances: The State Versus The Family in the
Battle for Childhood: Salarrué, Reinaldo Arenas, Julio Cortázar,
Alfredo Bryce Echenique, Cristina Peri Rossi, Isabel Allende

> ...we must ... take control of the con-
> sciousness of the youth, because it ...
> must belong to the revolution .... The
> reactionaries mislead us when they
> claim that the child belongs to the
> home, and the youth to the family; ...
> it is the revolution which has a com-
> pelling obligation towards the con-
> sciousness, to banish prejudice and to
> form the national soul.
> —Plutarco Elías Calles[1]

In Jean Franco's discussion of several mid-twentieth-century Mexican literary and cinematic works, she makes the point that the independent, "mas-

culinized" woman must be integrated into the holy family of the nation, characterized by a subordinate female, but subordinate now to the paternal state, not to a biological father (*Plotting* 147–48). One of the ideological problems Franco underscores in her chapter "Oedipus Modernized," is "how to uphold [the] need for family life without sacrificing revolutionary nationalism" (151–52). She notes in the film "Los Olvidados" ("The Forgotten"), for example, that all of the characters, except the victim, Julián, are fatherless, and the state finds itself attempting to become a surrogate father (154). In these works, women are aligned with the cycles of nature, and modernization exacerbates this problematic linkage by lodging paternal functions in the state. Woman then comes to represent a "Trojan horse" for the state, however, as she is the desire and "mothering" that the state cannot provide (158). Franco's comments here show a continuation of the displacement of the role of mother in the family, and in the perception of the state's role in one's life. We outlined this displacement in Chapter One, where we noted the prominence of fictive fraternal and paternal relationships, in particular the former, over those of biological parents, especially the maternal relationship. The works of Galván and Gamboa strongly support, and we would add that Galván's lays the foundations for, a nation based on a fluid, diverse family structure in which biological parents are highly fungible. This would seem reasonable given the positivist underpinnings of the late-nineteenth century when function, and scientific cause and effect were to reign over the more nebulous, less reliable and romantic governance by the emotions or the spiritual; in such an atmosphere, allegiance to the state or to some other institution, or to whomever can provide for one's well-being, would take precedence over allegiance to one's parents or other family members.

In the works to be examined in this chapter, we see twentieth-century authors who take several stances with regard to the child and the family while exploring this battle between the state and the family over control of the child, and indeed over control of the concept of childhood. In some works, such as Peri Rossi's stories, there is an impressive criticism of a regime's expropriation of the family and of its politicization of family ideology, in the state's drive for power and control in society; in others, such as Arenas's novel of 1950's Cuba, we see a desperate uncovering of the evils committed by family members under an oppressive socio-economic and political system. Some works criticize the entire idea of the family[2], whereas others, such as the Bryce Echenique novel *La Vida Exagerada de Martín Romaña* (1985) (*The Exaggerated Life of Martín Romaña*), recognize the family's value, criticizing its use by political regimes as a means of control, and also, perhaps, its at times stifling control over the artistic development of the individual. The state may be perceived as a parent in such works; not necessarily as a caregiver, but rather as an all-powerful patriarch and/or cooperative brother, or as an abusive relative. There is a rejection in such critical works of the nation's insistence on fictive fraternity over real familial relationships, a rejection of the state's expropriation of familial relationships, but not necessarily a rejection of the nature of traditional familial ties themselves. Most of the works treated here, we would argue, do not support the idea that biological parents, or even the traditional family structure, are replaceable. Indeed, for all its faults, the family is the place where the individual learns, and may also challenge, societal norms (Lomnitz and Pérez-Lizaur 9–10). As the anthropologist Oscar Lewis writes:

> The family is the natural unit for the study of the satisfactions, frustrations, and maladjustments of individuals who live under a specific type of family organization; the reactions of the individuals to expected behavior patterns; the effects of conformity or deviation upon the development of the personality. (86)

Kuznesof and Oppenheimer see the Latin American family as the "central complex of relationships through which political, entrepreneurial, and agrarian history may be viewed to make societal sense out of seemingly impersonal phenomena" (220).[3] Thus, the family and the individual's dealings within it are of interest to the historian. The family is also the place where the artist first experiments with the violation of boundaries, and with attempts to understand the complex web of relationships which form a family and may serve as a training ground of sorts for efforts to comprehend the greater society. The family is important to the author if for no other reason than its role as something against which to write, an oppressive regime which had previously stifled his or her expression.

The above-mentioned battle for childhood, for the allegiance of the individual to entities such as the state or the family, has a very long history. Indeed, since the inception of the modern nation-state, political hierarchies have battled over such allegiances. Ferdinand Mount traces the history of these "family-haters" from Plato to the contemporary period. He calls the family the "ultimate and only consistently subversive organization" as it undermines the state and is the enemy of all hierarchies (1). Mount outlines how the state attempts to downgrade the importance of the family, but then co-opts family ideology, thus accepting the enduring importance of the family and giving it a high place in its dogma. The state then goes on to define what is good for the family, and to link acts of patriotism to family preservation (3–4, 38–39). Mount says that it is the emotional ties between parent and child, and between spouses, which are dangerous to the survival of the state, though we would add that it is also the family's propensity to incite its youth to rebel and to seek freedom which also poses a danger. Socrates in Plato's *Republic* notes these split loyalties, saying that devotion to the family is selfish, as is devotion to the self, and that both come at the expense of the wider community (Mount 42–43). In Latin America, the Catholic Church, the Crown, and later the modern political regimes, have confronted each other on the domestic level. The Spanish colonial rulers, for example, tried hard to limit the power of the "conquistadores" and their families in order to limit political competition; the Catholic church selectively enforced its free-will edict where the selection of marriage partners was concerned; and politicians, as the above quotation by Calles demonstrates, unabashedly have declared their right to the allegiance of the nation's youth, declaring the state's "holy family," to use Jean Franco's term, superior to the traditional domestic unit. In that "feminine" space of the home, however, the family breeds resistance to such rhetoric: "Families thus inherited opposition as others inherited positions in the government and bureaucracy" (Franco, "Killing" 414).

In such battles, children find themselves caught in the middle, of course. Florencia Mallón, for example, has described how such a conflict festers and plays itself out in provincial Mexico where she sees "democratic patriarchy" developing in the early twentieth century, thanks to the state's ability to exploit generational conflict in the villages (19–20). A principal point of contention in these situations is the conflict between the ideologies presented in public education versus those taught in the home or the traditional community. Vaughan has noted the way the introduction of female teachers in rural Mexico, for example, threatened the local patriarchy, when the state's great hope for universal education was to recruit disciples for the new nationalism (106–7). Not unlike the children who dared to bury teachers murdered during the Cristero War in Mexico (see Rockwell), the nation's progeny find themselves forced to choose among church, state, family and individual expression. Insanally and Godoy Gallardo emphasize that war leads to a nostalgia for childhood, thus in post-war literature they expect to see a greater preoccupation with that life stage, especially as authors recuperate some idyllic past to compare with the trauma of war and its aftermath (Insanally 36–37; Godoy Gallardo 9–10). Our analysis, however, makes clear the ubiquitousness of the choices noted above, whether the nation faces an armed conflict or is simply debating moral values. After a brief explanation of some of the underlying ideology of the Latin American family, we will examine below how authors have explored these difficult choices.

One of the major principles underlying Latin American family ideology is that "parents represent God on earth vis-à-vis their children." Parents have a "divine mission" in the raising of children and are therefore responsible for their offspring's physical and moral deficiencies. Godparents, aunts, uncles and other members of the kin network share in the parents' mission and responsibilities, and are to receive from the children the respect and obedience accorded to parents (de la Peña 204–6, 210–12, 225). There are inherent contradictions in this and other principles outlined by de la Peña, including the idea that paternal love should be equal for all progeny, when in fact the eldest is often favored over the younger children, and males are favored over females (210–12, 228). Mount notes another contradiction in that the Church has consistently insisted on the supremacy of one's love of God over that shown one's spouse or progeny. Confessor's manuals of the seventeenth century, for example, encouraged friendship between parents and children, but not love. Parents would be "like monkeys" if they loved their children too much; only God is to be loved immoderately and boundlessly (23–25). Mount argues that the Protestants, on the other hand, instigated the Reformation, in part, out of a rejection of celibacy; the Puritans saw marriage as a better or fuller way to glorify God (19–20).

Additionally, the Latin American family's reality is often a far cry from the ideal established in the ideology. Families are often in flux, rarely "complete," in the sense that they may not be models of nuclear or extended families. They fit well the family organizations described by Rivera:

> The reality is so fluid that it may defy classification...[for] the nuclear family is a knot in a network of blood relationships. There is...a continuing transformation of the nuclear into the extended family, and vice versa. It is not unusual for members to drop into other nuclear families for extended periods (57).

Add to this the apparently growing preference in Latin America for mutual aid among acquaintances rather than hierarchical and authoritarian positions among kin (de la Peña 229), and the long-standing Latin tradition of *compadrazgo* and its ability to increase one's familial network, and we find ourselves in a complex world when we attempt to speak of the "Latin American family." More importantly for our study, these inherent contradictions and this acceptance of such fluid relationships, like those outlined in Chapter One, would seem to make more acceptable the idea of the state as family in Latin America.

Indeed, according to Gelpí, in the rhetoric of nationalism, the paternal figure's subordinates are infantilized creating a parent-child relationship. The "infants" are often turned into pupils so that the pedantic paternal voice may dominate and indoctrinate them. He becomes a "figura tutelar" (2, 90). As we have shown with Galván in Chapter One, some writers, seek the lost father in nationalistic writing, a paternal and magisterial voice "who will dictate a story to a group of young men" (Gelpí 24). The children, or figurative infants of paternalistic nationalism, are to be mute, docile, and faithful. This hierarchy allows the leader of the moment to proclaim himself (or his party, as in the case of the PRI in Mexico) the nation's figurative father. (In these writings, colonialism, neo-colonialism, and vestiges of European colonialism are all associated with illness, the other great metaphor of nationalistic writing) (Gelpí 7). The writings of both the left and the right in 1970's Chile, for example, make use of these metaphors. Both Augusto Pinochet and Salvador Allende claimed that their actions and policies would benefit the Chilean family, the backbone of the society and "culture," whereas their opponents' ideologies were characterized as specifically meant to destabilize the family (Loveman and Davies 427, 433).

The right is especially vehement in reclaiming for itself a role as protector of the nation and the family, which it considers to be one in the same. The Pinochet regime's 1981 constitution, for example, proscribed "all parties and movements spreading doctrines undermining the family..." (Loveman and Davies 427), and Pinochet's own words from a 1975 speech emphasize family in explaining the regime's concept of liberty:

> Freedom is an innate attribute of man which enables the human being to defend the inviolability of his own conscience, as well as to exercise the right of unconfined choice for himself and his family, free from the oppressive interference of the state. (Loveman and Davies 244)

Perhaps the most explicit expression of this concept from contemporary military leaders is found in a 1980 speech by the Argentine General Leopoldo Fortunato Galtieri, one of the leaders later jailed for his role in that country's "Dirty War":

> The entire country knows and should not forget, I repeat, the entire country knows and should not forget, that in that dark period of terror and crime—during which sons were indoctrinated to assassinate their parents—parents abandoned their children in order to engage in criminal nihilism, and Argentine families were the innocent victims of an unmerciful aggression and a systematic attempt at dissolution of the family. (Loveman and Davies 201)

Galtieri raises the specter of parricide and infanticide in his comments, acts which would violate moral values as well as signal a state of chaos for Argentine society. Controlling adults is clearly not enough, the regime must exercise control over the nation's youth for parents cannot be trusted with that all-important task. We emphasize in our analysis the tension between oligarchic powers and parents in their struggles to control children and the family, and how family members react under that pressure. We investigate the inherent contradiction between the hierarchical requirements of the politics of nationalism, where subordinates are infantilized, and the valorization of the innocence and creative potential of the child; the latter always seems to be sacrificed to the former, even as it is said to be supported by the nationalist politics. We will first consider the confusion of real parents with those figured parents from the oligarchy in two stories by Salarrué.

In Salarrué's "El Padre" and "El Maishtro," we see two local representatives of sectors of the oligarchy—a priest, representing the Catholic Church, and a teacher, the state's most visible representative at the local level—whose roles as fathers become confused by sexual desire. The spiritual incest committed by these two can be read as an indictment of the oligarchy's usurpation of familial roles, an acknowledgment that these self-proclaimed fictive kin are capable of violating their charges. In "El Padre," the reader is led to believe that a priest has had sexual relations with a young adolescent whom he has raised in his home. We say "led to believe" because from the story it is impossible to know for sure whether the priest's sexual desires were consummated. It is also difficult to ascertain the girl's feelings about the relationship; the child's silence stands out as we are left straining to understand exactly what has happened, and we find ourselves with only the priest's emotional, yet vague lamentations. The author signals a confusion in the roles of father, lover and priest when the cleric, interrogated by the bishop, responds that he just had a "vague desire to be a father," and that the girl is like a daughter to him. (103) It is possible that he is expressing a long-held desire to have a daughter, or that he has always tried to treat the girl as his own child. We do not know from the text whether he regrets his actions, or whether he might even be trying to justify them. The priest's words can also be read as a sign of his confusion regarding his, and the Church's, role as a figured father in society. The silence of the girl in the narrative contributes to the ambiguous meanings. Carolyn Steedman writes that the silence of such child-figures as Goethe's Mignon is a tool of melodrama, and is interpreted in the twentieth century, in the reader's search for such drama (and under the influence of Freud), as evidence of sexual abuse: "We know by the sign of her silence that damage has been done to her" (164). We believe Salarrué puts the girl's silence to a similar use, melodramatically leaving the reader to assume that the spiritual incest has occurred. The author has thus worked a double ambiguity in that the girl's silence is coupled with the vagueness of the "father's" words.

There is a similar confusion of roles in the tale "El Maishtro" ("The Teacher"). An elderly teacher is the friend of a neighbor's daughter. One day the old man comes to his garden, tired from a long day at school. The relationship between the man and the girl seems to be one of simple friendship, until the teacher begins to feel sexual desire for her: He becomes sexually stimulated while reading the girl's palm. At the point of telling her of his feelings, he suddenly feels his age and, with "paternal sweetness," tells her so: "Volvió a correr por sus dientes una miel paternal y dijo, señalando con firmeza: ¡Eso, eso, hija mía..., es el río del tiempo...'" (125). The narrator shows us that the girl was "hopelessly nailed to her spot" as the old man spoke and read her palm, giving the impression of the child's vulnerability. Once again, it is unclear whether the teacher has realized that he has over-stepped his bounds and blames such a transgression on his old age, or whether he regrets that he cannot produce the romantic words—or sexual deeds—because of his age.

In any case, in "El Padre" and "El Maishtro," while the vulnerability of the children is clear, there is a powerful sense of ambiguity in these relation-ships with regard to the males' perception of right and wrong. The desire that these men feel for the girls collides with their roles as father figures, setting up a moral dilemma whose resolution, at least in the males' minds, the text leaves open to interpretation. The endings of both stories seem to be remind-ers, however, of the males' responsibilities as figured fathers: The priest is interrogated by his superior, thus signaling official disapproval of the relation-ship; and the teacher's desires recede as he feels his age, his words then reaf-firming the father-daughter aspect of their relationship. Salarrué's writing in this regard can be read as pointing up the dangers of the state's use of such familial rhetoric, and of the oligarchy's displacement of the family. It is sig-nificant that actual incest does not occur in the collection, only this spiritual incest. We believe that Salarrué sees the latter as somehow more destructive due to its implications for the broader society; although the violation of trust inherent in real incest may be more significant on an individual or familial level, it is this spiritual incest which warns the reader of the falseness of the oligarchy's expropriation of familial roles, and of the weakness of the extra-familial ties. The girls' relative silence aligns them with other "figured chil-dren" of the patriarchy who are required to remain mute and faithful. It is interesting that in the two Salarrué stories the children's biological fathers are absent, thus there is a lack of biological paternal authority (see our Chapter Three for a more expansive treatment of this Salarrué anthology). There is no apparent confrontation between the regime and parents, but rather the sub-stitution described above, which leaves the figured fathers in an easily con-strued, ambiguous relationship with the girls. Though the text does not refer directly to the missing biological fathers, it is clear that their absence leaves open a power and desire vacuum into which the state's figured fathers insert themselves. Such a substitution at the domestic level, and the ambiguity with which it is presented, easily disturbs the reader. The implications for the na-tion of such a substitution are equally disconcerting, as these figured fathers have the paternal authority to enter the domestic sphere and to demand obedience and to inspire silence, yet they are not bound by the incest taboo. Their spiritual incest, however, signifies in our reading a violation of trust on the personal and national levels, and seems to say that the usurpation of familial rhetoric by the state will result in the violation of what Franco has called those "immune" spaces. The next work to be considered, Reinaldo Arenas's novel *El Palacio de las Blanquísimas Mofetas* (1975), has as a major theme the absence of paternal authority and the search to recover it.

Roberto Valero notes this absence of paternal authority and this search in Arenas's work (136). In our reading, however, there is no such absence because paternal authority is present in the numerous flashbacks to the childhoods of the characters explored by Fortunato, the protagonist. The ultimate authority of the male father figure is an overriding presence; therefore, even though the male parent may not be present physically, his absence makes paternal authority a preoccupation of the protagonist and the personages he occupies. It is possible to read, however, the narrator's comment that there are no longer big trees around the old family homestead, only small, "twisted" ones that do not give enough shade to protect a person from the sun (77–78), as a lamentation on the lack of right-living, protective males in the present. This would indicate a certain nostalgia for a time of positive paternal presence, but the only other descriptions of the past in which a father has a significant role are rife with abuse and abandonment; thus, it is not clear whether there ever was a paternal authority other than the violent, oppressive one that Polo represents, or the neglectful, absent one represented by Fortunato's own father and uncles. We read in *El Palacio* not so much a lack of paternal authority, as a lack of paternal—and maternal—*affection*. The authority of the male is present if only in what the society says the male should be, if only in the description of the male's power. Paternal authority bases its power, in this novel, in violence, intimidation and the freedom to leave; not in justice or love—it is a cold, morally empty authority, but it is not absent. Fortunato's search, then, is not for a paternal authority, but rather for a flesh and blood manifestation of the ideal father. He believes he has found that body in the person of an officer who orders the protagonist's torture and murder. This officer completes a cycle of abandonment by males that Fortunato experiences throughout the novel, both in the first person, as well as vicariously through his empathetic assumption of the histories of other characters. The cycle begins with Polo's father hanging dead in a tree, is continued by the abandonment of the cousins, and that of Fortunato, and is followed by Polo's abandonment through silence. The novel does not attempt to re-write the nation's beginnings with a new figured father, as we have seen in Galván's work, but only points out the deceptiveness of the father's presence, or lack thereof. In the end, Fortunato's locating of a paternal figure in the army officer translates to the boy's death, a clear warning, as we have also seen in Salarrué's stories, against such a displacement.

The novel, besides underscoring the emptiness and danger of society's emphasis on paternal authority, also lampoons, or laments, depending on one's sense of humor, the society's overburdening of women with the responsibilities and empty promises of child rearing and marriage. Valero says that the desolation of the novel is concentrated in these lower-class women (111). Indeed, as we see in Fortunato's empathetic flashbacks, they are severely abused, physically and psychologically. Later, their attitudes toward children reflect the frustrations of these women. One of the narrators notes how his mother knows only how to embarrass him in front of other people (18–19). Fortunato's grandmother berates him for being effeminate, lazy and for secluding himself, noting that it would be better if he were not alive, given his state: "Qué haces acostado a estas alturas. Zanaco, encerrado como una mujer. So babieca, so faino, so marica [...] De todos modos como vives es igual que si no lo hicieras" (20). His grandmother later calls him "a piece of meat with an eye" (102–3).

The point here is that neither father nor mother seems capable of nurturing children, with the exception of Celia, who was close to her daughter Esther; however, even in this lone case of parent-child intimacy, the family seeks to destroy the happiness between mother and daughter (65–66). We read the novel as blaming such a failure of the family on the frustrations caused by the difficulties of life in the countryside[4] and later in the alienating city; but, the failure is also blamed on the over reliance on the image of the paternal authority: The family is no match for the economics of industrialization, urbanization and large-scale farming, or for the myth of the stability of patriarchy. (As the narrator says, their hunger is so great that they have begun to eat each other (12).) Elena Poniatowska, writing about Mexico, notes a possible purpose behind that reliance on the dominant male that we see in this Arenas novel: What would become of the nation, she asks, without this father who disguises himself so that everyone else might hide their true faces as well? (34). Fortunato's empathetic activities and his ability to become a voice for the other members of the family is an attempt to break free of that reliance on the abstract patriarch as the front for the entire family, indeed for the society. As one of the cousins says sarcastically during a more ludicrous moment in the novel, significantly, a playful theatrical segment: "aquí tienen a la gran familia" (363) as the doors swing open into the family's home. Adolfina asks what one could possibly expect from a family of islanders, from people who live amongst the beasts (12). Fortunato, in the end, turns away from that family, from his writing, which had served "as a means to survive the continual state of oppression he faces from his family, as well as [his] town" (Soto, 62), and toward the army in an attempt to give shape to that abstract authority, with fatal results.

The boy cannot look to an older generation for guidance, there is no "figura tutelar" as Gelpí says, to serve as mentor. Indeed, the expectation is that children will grow up to kill their parents, and there is some fantasizing to that end in the novel, while parents also attempt to kill their children. In the "Fifth Agony" of the novel, Fortunato remembers a story that his grandmother used to tell him, a story in which a boy kills his father, who had "tricked" the boy's mother, and thus the boy becomes a man, a son who knows how to love: "Así hacen los hijos que saben amar" (260), the grandmother would say. The promise of the nurturing mother is demystified as well, and there is nearly equal denigration of mothers, as Adolfina comments that the world has been "adrift" ever since the invention of motherhood (169). She also was the hated second mother for her siblings when she aged and did not leave home. In this role as a substitute mother, as someone "useful" and worthy of scorn, she is detested like "all substitutes" (30). We see that at the extra-domestic, political level, then, fathers are not fungible, and on the domestic level mothers are not either. There is a painful awareness in this novel of a nostalgia for something that has never really existed: The nurturing, stable, traditional family. The protagonist's empathetic journeys back into the childhoods of his fellow family members serve to underscore the real absence of this omnipresent ideal; and he discovers in the process that even childhood is a lie, that the grand return to the site of childhood is at best disappointing, and at worst nightmarish.

When the Cuban revolution of the late 1950's makes an appearance in the novel, the point is made that a young Fortunato must decide between his family and the rebels. Choosing to rebel is more than a political act directed against a government. A mother tries to make him feel guilty by saying that his mother will fall apart when she finds out that he has joined the rebellion. She tells of young people who denounce each other, or even their parents, to the government (306-7), thus signaling a time of distrust, and a search for what we have noted above as a physical manifestation of the paternal authority. It could be argued that once Fortunato has thoroughly investigated his family members' pasts, he ventures forth to locate some form of the ideal family in the revolution itself, in a new regime. He decides to stop being a child and to try to free himself from the house and become a man.

Fortunato is easily captured in his attempt to steal a guard's gun. In the holding cell after his capture, he has become an important person, worthy of the attention, even the work, of several men (384). As a child, as an adolescent, as the writer, the factory worker, the son, the grandson, he was unworthy of such attention. But, as they torture him, he is the most important person on earth. Interestingly, Fortunato fixates on the lieutenant in charge of his torturers. It might seem that he seeks paternal authority in the officer, as he is called the "only man" amongst that group, but Fortunato also draws our attention to the soldiers as being "machines" (386–87). He seems to imply that the lieutenant is capable of sentiment, while the soldiers are not; or, perhaps, it is that as the paternal authority, Fortunato expects—or hopes—that to be the case. Tragically, he dies at the hands of the soldiers, at first being abandoned by the lieutenant, just as he has been abandoned before. The lieutenant does not adequately replace the physically absent paternal figure; the father is not replaceable; and if we see the paternal/familial ideal as reality, we find that it is not fungible either, as Fortunato does not locate a substitute for it in revolutionary ideology.

Neither pre-revolutionary society nor the revolution itself has valued the young writer, nor have they valued the children whose histories he has brought to the fore through his empathetic narrative; there is no benevolent dictator here, no "figura tutelar." Both social systems have stifled the young writer's, and others', efforts at self-expression. Francisco Soto notes that this oppression of creativity is a dominant theme of Arenas's writing:

> . . .one thing remains constant in the protagonist [of the author's "quintet" of works]: an unwavering defense of individual creativity. This positive spirit indomitably rebels against all hierarchical systems of power that attempt to prevent or limit human creativity. (60)

Reinaldo Arenas utilizes childhood to trace the history of that oppression and of the individual's struggle against it. He demonstrates just how trapped we are by the "lie" of the romantic childhood; for this protagonist there is no idyllic childhood to recuperate when faced with an unpleasant present reality; there is nothing but trauma out of which to build the nation. Fortunato even abuses the ideal, imaginary child he creates in his fantasies. The battle for childhood, for the control of the next generation and for the memory of childhood, leaves the child traumatized. The reader suspects that trauma is behind the silence of the child (Steedman 164), and this novel attempts to give voice to that child.

In the next two works to be considered, Julio Cortázar's *Rayuela* and Alfredo Bryce Echenique's *La Vida Exagerada de Martín Romaña*, we examine the perceptions of childhood and family among Latin American intellectuals who are engaged in youthful revolutionary exercises in Europe. Both novels present the problem of the intellectual who tries to escape from the inherited paradigms of bourgeois culture, principally its family life and literature. We find that just as Fortunato does not locate a substitute for family within revolutionary ideology, neither do the projects of these two novels escape the constraints of paternalism. We read *Rayuela* as, ultimately, a paternal text which, in its search for the perfect reader (and originality of expression) must finally turn to paternity itself—the creation of the child-like figure of Oliveira at the end of the novel, and of an omnipresent baby, Rocamadour, throughout the text—in order to bring the project to a close. *La Vida Exagerada* similarly realizes the inescapability of the paternal paradigm, but the protagonist chooses to exploit its positive points and to avoid, through exile, his re-insertion into its banal hierarchy; Martín Romaña, however, never abandons the past entirely. Jean Franco has noted that in Cortázar's work "individuals [are] bound by friendship not by the social practice of the workplace; and revolution is the combination of a series of individual decisions" rather than a cooperative project driven by a common ideal ("Crisis" 17). *La Vida Exagerada*, on the other hand, stresses the interconnectedness of individual exploration and the social order. While Cortázar's Oliveira believes that it is possible to free himself from paradigms and from the past that created them, Martín Romaña, on the other hand, accepts the inevitability of the past and of hierarchies, and struggles with the search for a niche from which he can practice his self-expression.

Alfredo Bryce Echenique may have realized the validity of Franco's analysis of the new novelists of the 1960's. She finds that they are, in a sense, behind the times as they continue to write against a "bourgeois stereotype" that actually valued the qualities, "the mobile, the gratuitousness, the infinitely changeable," which the authors themselves were utilizing in their writing. Bryce Echenique seems to realize that, as Franco says about Cortázar, Sarduy and Fuentes:

> To attack such an individual is anachronistic at the present time when the global system has taken on quite different characteristics. The dominant ideology is now reproduced in every facet of daily life, in the very pursuit of pleasure. It encourages the setting up of private worlds but sets taboos around politics, compartmentalizes information and, in general, flourishes on the suppression of history. ("Crisis" 22)

We shall examine how family and childhood are implicated in the works considered here as part of the battle for childhood within the intellectual sphere.

As we will explore more profoundly in Chapter Four, we read in *Rayuela* the death of Rocamadour as an attempt to recreate the child through Oliveira's "letters to Rocamadour." Cortázar sets up what for us is a major paradox in *Rayuela*, that of the intellectual who flees from family and children, but who becomes a father figure for his pupils, for his molded child-readers. The (pseudo-)intellectuals of "el grupo" of *La Vida Exagerada* and "el club de la serpiente" in *Rayuela* consider the child to be a hindrance to their creativity and their "revolutionary" activities. The members of the two circles of friends are participating in a long tradition among artists, ascetics, philosophers and the religious who consider the family to be a competitor for the faithfulness of their members. Ferdinand Mount concludes, regarding the adult artist's relationship with the family, that "artists simply cannot afford to dissipate on spouse and children their scant resources of time, emotion and concentration, which must be exclusively devoted to their art" (157). Leaders of utopian movements have expressed their resentment for the "selfishness" of the family, which competes with the utopian hierarchy and ideals. As the narrator says in *Rayuela* when Morelli is run over by a car: "No tiene familia, es un escritor" (238). Even when he finds himself in a domestic arrangement, the artist seems indifferent to it; he participates in a "public" dialogue, in public places, with other artists and often ignores in his works the family which surrounds him (Mount 153–56; and see Puleo 205; and Franco, "Julio" 115). The inherent contradiction and ultimate frustration of attempting to create a reader with the innocence, open-mindedness and incorruptibility of the child, while at the same time distancing oneself from family and children, is apparent.

In *La Vida Exagerada* we see one of the paradoxes of this attitude toward the family as it becomes difficult, even for the young intellectuals in Paris, to ignore its presence. During a party, for example, as Martín narrates, the women care for their babies:

> . . . no tenían con quien dejar a los futuros hijos de la revolución, los que ya crecerían sin ninguno de los traumas burgueses de los que yo parecía víctima insalvable, los traían en ataditos andinos sobre la espalda y los colocaban en una especie de barriadita que se instalaba en algún rincón de la fiesta. Era enternecedor el asunto . . . . (127)

Children are a burden (Inés mentions that it is impossible for a female guerrilla to carry one), the partygoers do not want them there and they separate them into a "kind of slum." However, these children are the very beings who would live in the utopian future; they are future revolutionary leaders; these are the children for whom the revolutionaries supposedly struggle. At the same time, Martín alludes to the fact that if there were a place to leave the children, they would not have to be brought to the party, but only the bourgeoisie, or some utopian commune, could provide such a child-care facility. At this point, however, the members, would not condone the bourgeois lifestyle, and the communal paradise they seek does not exist. Those young intellectuals will end up as stalwarts of the bourgeoisie, as they find it impossible to convert "the individual lifestyle into revolutionary movement or even into a significant transgression of the present," as Franco says regarding

Cortázar's work ("Crisis" 22). Indeed, the separation of the children into a "kind of slum," reflects not only the intellectuals' inability to integrate children into the revolutionary lifestyle, it also presages their future participation in a class system upon returning to their own nations. In Chapter Three we will explore further this concept of viewing children as a separate class, as well as the use of children as representatives of the marginalized.

While the revolutionaries (and Oliveira) in both novels would like to avoid paternal responsibilities, Martín would gladly accept the role of father, although he recognizes its inherent difficulties. As he says in the autobiography he writes for his psychiatrist, it is more difficult to fulfill the responsibilities of "father," than those of "daddy" (129). He pays homage, in a sense, to those who take on those more mundane requirements of a parent such as the setting of limits and the financial support of the family, and who accept the pain of parenting. While the young revolutionaries have tried to forget everything related to their families—"no recordaban a nadie por ninguna parte, no se les había perdido nada, no recordaban nada, y no habían sufrido nunca por nadie" (129)—the young Martín has attempted to maintain alive his memories and to reconcile himself with them, utilizing them in his present life and guarding them for the future. The quotations above show that Martín recognizes that it is possible to respect and love one's parents and ancestors without necessarily agreeing with all aspects of their lives, even their more odious characteristics. We note this as well in Martín's response to Inés's criticism of the Romaña family:

> Francamente me dolió. Que mi bisabuelo y mi tatarabuelo fueran ladrones de plusvalías, de acuerdo.... Pero yo a mi abuelo lo quise muchísimo, y mi padre acababa de morir [...] Inés, ya sé que hace cosa de una semana que dejaste de creer en el abate Pierre y en el cielo. Pero te aseguro que si todavía hay cielo, mi padre y mi abuelo se fueron derechito de la cama al cielo, con plusvalía y todo. (116–17)

Earlier in the novel, we see some of the hypocritical and elitist attitudes of his family, particularly of his father, which Martín dislikes (95). Toward the end of the novel, Dr. Llobera, Martín's psychiatrist, applauds his client's more mature, balanced attitude toward the family: Que no le vengan a decir a quien ha escrito una frase así que no ha tomado sus distancias frente a su familia. Y que tampoco se la insulten, porque precisamente usted ha establecido un equilibrio ante ella que no excluye un afecto natural. (517–18). This "equilibrium" reflects Martín's acceptance of the family as an integral part of western society that one cannot deny by simply considering it to be evil, or the source of all evil, and writing against it. Martín Romaña does not have a family with Inés, but he does wish to have one. The balance that Martín strikes with regard to his family is much more complex than the explicit rejection of the bourgeois family attempted by his cohorts. He praises certain individuals from his family and does not denounce the emotional ties he has with them. His stance does not attempt to wipe the slate clean, but rather is more of an effort at reconciliation. Martín's ability to accept the past, his family's bourgeois history, while at the same time making an effort to transcend it, is not well accepted by his more radical cohorts. Martín Romaña appears to realize that the trip to Europe for all of the young Latin American revolutionaries, and their concomitant *temporary* rejection of bourgeois life, is actually part of modern bourgeois life, just as the mobility and propensity for change that Franco identifies in these novelists are actually qualities valued by the contemporary bourgeoisie. Upon returning to their homelands, these young revolutionaries will take positions in the oligarchy and buy homes in the suburbs; whereas Martín will continue to live in exile where he might keep writing. He remains truer to his criticism of society and of family life as he would like to have a family, but is not able to accept re-integration as his cohorts do.

Martín's character contrasts with that of the mainstream intellectuals who appear in the two novels. He instead reflects more closely the romantics' ideals in that he attempts to keep alive his child-like qualities of spontaneity and creativity. The romantics also delighted in observing and admiring their children; they not only found inspiration in the child, but they also described and were worried about the children's daily life struggles, both successful and failed. In spite of his "familial" pangs, however, Martín does not create a family with Inés; he has no children of his own to observe. Like Morelli, he remains childless, although perhaps for different reasons. While the intellectuals of the two circles described in the novels do not want to live under the weight of the responsibilities of the bourgeois family, for Martín it would be practically impossible to live with a family: While society needs and desires artists, it is often difficult to live with them. We see repeatedly how Martín finds "exaggerated situations" (and "infantile," we would add, since exaggeration is one of the characteristics of artists and children) wherever he goes; but only another artist, perhaps, would be able to endure such a life.

If the bourgeois family will not suffice, the intellectual will seek a new constellation of relationships to take its place. Puleo notes in Cortázar's work that only in male friendships does one find a union of conscience as well as affectivity "without confrontations," and not in any familial relationship in the traditional sense of the word (209–10). The male artist supposedly finds affectivity in his communion with other writers, his "brothers." In *Rayuela* a fraternity of intellectuals meets in an apartment in a building that is not, in the main, populated by individual intellectuals or students, but rather by families and couples. However, it seems that the family, through the constant interruptions due to the baby's crying, the administering of medicines and the complaints of the neighbors, is trying to invade or re-insert itself into the intellectuals' world. Throughout chapters twenty-four through twenty-eight, the presence of Rocamadour permeates everything that the members of the club do, and at times what they think and what they say: They ponder on how their voices, the music, the light are going to affect Rocamadour's sleep; the sounds the sick child makes remind them of his presence; and in chapter twenty-eight, death enters the members' conversation as the baby's death begins to occupy their minds.

Their brotherhood possesses those qualities of equality, diluted sentiments, and a lack of responsibility or reciprocity that characterize such a group (Mount 180). Childhood and memory are linked in *Rayuela*—as we have shown in Chapter One regarding the formation of communities—sometimes at the national level. La Maga would like to establish more affective and historical relationships with members of the club through the sharing of personal histories. She attempts this by relating to them events from her own childhood (chapters 12, 15 and 16), but her cohorts reject any show of empathy or sentiment (chapter 16). It is only at the death of the child that Oliveira mentions the friendship of his fellow club members (316). After the death, the group disperses, incapable of maintaining the apparently affectiveless relationships that they have known up to that point. We might also posit that it became impossible for them to come together without remembering such a painful, and probably shameful event, from which they, as reasoning intellectuals, should have been able to keep their emotional distance. When La Maga reacts violently to her son's death, Ronald, an American member of "el club," regrets their negligence and shame in not having taken care of the baby and Maga: "Qué joder, hubiéramos tenido que prepararla. . . . No hay derecho, es una infamia. Todo el mundo hablando de pavadas, y esto, esto. . ." (318). Oliveira tries to tell people to keep calm, but he, too, tosses a barb at Gregorovius as he leaves to get help, and himself trembles, though his shaking is referred to as "tics" (321). Etienne, as well, speaks sullenly as he also tries to keep the others calm (318). Unlike Martín Romaña, who displays a hypersensibility, the members of the Club in *Rayuela* express diluted sentiments toward those who would be their re-constituted, newly discovered, intellectually based family.

Rather than a member of a family or of the Club, Oliveira sees himself as a hero, and an anti-hero of a(n) (anti-)novel. If the "heroism" of the writer is to be found in his voyage of self-discovery (Franco, "Crisis" 10–11), and if we see the ideal reader in the child Rocamadour, then we must ask whether there is communicated here an element of heroism in paternity. Morelli and

Cortázar want to create a model work that will incite a revolution among the artistic masses, but the two demand perfection from their "children" when they themselves have not achieved it. This un-writing does not inspire revolution, but rather only slow changes in individuals and, through them, in the subsequent generations. In the end, the goal of this voyage of the intellectual continues to be that of many parents throughout history, and that of many mythologists in diverse cultures, to leave to their progeny the tools for the search, which implies an acceptance of the familial and intellectual hierarchies. It in fact signals a failure in the supposed project of Morelli—it is impossible to escape the inherited models. The "stimulating paradox" when speaking with the "seeing blind man" (125) ends up creating a paradoxical and paternalistic text. Therefore, although Morelli criticizes the millenarians and the messianic and their nostalgia (chapter 71), he and Oliveira position themselves as messiahs in the end: The intellectual attempts to liberate himself from literary conventions and the bourgeois family, but he must utilize a paternalistic text and offer himself as a model, a type of father, in the course of the effort. Martín, on the other hand, is not a paternalistic writer, but he does want to become a real father. Parents and the family are not fungible in *La Vida Exagerada*. For Oliveira, meanwhile, they are present as something against which to write (even though it is anachronistic to do so by the 1950's, as Franco says), thus the ideal is irreplaceable; nor can the romantic perception of childhood be displaced, a perception whose popularity surged ahead along with the growth of the bourgeoisie, as ultimately Oliveira retreats to childhood to find his "bridge." Nor are parents and family fungible for Martín Romaña, as he does not reject them entirely, though neither can he bring himself to integrate into that paradigm. The family continues as a controlling presence for him as his continued exile is partly inspired by his unwillingness to integrate. By remaining in Europe, he can perhaps avoid the battle for the grown-up child waged in his own country. What he does not seem to realize is that continued exile also has become a trope in the life of the Latin American intellectual. While Martín may have resented parental control as a child, he also resents the intellectuals' hypocritical expropriation of family as the target of their battle cry. As an artist he must recognize and protect in some way the family within which he learned resistance; his defense of his family, "plusvalía y todo," is a statement in defense of the immunity of the home, as Jean Franco would call it, from invasion and usurpation.

The battle for childhood becomes a more dangerous, explicit activity in Cristina Peri Rossi's short story collection, *La Rebelión de los Niños* (1980) (*The Rebellion of the Children*). While Verani (305–6) and other critics have correctly characterized much of Peri Rossi's writing to be concerned with the disintegration of society, and Gabriela Mora ("Mito") points out the vision of the decadent upper-class family of *El Libro de mis Primos* (1969) (*My Cousins' Book*), this is not what we read in "La Rebelión." Instead we see a concern for the replacement of the biological family, typically middle class, by the regime, the "holy family." Mora says *El Libro de mis Primos* presents a "devastating vision" ("Mito" 67) of the traditional family. It is the grandmother in that work who is charged with maintaining, at all costs, the traditional social forms, while children, in their thoughts and their play, serve the author as deconstructionists of those norms. At one point, the family chooses its economic interests over the life of one of its family members, one who has become a rebel (Mora, "Mito" 72-4). Mora's interpretation of the vision of the family in this Peri Rossi work is, we believe, reminiscent of that found in Arenas's novel; a family capable of great cruelty and neglect, living in an environment of despair, and dehumanized by the abuse of power:

> La intención desmitificadora de la institución burguesa familiar, por otro lado, es muy clara. El ambiente único, aislado que la autora creó magnifica la visión de un mundo que encierra sádicas crueldades, sexualidades desatadas, existencias que vegetan sin objeto; pero sobre todo, el deshumanizante efecto del poder. (Mora, "Mito" 75)

Although the family in *El Palacio de las Blanquísimas Mofetas* is from a lower socio-economic class, we see the same devastating dehumanization at work. The regime's expropriation of family rhetoric and its institutionalization contribute to this dehumanization.

We note in *La Rebelión de los Niños* that the gradual disintegration of the child's creative capacities leads to his or her integration into an established system, but then that system is scrutinized and critiqued as being in a state of disintegration. As the child ages, he or she loses the creativity and playfulness of childhood, and is at the same time progressively integrated into adult society. The child in these stories seems to understand the weaknesses of that into which they are moving, and then they act to expose those weaknesses. This is not unlike the woman, the Indian or the African-Latin American who has developed a sense of the weaknesses in the dominant culture, and has found ways to subvert it. Once childhood is lost, however, as Steedman and we have noted previously, the person enters a prolonged period of senescence.

No matter the political persuasion of the dominant regime, the child will undergo the "integration" to which the protagonist of the title story refers. The particular military regime in power in the story is making a concerted effort to cull from the social organism unhealthy fruits. Pinochet in Chile used the organic metaphor to characterize the "evil" foreign influences in his country as a "Marxist cancer" which needed "extirpating" (Loveman and Davies 427). Had the revolution triumphed in "La Rebelión," the children are told, they all would have been sent to Siberia, where it is, "as everyone knows," very cold and "full of bears" (123). But the current regime prunes the population, and redistributes the children in order to re-educate them and somehow save the whole at the expense of a few of its parts. Rolando's re-upholstered chair, covered with newspaper clippings, helps to emphasize the way the regime focuses on certain children at the expense of others. While he is living with a family that is part of the oligarchy, the clippings note that 640 out of every thousand children born on the continent die from curable diseases, and that some children are born headless (113). The regime perpetrates violence against certain individuals, then, to save the whole; it is a violence, not unlike surgery, which is meant to cure. (The perceived aggressiveness of a father feeding his daughter in the first story in *La Rebelión*, "Ulva Lactuca," is similar in this regard as the child sees as violent and repulsive an act which is meant to be nurturing and nourishing (5–6, 8, 10, 12–13).) The narrator's brother, Pico, has been sent to a reformatory, while Rolando has been placed with a new family. The regime obviously feels that the biological family is fungible here, easily replaced by institutions or foster families. By the end of the story, that perspective proves fatal for some members of the regime as Laura's art project douses them with gasoline which is then lit by a Molotov cocktail. The youths who mount this violent protest in effect cull a few members from the upper ranks of the oligarchy so that the resistance may continue. The subversives as well, then, destroy a few in an effort to save the whole, thus perpetuating the violent cycle.

The narrator has been placed with one of the "rankest" families in the country; a clan that has proved its faithfulness to the nation's institutions—and indeed are an institution themselves—for some fifty years or more. This elite family attempts to erase from the narrator any "seed" of the past; Pico, meanwhile, who is younger and is considered to be less rebellious, has been sent to a reformatory (122). Following up on the organic metaphor, the generals have broken up families in order to save them: "...nos han hecho separar de nuestras familias para que no nos separaran de nuestras familias" (123), says the narrator. The child is well aware of the hypocrisy in the government's policies, and communicates a belief in the humanity of his own biological family. His father, the boy notes, was not interested in sending anyone to Siberia, nor would he have wanted to separate any child from his family; indeed, he says, his father likes children and families (123). In place of the humanity of his parents, the state has created foster institutions which serve to "protect" the children from chaos and the subversive influences of art: "muchas veces, bajo el aspecto de la experimentación o la libertad creadoras, se introduce solapadamente el germen de la destrucción familiar"

(107). This is, of course, exactly what the two youths do in the end, as Laura's art project introduces the germ of destruction into the *official* family, the holy family, as Franco calls it, which has attempted to replace—indeed, to destroy—the children's biological families.

While Rolando's brother lives in a reformatory, the narrator sets up a fictive kinship with Laura. This is a slippery relationship, diluted, as fraternity tends to be, which he establishes in his imagination. It serves to bind them together during the period of their rebellion. Also, we read it as an effort to re-constitute the family in some sense, not unlike the members of the Club and the Grupo in the Cortázar and Bryce Echenique novels, or Fortunato and the revolutionaries in Arenas's work. The sibling relationship is not ideal for Laura and Rolando, and indeed it would seem to be a playful subversion of the regime's familial rhetoric, as Rolando imagines her as a sister with whom he is having a sexual relationship (120-21). It is clear, however, that this relationship cannot replace the biological ties of true siblings, as it is something which is created only in Rolando's mind, through his own imagination and private rhetoric, just as the regime creates or imagines for the populace, its own version of the family. To paraphrase a quote from *Rayuela*, a bridge cannot sustain itself from just one side, however, so this relationship, at least as Rolando has imagined it, is as temporary as those established by the oligarchy for these youths. Indeed, if it were not for the regime's usurpation of familial ties, Rolando and Laura would not find themselves in the position of having to create out of their shared exile this imaginary familial relationship.

As we note in our introduction, and later in Chapter Four, children have been seen as incomplete beings, highly pliable, soft and easily molded. This is precisely why they are such good candidates for re-education. They are also seen as in need of protection, therefore a family or a regime can mold and reshape a child citing the need to "protect" them, as the regime does in "La Rebelión"; children are seen as adaptable. Schmidt notes how exile causes a reversal in the family roles of father and daughter in Peri Rossi's "La Influencia de Edgar A. Poe en la Poesía de Raimundo Arias" ("The Influence of Edgar A. Poe in the Poetry of Raimundo Arias"). The displacement "results in disorientation, humiliation and loss of identity" (Schmidt 223). The goal of the regime's educational institutions and foster families is to exploit the slipperiness of identity caused by the displacement of the family. First the families are broken up, causing disorientation, and then the children are moved to a replacement structure where their identity can be rebuilt and integrated, through a type of homogenization process, into the whole of national identity. The daughter in "La Influencia," says Schmidt, matures overnight, and becomes a hard, unforgiving observer of society: "Their creative and unexpected self-transformations serve to both defy and parody the alienating structures of which they are victims" (226). The irony is that, just as exile causes a role reversal between father and daughter in the above-mentioned story, the substitution of one family for another leads to subversive activity in "La Rebelión." The regime has fooled itself with its image of children as pliable, completely re-programmable.

In two stories from *La Rebelión*, family members are engaged in a struggle with the dominant ideology to control the fate of their children; we see, however, that in "saving" their children, the parents save themselves as well. In "Vía Láctea," ("Milky Way"), a mother works to keep her son from growing up and attending school where he would learn the doctrines that men have created to define and divide reality. A more direct criticism of the painful imposition of—and disillusionment with—patriarchal dogma that takes place in educational institutions can be found in works such as Mario Vargas Llosa's *La Ciudad y los Perros* (1963) (*The City and the Dogs*) or the Julio Cortázar short story "Escuela de Noche" ("Night School"). Nancy Kason, in an analysis of the latter work, notes that the educational mission of the school is simply a mask for the abuses, violence and perversion that go on inside (190). The school in such works is seen as a symbol of all of those governmental institutions that are directed by a man whose outward appearance does not reveal his true personality (191). Much of Peri Rossi's "Vía Láctea" is devoted to outlining the distinctions between the world views of the mother and father. It is clear that she does not want the boy to be educated to follow the "way of the father," thus the title refers not only to the Milky Way, but also to the "way" of the mother, the giver of milk. Though the mother seeks a way to detain the advance of time, she recognizes the inevitability of her son's indoctrination. Indeed, in the debates with her husband about their distinct world views, it is revealed that the father sees reality as a rigid square, while the mother sees it as a circle without a beginning or an end, and which is intertwined with a multitude of other spheres rotating throughout the world. The father sees marriage under such circumstances as possible only if the sphere subsumes itself to the square (67). The mother sees in the father's view rigidity and entrapment, while the father sees her version as leading to chaos, to an uncontrolled integration of distinct "molecules," and a lack of progress (72–73). The mother's efforts to keep her son out of school are meant to keep him from being integrated into the father's world view, into his perception of reality, into the "fishbowl" that the rigid square imposes (72).

Later in the story, the child, Mauricio, spends his time trying to count the stars in an attempt to capture the infinite within his finite system of numbers (69). It is his father who has introduced Mauricio to the infinite, an event which sends the boy off on a treadmill-like attempt to count all of the stars.

The numbering system, however, is insufficient to count the stars, which go on infinitely—similar to the mother's circular view of the world. Those innumerable stars lead to a fainting spell because, like the protagonist of Borges's "El Aleph" (1949), his effort to comprehend everything at once overwhelms him. Mauricio retreats, then, sectioning off the sky in order to verify the content of a smaller portion of it. The mother had argued that the father's view of reality as a square would always lead to such retreat and a reliance on arbitrary limitations; one would always crash into the borders and one would not be able to transgress its boundaries:

"Si fuera un cuadrado. . .siempre existiría el riesgo de golpearse contra los bordes, de chocar contra ellos. . .no habría posibilidad de transgredir esos límites específicos marcados por no sé quién. . .siempre se daría de lleno contra la indefectible rigidez de los lados del cuadrado" (72–73).

We read the mother's struggle to keep the child out of school as an effort to save him from the rigidity of the doctrines that are taught in an effort to control and limit the world's reality, a reality the mother accepts in its highly integrated and unlimited form.

In "Feliz Cumpleaños" ("Happy Birthday"), a boy strives to find a machine that will stop time so that he can grow and marry his mother, thus bond between mother and son is explored from the latter's point of view. In this conscious re-working of the Oedipus myth, the boy is disillusioned by the inability of technology and science—of knowledge—to give him the means to fulfill his desire, which parallels the efforts and disappointment of the mother of "Vía Láctea":

Entonces, ¿de qué sirven todas las experiencias realizadas con negros, indios, anarquistas y demás presos políticos? –preguntó la mujer, que, aunque carecía de datos precisos, tenía idea de que en los gigantescos laboratorios norteamericanos del desierto de Nevada y Oklahoma se habían consumido, en pruebas científicas, miles de reservas de búfalos, chilenos, chimpancés, uruguayos y otros animales. (66)

In "Pico Blanco y Alas Azules" ("White Beak and Blue Wings"), the parents struggle to stay ahead of the regime's shifting interpretations of reality in order not to be accused of being subversive. The fight here is over language and meaning. The parents find themselves in an infantilized state as they must re-learn meanings for objects at the same time that their son is learning language. The child is searching the world, just as the soldiers do (82), trying to assign words and meaning to objects. They fear that the military's searches will become commonplace to their son, and also that the child will not grow to see the world as they had hoped he would, but rather as the military interprets the world. The parents are in danger of losing their most basic, and most powerful, task with regard to childrearing: The teaching of a world view through the assignment of words and meanings. The state, of course, attempts to impose a uniform code of interpretation.

The mother makes an effort to recuperate that power in "Pico Blanco y Alas Azules" through a subversive act.· The child sees a bird at the beginning of the story and is fascinated and obsessed by it, he wants to share his joy with his parents, but he does not have the vocabulary to describe the bird or name it. The blue bird is like good art to him: It may be indescribable, but it is recognizable to the viewer. The bird departs, however, and does not make another appearance until the mother performs the potentially subversive act of saving, and not burning, a work of art by an unknown artist (91). It takes a consciously subversive act for the mother to regain control of the child's development, to wrest it from the state, if only for a time. The mother's own abilities to interpret signs, and to see the details in life have also faded; the act of saving the painting may be self-serving as well then, as she grasps at the opportunity to preserve an image when so many images have been slipping away from her. In both of these stories, the mother makes an attempt to save her son from his integration into the male dominated world where arbitrary limits are set, and where meanings are changed in the name of political expediency. The efforts cannot lead to permanent control of the child, however, as the boy in "Vía Láctea" must eventually grow up, and in "Pico Blanco" the mother's victory certainly seems precarious.

It would appear that subversion itself will have to be left up to the young. In "Pico Blanco," the mother who helps the child to see the return of the blue bird is fomenting that very rebellion as she allows the boy to continue his own process of interpreting the world. At the end of "La Rebelión de los Niños," we see the ironic culmination of a child's development and the battle between the state, the family and the individual will for control of her thoughts and creativity. As Laura receives from the regime her award for artistic achievement, it is significant that the "máximo general" is cited as being a savior of, not just the nation and its citizens, but people who are identified by their membership in a generation and within families: "había aplastado la sublevación, salvado a la patria, a los niños, a los jóvenes, a los adultos y a los ancianos, a las abuelas y a los abuelos, también a los nietecitos" (135). The general's accomplishments are couched in terms which equate the nation with the family. This is reminiscent of the Argentine "Final Document of the Military Junta Regarding the War Against Subversion and Terrorism: The Fundamental Concepts, 1983" in which the authors emphasize their self-appointed roles as saviors of the family, individual families and the metaphorical national family: "Those who placed their intelligence, goodwill, solidarity, and piety, indeed, the whole weight of their being, at the service of the reconciliation of the Argentine family are worthy of recognition and respect. . ." (Loveman and Davies 210). Laura receives her recognition as a good daughter of the "family," and the regime praises itself as a paternal authority, as a good "parent."

As we have seen in the works of Arenas and Peri Rossi, these authors do not write so much against the family per se, as against the expropriation of familial roles and rhetoric by the state. In the last work to be considered here, "De Barro Estamos Hechos" ("We Are Made of Clay"), the last story in Isabel Allende's collection *Cuentos de Eva Luna* (1990) (*Stories of Eva Luna*), the author exposes an exploitation of the child by the state at the same time that she imitates it. Allende uncovers for the reader the shameless use of the suffering child by the government as a means of presenting itself as a caring entity, a guardian of the helpless. At the same time, the author utilizes that child as a focal point for the nation's re-examination of its history.

Gabriela Mora has criticized Allende for allowing stereotypical clichés to be part of the ideologies of even her liberal characters ("Novelas" 56–58). Indeed, Allende's characters do seem to fit Romano's definition of a "liberal" author, one who wishes to choose his or her master, but not to face and revolutionize the capitalist system (180–81). Such a confusion of stereotype with subversion makes Allende's characters more human, we would say, and they also are part of her efforts to reconcile disparate forces within Latin American societies, what Shields calls the "myth of disunity" which "must find some way to bring together what we usually consider to be irreconcilable elements, violence and love (79). Isabel Allende has often played out those efforts at reconciliation in a familial setting in her works. We identify in those works a progression of family structures, from the extended patriarchal family in decay of *La Casa de los Espíritus* (1982) (*The House of the Spirits*), through the three disparate families of *De Amor y de Sombra* (1984) (*Of Love and Shadows*), the variations on traditional nuclear and extended families of her novel *Eva Luna* (1987), and finally terminating in the variously founded and reconstituted families of rural, urban and suburban Latin America found in the twenty-three stories of *Cuentos de Eva Luna*. The families in the latter work are often in flux, rarely "complete," in the sense that they are not models of nuclear or extended families. They fit well the family practice and ideology described above by Rivera and de la Peña.

As Helsper notes regarding *La Casa de los Espíritus*, "the traditional family as symbol is deconstructed and, simultaneously, the power of the family-as-image is reclaimed for the novelist's Utopian purpose" (220). "By the novel's end, following in the footsteps of her grandmothers and mother, Alba has begun to forge a new model family, which will include Chileans of all social classes and political tendencies. The family is the Utopian image which anchors the novel" (Helsper 217–18). In "De Barro Estamos Hechos," the author utilizes the image of the suffering child in a similar attempt to bind together at times antagonistic sectors of society. She has essentially reduced the problem to the question of how society can call itself advanced, in spite of all of its technology and military force, when it cannot save, or has not the will to save, one suffering child.

The protagonist of "De Barro Estamos Hechos" is the foreign-born television journalist Rolf Carlé. A general runs the oil-producing nation, probably Venezuela, where the story takes place. The action revolves around a flood and massive mudslides that have buried entire villages. The government and rescue agencies seem to be able to do little to help the victims, thanks mostly to bureaucratic inefficiency. Carlé is one of the first to arrive at the site of the disaster and soon finds himself with a child, Azucena (white lily), who is half-buried in the clay, and whose name suggests the innocence and purity so typically associated with the child. It is not possible to extricate her without a pump, but in spite of Carlé's efforts and those of his television station and the narrator, Carlé's lover, he is unable to obtain a pump.

Carlé accompanies the girl in her suffering, telling her stories to "cheat the hours," using his imagination to create tales to distract the girl from her suffering (276). On the second night he begins to tell her about his childhood in Austria, about the concentration camps, remembering everything but telling the girl only certain parts so as not to frighten her, and because she seems too pure to hear such tales. Azucena's purity has been marred by this tragedy, just as Carlé's was by the specter of the destruction of his family in Nazi-controlled Europe.

It is through his recognition of Azucena's suffering that Carlé begins to face his own past, which he has left buried for decades, a past in which he, his family, his entire people have suffered gravely. Although he is not Latin American by birth, it is obvious that Rolf Carlé represents here the Latin American middle class which has ignored the suffering of its own people—both the poor in their countries and their fellow members of the middle class who have been victimized by right-wing dictatorships. But this sector of society has been going through a process of consciousness-raising, as the end of the Argentine "Dirty War" of the 1970's and 1980's demonstrates. The narrator describes Carlé's work and his attitude about life in the country; he had used the camera, in a sense, to distance himself from events even while intimately observing them:

> Durante años lo había visto en los noticiarios, escarbando en batallas y catástro-
> fes, sin que nada le detuviera, con una perseverancia temeraria, y siempre me

asombró su actitud de calma ante el peligro y el sufrimiento, como si nada lograra sacudir su fortaleza ni desviar su curiosidad. . .Creo que el lente de la máquina tenía un efecto extraño en él, como si lo transportara a otro tiempo, desde el cual podía ver los acontecimientos sin participar realmente en ellos. (274)

The process of consciousness-raising, of leaving the lens to one side, is painful, and at the end of the story the process has not ended; Rolf Carlé continues to examine the videos of himself and Azucena, looking for some way in which he might have saved her, and also trying to look at himself as in a mirror. The narrator observes him and notes that he has to make this voyage to his interior in order to cure his old wounds (282). This seems to be Allende's prescription for reconciling opposing forces in Latin America without the violence which has been such a part of its history. (Similarly, in other stories in the collection, such as "Una Venganza" ("A Vengeance") and "Niña Perversa" ("Perverse Girl"), men who have wronged young girls in some way are made to suffer long lives where they are tormented by their memories of the girls.) Carlé's experiences in Austria are an extreme example of the state's efforts to control the population, of course, with the control of families and their offspring being a significant element of that effort. The protagonist's re-examination of his childhood is a first step in taking back from the past, and thus from the state in his case, control of his childhood. His journey of self-exploration, however, comes at the virtual silence of the girl, Azucena. Her history, outside of the current tragedy, remains a mystery. Allende is counting on the reader to assume that the girl's childhood has been some sort of age of innocence. Indeed, at the end of the story, Azucena laments that she will die at the age of thirteen without having been loved by a boy. Rolf Carlé declares his love for her at that moment, telling her that he loves her more than his own mother, more than all the women he has loved (282). The girl's life is given in the interest of uniting the nation and providing a focus for the re-examination of personal and cultural histories. In *El Palacio*, Fortunato's exploration of childhood is much more concerned with bringing to light the myriad experiences of the members of his clan, in particular their childhoods, as they occupy representative roles in society. Azucena, like her name, is rather more symbolic, she is a conduit, and is utilized as such in this Allende story.

It is obvious in "De Barro Estamos Hechos" that cooperation among various sectors of society is necessary to stop the historical cycle of violence, whether violence of the right wing, of rebels, of oppressive paternalistic mores, or of capitalist exploitation. In *Cuentos de Eva Luna*, Allende seems to be turning the reader's attention to the plight of children in modern(izing) Latin America, forcing the reader to examine his or her own commitment to children (and his or her own childhood as well), and to the future of the nation. In this sense, then, Allende is equating the nation with childhood. Before people such as Rolf Carlé and the narrator of "De Barro Estamos Hechos" can continue their lives, and populate the country with a new generation born in peace and with an expectation of justice, they must first examine their own violent pasts, including their complicity in the oppression of their infant and infantilized (marginalized) countrymen. In this collection, children are often doubly or triply marginalized: For being children, for being female, and for being retarded. The illness metaphor usually applied to the nation to show its colonized status is here applied to children, the most colonized sector of all.

Sommer reads heterosexual love and romance as an alternative chosen by nineteenth-century authors tired and fearful of the violent chaos of their period. In our Chapter One we note the offering of fluid, fraternal relationships, and the role of infantilization in achieving a similar sort of comforting resolution to conflict during the late-nineteenth century. We emphasized that for these authors, parents and siblings were fungible, as the state, the oligarchy, or the "intelligentsia" wished to replace them. In this chapter we have analyzed twentieth-century authors who have questioned that fungibility, even though some have at the same time severely criticized the traditional family. The major critique to come out of the works, from our reading, is that of the oligarchy's appropriation of familial rhetoric and roles. Carlos Fuentes has put this criticism thus: "el paternalismo, signo fehaciente de desconfianza en el pueblo, es hoy tan sistemático, aunque más sutil, que en tiempos de Porfirio Díaz" (qtd. in Boling 74). It is indeed a mistrust, a fear, which the regime has of the child, for it not only seeks to control the nation's real children, it infantilizes and controls the adult populace through its use of familial paradigms. Children are feared for their inherent capacity to cross boundaries and question authority, and the family is attacked because the state realizes that the home is the training ground for subversion. The patriarchal state, however, commits a dangerous and complex violation of the incest taboo when, in an attempt to gain control of the family and the child, it imposes itself as the figured father of the populace: The home is invaded, parents are displaced, and children are exposed to a "father" who has no emotional attachment to the child, seeing him or her only as a class to be manipulated, as a potential ally or enemy. Our analysis also brings to the fore the authors' own exploitation of the image of the child, as we see the "intelligentsia" as one sector of society which engages in a battle for childhood. As we will see in the next chapter, such a utilization of children requires a level of dehumanization of the child so that he or she may be manipulated as a group; this is not unlike the ways in which other marginalized sectors are homogenized and exploited.

NOTES

[1]From the Mexican President's "Grito de Guadalupe" speech (1934), cited in Jean A. Meyer, "Revolution and Reconstruction in the 1920s," *The Cambridge History of Latin America*, Vol. 5, NY: Cambridge UP, 1986, p. 163.

[2]Many critics have commented on mid-twentieth-century authors' criticism of the bourgeois family, using feminist, Marxist and psychoanalytical approaches, among others. One article on José Donoso's *El Obsceno Pájaro de la Noche* (1970) (*The Obscene Bird of Night*) makes a particularly bold statement in its title, and reflects the attitude of many works of criticism which deal with the family in Latin American literature: Jaime Martínez-Tolentino, "La Familia Como Fuente de Todo Mal en *El Obsceno Pájaro de la Noche*," *Revista de Crítica Literaria Latinoamericana* 11.23 (1986): 73–79.

[3]Becky Boling makes a similar point with regard to the literature of Carlos Fuentes and how its familial paradigms model the nation's history: "The classical dramatizations of the myths of Medea, Agamemon, Oedipus, etc. are firmly based upon the family as the structure in which desire and power are unmediated. The family, existing within the private and the public spheres, facilitates the study of human will, social structures and hierarchy. In much the same way that the classical stories centering upon the great families of mythology constitute an artistic representation of power and its use in a historical time, Fuentes' narratives reveal the political realities of twentieth-century Mexico" (80).

[4]As Polo says, it is the daily, mundane oppression that defeats one: "Pues no son las grandes derrotas las que aniquilan, son las frustraciones diarias, la cotidiana injuria, y la mezquindad de todos los días…" (280).

CHAPTER THREE

Always One Step Below: The Identification
of the Child with Marginalized Sectors of Society:
Salarrué, Juan Bosch, Silvina Ocampo

Children occupy a naturally dependent position in the human family, as
do the young of many species. Human children are perhaps unique, however,
in that they frequently labor within and outside of the family, often from a
very early age. The sight of a six-year-old girl carrying a younger sibling on
her back, or an eight-year-old boy selling chewing gum on buses, is common
enough in the developing world, just as young North American children can
be found operating large and dangerous farm equipment, or working behind
the scenes in family businesses.[1] The International Labor Organization esti-
mates that about eighty percent of child labor is unpaid help within the home;
whether the task be large or small, children are often taught that their work
is in exchange for food, shelter and clothing (Sawyer 133). It is reasonable,
then, that the child would be depicted in literature as a member of a marginalized class of citizens. We examine in this chapter, however, not only the
child as a dependent laborer, but also several other means by which children
are marginalized, means similar to those used with reference to other sectors
of society. We also examine certain authors' use of the child as a representative of the lower classes. In these works, the child's poor living conditions

and limited opportunities are a manifestation of a particular sector's marginalization. The child often becomes the symbol of a class's suffering as well as its hope for escape from such difficult conditions.

In general terms, we see the identity of the child as homogenized and exploited in the discourse of national identity, much like that of the Amerindian, as Amaryll Chanady outlines it: "The Amerindian is appropriated in order to differentiate between a national or supranational entity and an external hegemonic power . . . these discourses do not even portray the 'Indian' as a fictionalized object of representation, but merely as a pretext for a discursive practice of resistance and identization" (36). This appropriation, while bringing to light the effects of outside pressures on a particular class or on children themselves, thus giving them a "voice," is also frequently a dehumanizing process which primarily serves the political or esthetic goals of the writer.

Children, like priests, nuns and women (Franco, "Killing") are apt for this type of use because they have traditionally been considered as worthy of "immunity" from the negative effects of, for example, war and modernization. The violation of that immunity, then, heightens the reader's perception of the severity of the pressures brought to bear on that sector of society. This is the primary reasoning behind the use of the child narrator or child protagonist: The child's vision, supposedly imbued with innocence, makes the violence or privations of modern life all the more shocking. This attitude toward the use of the child's perspective has been explored in the works of a number of Hispanic American writers, such as Silvina Ocampo (Klingenberg, "Twisted") and Reinaldo Arenas (Rozencvaig 43–56).[2] Society is expected to react strongly to such child narrators as they are often meant to show the disintegration of the national community at the most basic level, that of the family and its weakest members.

Another aspect of their marginalization is the child's relative lack of comprehension of the language of the nation or community. Mary Louise Pratt notes how the nation is defined within a "speech community" constructed as a homogeneous social and linguistic universe:

> Detrás, o dentro del concepto de la comunidad lingüística yace el modelo idealizado de la nación, una totalidad discreta cuyos miembros comparten fraternal y discretamente una lengua nacional. Incluso la sintaxis abstracta, construida a base de modelos que parecen totalmente fuera de la dinámica social, presupone un hablante monolingüe que, como el ciudadano imaginario, habla el estandard nacional. ("Mujeres" 51–52)

Noting a lack of "literature", or, contrarily, the presence of a symbolic language that represented "perverse beliefs" (Adorno 22) was one of the ways in which members of the "learned city" of the colonial and post-colonial eras categorized as more barbarous the "other" of their society. Child speech is, in a sense, appropriated by the author who utilizes such protagonists or narrators in order to drive home a message regarding social conditions, or to experiment with the innovative speech patterns of the child.[3] The child's "freshness" of language allows for utilizing him or her "as a spokesman for the uneducated" (Lloyd 234). On the other hand, those who possess the skills and knowledge needed to manipulate the hegemonic national discourse become Gelpí's "figuras tutelares." We will question in this chapter whether there is a direct infantilization of the underclass in literature with such representations of children, as it is a child who comes to represent those marginalized sectors, or whether the child is chosen precisely because the author wishes to point out and critique, through metaphor, the "infantile," dependent position of a sector of society.

The works examined in this chapter make several points regarding the effects of poverty and societal upheaval, whether caused by war or rapid economic change, on a nation's children. The texts range from portraits of impoverished children to those caught up in war as witnesses, combatants or orphans. At times the children are more or less explicitly meant to demonstrate the suffering of the nation's people under a particular political or economic regime and often, therefore, warn of the society's bleak future, as well as its obviously painful present, under that system. Part of that warning regards the psychological damage done to the children, i.e. the society, by having witnessed internecine conflicts. We see family systems torn apart, the ideal relationships described in Chapter One violated, all under the pressure of forces beyond the control of family members and, certainly, of the children depicted.

Children in many of these works are, to varying degrees identified with other marginalized groups: Laborers, peasants, women, ethnic groups, artists and exiles. We will question in our analysis these identifications, as well as the extent to which the authors appear to exploit the qualities of the romantic image of the child in order to make a political point. There are no "Midnight's Children" in these works. In that Salman Rushdie novel, 1,001 babies were born during the first hour of India's independence from Great Britain, all with special talents, hopes and gifts, all of which were cruelly destroyed. Instead, here such potential is more implied, only the cruel destruction of romanticism's innocent child is displayed. Thus, the idea of children as special, talented, full of hope for the future is implicit, taken for granted as something which the reader and the narrator or author share. Rather than hopeful, many of the children treated in the following analysis would appear to be hopeless, at least from the authors' perspectives. In a sense, Enriquillo, the protagonist of the nineteenth-century Dominican novel discussed in Chapter One, was one of Midnight's Children. He was born not in the first hour of independence, however, but rather in the first hour of the colony, and invoked in the first moments of independence.

We begin to see in the works examined below the danger to the younger generation of the duplicitous image of the child, in which assigned qualities may be turned against the child, or to his or her favor, by those who exercise power over the young in a particular situation. A. Rivero, writing in Mexico in 1846, notes that one can say nearly anything, good or bad, about women— "todos en todo momento están dispuestos a decir mucho bueno y mucho malo de la muger (sic)" (57)—and that legislators were always disposed to using women for their own political designs (58). Similarly, the modern concept of childhood has often revolved around innocence versus original sin, around what is inherent versus what is learned. Solange Albeno notes how women are considered to be caught somewhere between the status of the child and the adult male; thus, they do not partake of the benefits of full adulthood (76–77). We will demonstrate in this chapter (and we will explore this further in Chapter Four) how this socially constructed and assigned ambiguity is a particularly important characteristic of the link between the subjugation of women, and the abuse of children. We begin with a discussion of several stories by El Salvador's Salarrué.

The collection *Cuentos de Barro* (1933) by Salarrué, has been analyzed and critiqued little outside of Central America, though more, perhaps, than any other work by this Salvadoran writer and artist. Criticism has tended to focus on the unique linguistic traits of the stories, on the author's *costumbrismo* techniques, and on the work as it belongs to the genres of *indigenismo* and regionalism. In this analysis, we examine the representation of the child and his or her relationships with parents or other family members and authority figures. It will be clear from this reading that Salarrué was concerned about the plight of the next generation of Izalco Indians, the main characters in the stories. The author, who utilized a nearly anthropological method in observing and writing about the Izalcos (Lara Martínez 8), paints a picture of the child as isolated and alienated not only from authority figures, but also from family members of all levels, and from the enjoyment of the simple pleasures that have come to be associated with childhood in the western tradition. Salarrué appears to warn that the child's alienation engenders violence, including intrafamiliar violence, and leads to the exclusion of the next generation from the mainstream of political and economic life. We suggest as well that this familial violence may serve as a metaphor for the military's violent repression of the Izalco Indians, who were the victims of a genocidal massacre in 1932 (regarding the massacre, see Thomas Anderson).

In addition to being concerned about the Indians and the nation, we might conjecture that Salarrué was exploring his own childhood alienation as he wrote about the Izalcans. The author was raised, for the most part, in the department of Sonsonante, the center of Izalcan culture. His family life likely gave him a useful perspective from which to observe the life of exclusion depicted in his stories. His parents separated when he was a child, at which time he went to live with an uncle in Santa Tecla (Ramírez xxv). In addition, Salarrué was always an observer and not much of a participant as a child (Ulloa), whether due to his natural inclination, or to the pain he likely suffered after the failure of his parents' marriage and his subsequent separation from them. In elementary school other children persecuted him for his reserved and quiet nature, although things changed when he entered high school and began to gain some attention for his artwork (Ulloa 91–92). Later, as a youth, Salarrué went to New York City, where he studied art. Being far from his homeland exposed him to new ideologies, but it also thrust him once again into the role of outsider. The young author, therefore, had experience living at the margins of society, and of his family, early in his life.

In Salarrué's writing about the Izalcans, we have an example of *costumbrismo*, but also of early *indigenismo*. Ramírez compares Salarrué with Arturo Ambrogui, the giant of Central American realism and *costumbrismo* (*El Libro del Trópico*), and asserts that before Ambrogui and Salarrué, the Indians represented in this genre in El Salvador had been little more than a shadow of themselves, "una invención, una realidad tan gaseosa como la de los planes astrales..." (xvi). Ramírez notes that Salarrué preserves in the stories of *Cuentos de Barro* the indigenous idiom, and their social organizations, including those of the family (xvii; and see Lara Martínez 8).

One could place Salarrué among the great *indigenista* authors of this century such as José María Arguedas, Jorge Icaza, Miguel Angel Asturias and Ciro Alegría. Arroyo has noted the realism of these authors (she does not include Salarrué in her study) and their tendency to denounce the deplorable living conditions of many indigenous peoples. She believes it is with Ciro Alegría's *El Mundo Es Ancho y Ajeno* (1941) that we begin to see a marked change from "a screaming denouncement" to a much more indirect social critique, which could be found by reading "between the lines" (69–70). We would argue that, while we see the violence, psychological primitivism and local dialects which Arroyo finds in other *indigenista* writers, we also note an indirect—rather than direct—criticism of the classist and racist Salvadoran society of the day, some eight years before Alegría's 1941 work.

In Salarrué, we see the Indian as an exploited human being, but the exploiter as outsider is nearly always absent from the narrative. This lack of an explicit oppressor contributes to our focusing on the family life of the Izalcos, where the exploited adults may become exploiters themselves, and where the exploited are often children. We see in the stories how the exclusion of the child is a major preoccupation of the narratives.[4] We will note the magical or revelatory nature of the child in the stories; we will see the child as the source of family honor, as well as the violence and tenderness with which the child is treated by his or her parents and others.[5]

The first characteristic to be explored here is that of the child as a source or conduit of what we might call magic. That is, the child is a focal point for the intangible, the secret sources of the power of nature. In "La Repunta" ("The Flash Flood") we see a girl, Santíos, who is constantly verbally abused by her mother. Santíos is called "stupid", "a shitty little Indian", "worthless", "an animal", and a "slug". In addition, her "nana," who is either her grandmother or some other caregiver, pulls her hair. After a heavy downpour, Santíos leaves to bring water from the river, and it is at this point that we begin to see the magic that the child possesses, and which protects her. When she walks, Santíos does not leave simple footprints in the mud, but rather magical flower prints; she walks "dejando pintada en el barro la flor de su patita" (107). While Santíos is filling the water jar, a man sees the advancing wall of water and shouts a warning to the girl. But Santíos does not hear him, continues her chore, and when the water, "altísima y solemne como un ángel de barro" (107) almost reaches her, it begins to crash down, but it haults its descent until the girl returns to her patio, "dejando pintada en el barro la flor de su patita" (107). Santíos either stops the crashing wave, or 'nature' does, thus protecting the girl.

However it is interpreted, this suspension of time and atmosphere of security contrast sharply with the oppression that the girl suffers at the hands of human society and her family. By contrast, in the story "El Sacristán" ("The Sacristan"), the adult title character does not have any control over the earthquake that destroys him. He can stop neither the earthquake nor the destruction of the saint's statue he adores. In "Semos Malos" it is people who kill the child, not some natural phenomenon.

Salarrué's stories often begin with a rather magical depiction of the natural world within which the characters are about to take the stage. The child in "La Repunta" appears to have a powerful connection to that natural world, signaling the romantic linking of the child and the inexplicable in nature. This perceived link to nature is not entirely unlike that perceived in women and indigenous groups. This linkage, of course, may have its source in the idea that children are less developed than adults are, and thus closer to the animal and plant realms in their development. It may also signal their status as property, thus they are to be possessed, cultivated and placed in commerce, not unlike women, slaves and the land. The link to nature, more exactly, to the unknown and misunderstood, makes children ripe for abuse and manipulation. Their ambiguous image as innocent, and yet linked to vast unseen powers can make of them dangerous and frightening beings to those who seek to maintain control over them and over society.[6] We might see this as a race between natural powers and societal ones to take control of the child.

We see the innocence of the child displayed in more than one story in *Cuentos de Barro*, but particularly so in "La Honra" ("Honor"), in which a boy misunderstands exactly what it means for his sister to "lose her honor" at the watering hole. He goes to the spot and, discovering a beautiful dagger, believes he has found his sister's honor. The frank optimism of the boy, and his own perceived success, contrast with "La Botija" ("The Jar"), in which an adult male is completely frustrated in his search for treasure. These two points—the child's connection to nature and his or her innocent optimism—are qualities of the child's image, which separate the child from the adult. As noted above, they are characteristics that can be manipulated by others, as indeed others to a certain extent create them.

A third quality assigned to the child, particularly to the female, and which is seen in at least three stories in the collection—"Hasta el Cacho" ("To the Hilt"), "La Honra," and "El Contagio" ("The Contagion")—is the way in which family honor is seen to reside in the child. Often, this honor is seen as the only contribution of the child to the family. While family honor, as it is interpreted to mean chastity of the female, is an important part of upper- and middle-class life, it is particularly so among the lower classes. As we saw in the previous chapter, the middle classes would leave to their children education rather than the great properties available to the elites; but the lower classes often have had even less to leave their progeny. While for the middle and upper classes control of the female members of a family might reflect directly on a male head-of-household's abilities in business and politics, for the impoverished male that control is more directly reflective of his personal manhood, his sense of self-worth in a world ruled by "machismo." The preservation of the female's chastity has its economic ramifications for the middle and lower classes as well: The middle class family may seek to marry well a daughter and thus cement ties between families, much the way the upper classes do; and the poor family might seek to marry off a girl who is seen as a burden, another mouth to feed (see Stevens for a discussion of *marianismo*).

Thus, in "La Honra," a father scolds and beats his daughter for having "lost" her honor, the only thing, he says, which she brought into this world. The girl was actually violated by a man at a watering hole. The father, after his son finds the rapist's dagger, considers avenging his daughter's loss, which can be interpreted, of course, as a loss to the family and to the father. He would avenge his own lost honor, not necessarily that of the girl. The girl in "La Petaca" ("The Hunchback") is also raped. Again, the father does not consider the violation to be significant, apparently due to the girl's lack of value as a bride given her deformity. We note that the girls' labor in these two tales is of little importance: The hunchback was only good for doing a few chores, and the girl in "La Honra" was collecting water when she was attacked. There is the perception that unless they can protect their honor and bring a male worker into the family, or leave the family themselves, they will be good for little; and, they will likely become pregnant, thereby increasing the economic burden on the family.

In a story that seems almost a comic aside in this discussion, "El Contagio," we note the hypocrisy of a married couple who set out to protect the purity of their daughter when they notice that she is behaving strangely. The father advises the young man who has been courting his daughter to be careful with her. But, the young man mocks the parents as he informs them that the young couple is actually already married, and that the daughter is one month pregnant. When the father returns home and gives his wife the news, she reminds him that they had done the same thing in their youth (65). The older generation's attempts to protect the honor of the daughter are certainly half-hearted, meant more to make the young man aware of the parents' vigilance, than to vehemently insist on "moral" behavior. The intergenerational conflict, inconsequential as it is within the story, serves to inform us of the tradition of the violation of certain moral tenets, in this case, the prohibition on pre-marital sex. The violation has been followed in both generations, however, by marriage (though "marriage" may not refer to legal ties, but rather to sexual and emotional ones, to the verbal agreement to establish a household or the actual setting up of such a home). Unlike the situation in "La Honra," the daughter's honor in "El Contagio" is recuperated by the marriage; in "La Petaca," the girl's honor does not seem to be worth recuperating.

We read a more complex example of how the child, in this case a boy, can come to represent the honor of the family, particularly that of the father, in the story "Hasta el Cacho." In this tale, the father and his son have what could be considered the best developed, the most tender of familial relations described in the collection. The mother is dead. The father and son work together, the father addressing the son with much more sensitivity and respect than is seen in the other stories. For example, the father hugs his son as they take shelter under a tree during a rainstorm, and later he is worried that the boy will become ill. The father also speaks kindly of his late wife.[7] However, when the father finds out that his son is not his, but rather the fruit of an affair between his late wife and another man, who lies moribund, the father curses his son and disowns him. He does not love the boy because he is no longer his, and because he represents the unfaithfulness of his late wife, his own "dishonor." The boy has to suffer for what adults have done: First, for the unfaithfulness of his mother, and then for the dishonor that the discovery of this act causes his father.

"Hasta el Cacho," however, presents a unique case. The father has sunk a dagger into the cadaver of the man with whom his wife had the affair. After going through an emotionally cathartic reconsideration of the events, the man returns and removes the dagger from the body. Thus the father forgives the adulterer and can then go back to loving his son as before. During the father's soul searching, the son remains resolute, crying, going without food, waiting for the return of his father's love. We see in this story the triumph of familial love over the father's *machista* pride. It is evident here, again, that the child in Salarrué has a tremendous capacity for optimism, for hope, and that those hopes can be turned into reality. We have seen, then, how the child can represent the family's honor, and how children who damage that honor are then excluded from the family, and how girls may be excluded by their parents' efforts to protect "la honra" of their daughters.

Parents in *Cuentos de Barro* rarely display what one could call physical or verbal kindness or tenderness. There are, however, numerous examples of physical and verbal violence in these relationships. Salarrué appears to warn that such violence can only engender bitterness in the individual, and another violent generation. In the story "Semos Malos" a child and his father, who are traveling on foot toward Honduras where they hope to earn money selling music played on a phonograph, are assassinated by a group of bandits. We do not see in the dialogue between father and son the brutality that is found in other stories in the collection: On the contrary, the night before their deaths, the father shows some kindness toward his son, who is complaining of the cold. The father hugs him as they try to sleep, and the narrator tells us that the father is caressing his son for the first time in his life (20). The next day, a group of bandits listens to a song on the phonograph as the father and son lie dead in a ditch. The narrator twice notes the alienation of the bandits and calls them children: First, "rieron como niños de un planeta extraño" (21) when they began to listen to the song; and later, "lloraron los ladrones de cosas y de vidas, como niños de un planeta extraño" (21) when the song has ended. In the song, the lyrics "lamented an injustice" (22). This we interpret not only as the injustice committed against the father and son who are assassinated in the story, but also that which has been committed against the bandits, the injustice of their alienation and exclusion as children, "niños de un planeta extraño," just as, perhaps, the boy was before he received the first caress from his father. We read in this act a warning for the reader: A lack of tenderness, of stable relations between parents and children is what leads the young people to stray, to become antisocial and violent, and the acts committed by these same marginalized children can put an end to any positive relations that may be developing, such as the one between the father and son just before their deaths. The tragedy of this continuation, from one generation to the next, of the acceptance of violence has been studied in Colombia. Intrafamilial violence there has been seen to be a result of several factors, including the incursion of political violence on the family—the state's violent acts, and those of its enemies, make violence a daily reality, an acceptable way of resolving conflicts—and extreme economic difficulty. In addition, the relationships of power within the patriarchal family itself, the apparent inequalities and contradictions we have noted previously, set the stage for familial violence. Rather than looking to such problems as alcoholism, poverty or single parenthood, then, as causes for familial violence, we must also look to the subordinate position of the child and the female in the family, as it is commonly constituted in Latin America (Uribe and Sánchez 15–17, 32–41).[8]

The exclusion noted above in "Semos Malos" is a recurring theme in *Cuentos de Barro*, particularly in "La Petaca", "Noche Buena" ("Christmas Eve") and "El Circo" ("The Circus"). This exclusion is noted both within and outside of the family unit. In "La Petaca," the girl's family members mistreat her for being malformed and, the narrator says, she was only good for fetching eggs, washing pots and for laughing at (77). Although she cannot see her own deformity, she feels it on her back like a "little story" (78).[9] Through a hole in the wall she peeks out at those who pass by her home, and we know that the family keeps her isolated not only physically, but also psychologically: The narrator notes at the beginning and the end of the story how she has always been a step below her fellow family members (81). After María dies, the *comadres* would say that she did not even feel. Even her emotions, then, were seen as having a lesser quality than those of a "real," or complete person: "Cuando todos estaban riendo, ella sonreía; cuando todos sonreían, ella estaba seria; cuando todos estaban serios, ella lloraba; y ahora, que ellos estaban llorando, ella no tuvo más remedio que estar muerta" (81). This perception of the girl's emotions makes her appear as less than human. She is, in this sense, a metaphor for the social situation of the entire Izalco people who may be considered by the dominant culture to be culturally "one step below," and who do certainly find themselves always in an inferior socioeconomic status. When the father takes her to a special healer, he abandons her there, running away as she protests. Once she is alone with the healer he sexually violates her. She is pregnant at the end of her stay with the healer, but the father, Tule, does not think about the honor of the family, just as he did not consider it upon leaving the girl with the healer—it seems that there is no need to worry about the lost honor of a deformed girl. Tule thinks only about the money he paid the healer and wonders where it has gone, since the girl still has her hunchback. María has obviously served only as a servant and scapegoat for the family.

The girl's deformity makes her physically different from others, just as the Izalco Indians are physically distinct from the *mestizos* and Salvadorans of European descent; in a sense, however, all children are physically disadvantaged as they are smaller and weaker than adults. During the seventeenth and eighteenth centuries, they were seen as incomplete and unhealthy beings who were not quite human; their bodies only loosely held together, their emotions and bodies overly sensitive to maladies and upsets. In this sense, children were compared to women and the lower classes (Sherwood 127–28, 166–69). Children were considered to be highly vulnerable and childhood was a dangerous time. As more attention was paid to them, children were progressively differentiated from adults in more scientific ways: "The call for descriptions of the 'physiologic...peculiarities' of children was answered, and as physiological exegesis developed throughout the [nineteenth] century, it isolated childhood from adulthood through its depiction of the nature of the interactions taking place within the child's body" (Steedman 71–72). There was a marked emphasis on observation during the nineteenth century, thus the child's "symptoms" were to be read for internal problems; this was later extended into psychology (Steedman 68–70). The girl in "La Petaca," then, is differentiated from others, physically and emotionally; and these differences reveal not only her status as a child, but also stand as mute testimony to previous harm done to her and, metaphorically, to her entire people. This incomplete, malformed, hypersensitive being serves only to do menial tasks, and to be the object of others' derision. Her deformity makes her unfit even for marrying, thus the tacit approval of her violation at the hands of the healer, as she lacks the commodity of honor which should have been her most esteemed "natural" quality.

In the next two tales to be considered, "Noche Buena," and "El Circo," two major themes emerge related to the child's position as a marginalized sector: First, children suffer due to a disagreement between adults, specifically due to the power that one adult wields over another, thus they are affected as a class by the discord and decisions of other sectors; second, children are denied entry into scenes which would offer them a form of happiness and a temporary respite from the hardships of life.

In "Noche Buena," the children of a peasant woman, after a long walk from the countryside into town, are not permitted to receive Christmas gifts given out by the local priest because they have not been coming to catechism classes (47). These children live an isolated existence in the countryside, and then are excluded from the dispersal of gifts by the priest. When the mother and children arrive, his rejection is curt and expressed with little emotion. The children, in the church amidst a cacophony of toy instruments and happy children, silently stand by as the Church's representative denies them what would have been their first toys. The children are the picture of poor health and poverty, with their swollen bellies, coughs and runny noses, and ill-fitting clothes. From the beginning of the story the author has created an environment of far-off lights, including the stars, candles in windows, light stretching out from the open door of a house and the distant lights of town, all of which possess a warmth and happiness unreachable for the young children and their tuberculin mother. Nacho and his sister, Tina, are silent in their poverty, as they are later among the other happy children in the church, until the end of the story when the five-year-old boy, Nacho, asks what has happened with the toys as the family makes the long walk home. In addition to the marginalizing effect of the distant light contrasted with the darkness in which they walk, the narrator also uses language and images which link the children to animals. Nacho is being pulled along with a chain; his face is *careto*, which can be translated as stained, blemished or discolored, or dirty, and which the author's glossary says was used to refer to certain horses. The road they travel is like a snake, its skin "stained," perhaps like Nacho's skin, with light and shadow. The small family of three shares the countryside with some cattle, the mention of which leads to a confusion of antecedents, which in itself contributes to the family's connection to the animals: "Unos toros pasaban por el llano, empujando la soledad con sus mugidos de brama. Al pasar por La Canoga, frente al rancho de ño Tito, la puerta de luz les cayó encima, asustándoles los ojos, y oyeron la risa de la guitarra" (46). As the second sentence begins, it is unclear whether the subject has changed from the bulls back to the family; and, in the second sentence, the family is frightened by the light, like animals. With regard to the priest, the message is clear: Follow the Church's doctrine or risk being isolated from even its charitable acts. But the family is isolated as well from the secular celebration of Señor Tito's house: Music, light, laughter are all reserved for someone else.

As in "Noche Buena," the children of "El Circo" find themselves on the outside looking in on a world of happiness to which they are denied entry. This tale expresses most explicitly the author's perception of the exclusion of the child. In this case, they are not permitted to enter the circus tent, so they spy through holes in the canvas, unable to experience "happiness": "Los niños ajuera (sic), los grandes adentro.... El circo era como la felicidad, que se la cogen aquellos que menos la quieren" (111). Thus, happiness is allowed for those who need it the least. When the circus workers grab the spying children, they are trapped like "defenseless dreamers" (112). Salarrué, once again, displays the child's persistent optimism in this story. When a mother scolds one of the children, saying he will "pay in hell" for his misdeeds (112), the child asks whether there will be holes in hell, like those in the circus tent, so that he can see what is going on in heaven (112). It would be a comical remark if it were not such a strong metaphor for the life of the child, indeed for the entire social class from which the child comes: The children's lives are hell, while those of the adults are heaven. The child's question, following the mother's comment, makes clear their acceptance of their hellish life. The younger generation has accepted their status as dwellers of a harsh land where they can only dream, defenselessly, of the happiness enjoyed by others. Theirs is the voyeurism of the impoverished, of the marginalized. Additionally, by putting such criticism in the mouths of children, by plying their innocence, Salarrué is able to criticize, from a relatively safe place, the class structure of an oppressive society.

In addition to the threat of sexual violation discussed in Chapter Two, we have seen other examples of physical violence against children and women in this collection. Such actions, according to an intercultural study by Levinson, are more common in a society where the male controls the life of the female, where it is acceptable to resolve conflicts violently, and where the mother has the majority of the responsibility for the care of the children. There is also, generally, more familial violence in a society which is experiencing outside pressures to change its customs, values, and even its family structure (Levinson 63, 106). Extreme economic difficulties are also blamed for violence against children (Henríquez). It is certain that the Izalcos depicted in the stories were living under overwhelming pressure at the time that Salarrué was writing in the early 1930's. It seems clear that the author is issuing a warning with his intense portrayals of family life, especially of the plight of children in the society, which is meant to call attention to a cycle of violence in El Salvador.

In general, we have demonstrated the author's preoccupation with the exclusion of children from the opportunity to achieve some form of happiness. The child is frequently abused verbally and physically, and suffers for the failures and inequities in the relationships between adults. The son or daughter is also the site of family honor. There are in these stories, however, relationships where love and tenderness are displayed, and where they even overcome considerations of familial and male honor. Salarrué, mining the perceived innocence of children, also portrays the ability of the child to believe in his or her ultimate happiness, even in the face of tremendous obstacles. In our reading, the author signals that the child will continue to wait for and believe in that happiness, and that it is the responsibility of parents and of the larger society to change their behavior and provide children with a stable environment in which they may grow and, perhaps, break the cycle of violence.

The vision of the family and of the child that is presented here is precisely what one would expect in a society that is oppressed and experiencing the brutal social changes occurring at the time in the Izalcos' lands. Salarrué obviously has wanted to make a political point here, and he has generally been praised, as noted above, for presenting more "humane" indigenous characters than those of his predecessors. While we agree with that assessment in general terms, we also find that in his attempt to "humanize" the Izalcans, he has appropriated the identity of the child, homogenizing him into a type, making him stand often in silence as a mute victim of the ravages of the genocidal and economic wars of the Salvadoran countryside. On the one hand, then, we do not see the children who appear in *Cuentos de Barro* as necessarily drawing attention to the plight of children, but rather as stereotypically acting as a symbol of the destiny of their ethnic group as a whole. On the other hand, in so using children, Salarrué enunciates for us his perception of childhood as a time deserving of a certain innocence, happiness and stability.

The short stories of the Dominican Juan Bosch to be examined briefly here, similarly utilize children to send a pessimistic message about the future of society under the pressures of outside influences; however, in Bosch's work, children are perhaps more explicitly linked to marginalized populations and certainly to political activities in their nation than we have seen in Salarrué's collection as it is analyzed above. This may be due in part to Bosch's having written many of his tales while in exile, whereas Salarrué wrote and published in El Salvador where he faced the specter of censorship. In addition, Bosch was a political figure who might very well put his literature to a political task. Not all of Bosch's stories to be examined here are so transparently political; some, like Salarrué's "La Honra," seem meant to elucidate concepts of family honor and to portray family life among the lower classes of Latin America, particularly of rural peoples. Choosing to portray figures from such sectors of society is, of course, a political choice on the part of the author.

Margarita Fernández Olmos notes that Bosch frequently combines an ironic ending and a personal tragedy within the context of a greater social tragedy in his works (113). Often, these personal tragedies involve relationships between family members, particularly between fathers and sons, while the social tragedies are frequently civil wars or revolutionary activities, or extreme economic pressures. Fernández Olmos observes that Bosch's story "Revolución," from the collection *Camino Real* (*Royal Road*), reveals the personal and social complexities of political struggle, where relationships and loyalties to family and friends may be in conflict with the urgency and responsibilities of a revolution (113). As we see in the following analysis, Bosch makes the familial relationships analogous to the political and social conflicts of the nation, and often utilizes the suffering of children to portray the damage to the nation and to individual lives that those conflicts cause. As Fernández Olmos diagrams in her book, Bosch had first-hand knowledge of such conflicts from his childhood onward as he experienced the United States' intervention in the Dominican Republic, later became politically active, and lived some time in exile (97–98). Imperialists at times attempted to justify the intervention as a "pedagogical vocation," with the Dominican people classified as children in need of schooling (Fernández Olmos 101). So, while Bosch may be taking advantage of the emotional reaction of a reader to the suffering of a child, or to the loss of a child's innocence, he may also be responding in kind to the imperialists' use of the child metaphor, portraying how their economic, military and cultural imperialism are affecting the nation's real children. In any case, in many stories children come to be the representatives of the poor and the displaced.

In the tale "Un Niño" ("A Child"), from the collection *Más Cuentos Escritos en el Exilio* (1976) (*More Stories Written in Exile*), Bosch addresses the problem of uneven modernization in Latin America, and utilizes a crippled child as the representative of the classes who struggle to survive in a countryside left behind in the rush to modernize. Three young travelers from the city have car trouble in the mountains and stop to make repairs near the only house in the area. They sustain a brief conversation about the disadvantages of country life, and the great advantages of the modern life of the urban zone. From within the shack they hear a cough and inside they find a small boy, ill with fever. The home is described as filthy and impoverished. The boy is alone; his mother is dead and the father works during the day, returning in the evening to feed his son. This child is described as being full of sweetness as he talks with the visitors. One of the young men tries to convince the boy to come to the city where he would enjoy modernity, civilization, and he could be cured of his illness. The boy resists the idea and, in a dramatic moment, the man lifts the boy and discovers that the child does not have any legs: A vehicle in the city amputated them, the boy explains.

As the travelers leave, one of them continues to talk of the advantages of 'civilization', but the youth who had lifted up the child seems to have learned the lesson as he states that civilization also means pain (56). Bosch attempts here to close the distance between the urban middle class and the rural poor, and it would appear that it is the former who have been changed by the experience as they realize that the very conveniences they enjoy have caused the pain and suffering of the child. Bosch also makes a point about the respect which children's opinions deserve. When the young man is trying to convince the child to go to the city, the narrator notes that the man was confused, that it seemed impossible to him that someone would prefer solitude; but children, the narrator says, do not know what they want (55). It is clear that the child is wiser than his urbane visitors are. Children, and a large sector of the adult population, are learning lessons about the effects of the modernization process which, up till now, were lost on the young travelers. This modernization, rather than uniting the nation, is serving to maintain or even accentuate the lack of comprehension between sectors of the population. It is a failure in a modern machine, the automobile, which provides the opportunity for contact. The child here becomes a focal point of that contact, the conduit for an improvement in communication between classes and between regions of the country. The author is obviously sharing in a belief in the universality of the emotive power of the suffering child as he makes his point.

The story "Mal Tiempo" ("Bad Weather"), from *Más Cuentos Escritos en el Exilio*, makes a similarly explicit linkage between childhood and the exploited working class. While Fernández Olmos has adequately analyzed the significance of man's struggle with nature in this work, and the particular significance of man's defeat in this struggle in an "underdeveloped" nation (147–51), we wish to emphasize here the portrayal of the nineteen-year-old protagonist as a child and a son, and as an exploited class of society. The tale is of a family of charcoal makers consisting of a mother, a father and their only surviving child, Julián. As a hurricane ravages the area, the parents remain at home while Julián, alone in the forest, attempts to escort a huge mahogany trunk into and down the river so that he and his father can convert it to charcoal. The storm's heavy rains are helpful to the charcoal makers as they wash trees downstream.

Stereotypically, the mother is afraid of the storm and frets for her son, who has not returned from the forest, while the father is obsessed with thoughts of the money to be made from the windfall of trees. Venancio, the father, lists the names of his dead children at one point, with the mother adding in an interior monologue that he is probably only thinking of the quantity of charcoal the children might have produced for him. Bosch clearly favors the more humane "female" concern for the child's well-being over the father's materialistic desires. Her role, precisely like that of the nineteenth-century mother outlined in Chapter One, is to temper the father's avaricious, "public" personality. She tries to elicit from the man some show of concern for their son, saying that Julián is a good son, "no le parece, Venancio?" (181–82); but, the father can only comment on the trees that the flash flood has brought them. Julián, meanwhile, thinks only of pleasing his father with the gift of the tree trunk, and of buying his suffering and self-denying mother a new blouse. The young Julián is clearly not a co-worker in this story, but rather an exploited child-laborer, while his father is cast as the obsessed capitalist, the boss who literally works his laborers to death.

In a typical Boschian ironic ending, the boy breaks his leg and drowns in the river, while his parents find the huge tree the teenager had been shepherding down the river; the father notes how God does not leave the poor man wanting, and how He has brought this storm in order to help the family (182). The family will ostensibly experience an improvement in their living standard from the windfall charcoal production, and from the fact that they have one less mouth to feed. The material improvements, however, will have come at the cost of the continuation of the family line. The victory over nature has been costly: The last of their children is dead; the couple has a sterile future. Our reading of this story points to a criticism of man's zealous exploitation both of the natural environment and of children—indeed, children are equated with the environment as they are creatures whose worth is measured only in the value of what may be extracted from them, in this case, in the quantity of charcoal they might produce. This exploitation is allied with the desires of the dominant male in the family, thus the extractive economy and patriarchy are connected. The tale is a powerful warning of the consequences for the nation of such economics, and of the continued disregard for the environment and the nation's children. Such disregard threatens the very existence of the nation as it may die out, washed out to sea with Julián, with nothing remaining but the empty promise of the profit to be made from the natural resources the boy has dislodged from the land, and a vague memory of children who have died in an effort to fulfill the promise.[10]

Sawyer sees the exploitation of children, whether as domestic, industrial or street labor, to be "the consequences of a breakdown in humanity's greatest influence for personal integrity: the family" (196). He blames that breakdown primarily on urbanization and hasty modernization. "Mal Tiempo" certainly shares this thesis, as does "En un Bohío" ("In a Hut"), from the collection *Cuentos*. While in "Mal Tiempo" both the husband and wife survive the storm, the two of them linked by fate and purpose to a sterile future, "En un Bohío" more strongly ties together children and women as sectors which must share the brunt of the effects of poverty. We see a desperately poor woman and her sick children who have been left alone as the husband/father has left to give himself up to the authorities. His absence impoverishes the family. The woman has decided to prostitute herself, and attracts a passing stranger into the hut for that purpose. But a daughter, who has been sent to trade eggs for rice and salt, arrives and interrupts. As the man leaves, the mother laments the lost half peso that the man would have paid her. In addition, the girl, while walking home from the store, has dropped the rice. The story shows how the result of a child's simple and common error—dropping an object—is magnified many times for a family living in such poverty. It is clear that the husband's absence and the ensuing poverty have forced the mother's breakdown in "personal integrity." That the children and their mother should be so linked has become a common object of study among sociologists and anthropologists in recent years.[11] Mothers may even teach their male children that they are the only females who will never abandon them, thus trying to limit the male child's search for a spouse and, in the case of a poorer family, keep the earning potential of the child at home (Romanucci-Ross 56). "En un Bohío," however, not only displays the situation shared by mothers and their children, it also forebodes a similar fate for the daughter who has returned home from the store. The story utilizes the child's innocence to hide from her, but make clear to the reader, that prostitution is a likely outcome for her.

A continuation of this tale, in a sense, is found in "Fragata" ("Frigate" *Más Cuentos Escritos en el Exilio*). The title character is a fat, ugly, "painted" woman who arrives in town a stranger, but possessing keys to a house. She proceeds to shock her neighbors with her childish behavior, playing and fighting with the local children, tying ribbons in her hair as if she were a young girl (22), as well as holding "parties" at her home as she is, apparently, a prostitute. She sometimes even leaves off arguing with an adult in order to run off and play with a child. She is an infantilized adult in a strange town. But this energetic character at times is depressed and suffers anguish; she becomes, at those moments "worthy of compassion" (25). The source of her depression is that she does not have, and apparently cannot have, children. Her desperate desire to be a mother is obviously admired by the narrator. At the end of the story a group of local adults asks her to leave since she is setting a bad example for the children. She bursts into tears and leaves town that very day as she does not wish to be a bad example for the children.

Fragata is at once an infantilized character, as the adults see her exuberance and playfulness as inappropriate; but she is also tormented by the adult desire to have children of her own. Since her age is not clear in the story, the arrested development of the child-prostitute is emphasized; she carries her child-like behavior with her as she ages, in spite of the very adult business in which she is engaged. Not unlike the protagonists and writers to be discussed in the next chapter, she is caught between two worlds, and the adult world persecutes her for that ambiguity. Bosch points to a sterile future for the nation once again, for those who have been trapped by poverty and, in the case of the protagonists of "Fragata" and "En un Bohío," find themselves engaged in prostitution in order to survive.

Survival is also the main concern of the protagonists in "Luis Pie" ("Louis Foot" *Cuentos*). Contrary to what we have seen in "Mal Tiempo" (and also in "El Difunto Estaba Vivo"), in "Luis Pie" we have a father who is driven by his desire to provide for his children and to end their suffering. In this story a parent is missing, but in this case it is the mother. Significantly, Luis is a Haitian working in the Dominican Republic. Fernández Olmos states that this story and the novel *Over*, by Ramón Marrero Aristy, represent the literature of the compassionate Haitian. "Luis Pie," with the introduction at the end of the twelve-year-old Black girl of unknown nationality who witnesses Luis Pie's beating by the police, attempts to transcend the barriers between Haitians and Dominicans. This all takes place in a climate in which Dominican leaders freely expressed their racism, their contempt for Haitians, and their own pride in their Spanish heritage (Fernández Olmos 141–46). For our study, however, it is important to note the way in which Bosch has, once again, focalized through the child his comments on social injustice. On the one hand, Luis Pie is a more sympathetic character because of his love for his children and his concern for the health of his eldest (a six-year-old). Their mother has died, and he acutely feels his responsibility to them; he has brought them to the Dominican Republic to make a better life for them; as he struggles, lost and injured in a cane field, he thinks only of how the children will starve, perhaps become ill and die without him. The story seems to be asking the question of how one can discriminate against a people who are capable of accepting such parental responsibility and expressing such parental love. On the other hand, Bosch, like Salarrué, is portraying the way in which children suffer for the errors, disagreements and prejudices of adults. Luis Pie is ostensibly being punished for starting a fire in a cane field, a fire that was actually sparked by a rich man's cigar. The immigrant here is the scapegoat for the catastrophes that occur in the community. At the end of the story, as Luis Pie is being dragged through town by the authorities, they pass by his own hut, and his three naked children come to the doorway and see him pass. He attempts to speak to them, asking how they are, and the oldest, crying, answers that they are fine. But his captors, Dominicans, are those least concerned about the children and the family as they torment the protagonist when he tries to communicate with his children: "Luis Pie había vuelto el rostro, sin duda para ver una vez más a sus hijos, y uno de los soldados pareció llenarse de ira. –Ya ta bueno de hablar con la familia! – rugía el soldado" (16–17). Bosch portrays his countrymen as the insensitive abusers, and the immigrant as the caring father. The proof of their "(in)humanity" lies in their attitude toward the suffering children, much as Hugh Cunningham has pointed out with regard to British society and literature of the nineteenth century (61–63, 133–34, 138). Thus Bosch emphasizes childhood as a time of innocence and weakness, when one's needs should be met by one's parents, and not by resorting to child labor or to other unhealthy labor such as prostitution.

As noted by Fernández Olmos, Bosch expertly weaves together the social and personal tragedies of his protagonists and their nations, particularly in such stories as "Revolución," "El Cobarde" ("The Coward" *Cuentos Escritos Antes del Exilio*) and "Luis Pie." In the story "El Hombre que Lloró" ("The Man Who Cried" *Cuentos*), the child is at once the symbol of the nation for which a subversive is fighting, and also of the sacrifice that he is making by pursuing the life of the revolutionary. The spy, Régulo, while hiding out from the National Police, can see across the street a boy passionately riding his bicycle in front of a house called Mercedes. The boy's freedom contrasts with the spy's self-imposed incarceration, paranoia and general fear. At the end of the story, as he is heading off to exile in Colombia, disguised as a soldier, a cohort informs him that his wife and son, Regulito, have been moved from Valencia to Caracas. He realizes from the address given to him that the boy he saw playing on his bicycle was his own son, and thus he cries. It is for the next generation of exuberant children for whom the revolutionary is fighting, but in so doing he leads a life which leaves him unable to recognize his own son. This father also contrasts with the mob that dragged Luis Pie through the street, and with the father of Julián, the boy who drowned while trying to secure a tree for his family's charcoal making business. It is the politically active, committed, educated father who is capable of crying for the children, and of recognizing the value to childhood, and by extension to society, of freedom and play. In our reading, this subversive is allied with such marginalized characters as Luis Pie and the mothers from "En un Bohío" and "Mal Tiempo." The axis around which this alliance revolves is their concern for and solidarity with children. Thus, the downtrodden, the marginalized and the intellectual subversives are united to secure a better future for children and for the nation.

We have seen in the above analysis a depiction of the very real suffering of children under chaotic political systems, foreign intervention, changes in the economic structure, and the resultant precariousness in the lives of the lower classes represented in these stories. We have seen Bosch's use of children as a symbol of the nation's suffering under these conditions, and of children as symbols or representatives of entire sectors of society. In Europe, as children became progressively less economically important in the late-nineteenth century (at least for the growing middle class), they became more emotionally important, thus they entered into the national consciousness as a population to be protected (Steedman 133). Protecting children (or at least arguing for their protection) became a source of national pride, one of the factors determining the level of 'civilization' of a society; and, discussed as early as 1785, it became generally involved in the debate on Black slavery in the early 1800's in England. One aspect of this attention which came to the fore was the "perception that childhood was a special state in which innocence and freedom from care should flourish and be protected (H. Cunningham 61–63). In Latin America, writers began to mine the emotive power of the suffering child at the end of the nineteenth century, but it did not become a significant strategy until the 1930's and beyond. Perhaps due to the very real history of the region's uneven and "under"-development, these nations did not experience the trend of the child becoming less economically important and more emotionally important until a later date. In the works of both Salarrué and Bosch, however, this perception of the child as deserving of such freedom and protection is evident.

In the next section, we will examine a work by the Argentine Silvina Ocampo, which is more concerned with middle-class life. This work, rather than evoking the reader's emotional connection to child protagonists, shocks the reader with the grotesque, violent or sexual acts of a portion of the human population which the reader expects to display supreme innocence. We will also show how her work makes a strong connection between children, or childhood, and the working classes or other marginalized sectors of society.

The works of Juan Bosch and Salarrué clearly exploit the concept of the child as an innocent, nearly helpless and passive member of society; the child is thus aligned with the oppressed sectors of societies in which those marginalized peoples are viewed by the author as having little public power, or even the means to prevent the powerful from influencing their domestic lives. In the work of Silvina Ocampo to be examined here, we make some of the same points made above, particularly with regard to the effects of childhood experiences on one's adult life; however, in the stories from *La Furia y Otros Cuentos* (1959) (*The Fury and Other Stories*) there can be read an exploration of society's construction of beings with supposedly ambiguous natures, and how that ambiguity or ambivalence is used by society to foment oppression. This Argentine author's work underscores the good-evil dichotomy, in particular, as one of the ways in which societies communicate to the younger generation the limits on their behavior and on their future in that society. We see in Ocampo's work, particularly in the stories "La Furia" and "Los Amigos" ("The Friends"), how the all too familiar belief in the cruelty of children is, on the one hand, a trap with which society can categorize these beings as less than human; on the other hand, however, these acts of cruelty can be interpreted as the child's reaction to the limits, seen as unjust, which society puts on them due to their age, race or gender, limits of which a maturing child becomes progressively more aware. These acts of cruelty, or rebellion, only fuel the extant belief in the good-evil dichotomy, however. In addition to this major point, we will also explore briefly the complex manifesto on childhood and society laid out in "La Raza Inextinguible" ("The Inextinguishable Race"), the final story of *La Furia*. This story clearly points to an identification of the child with the working classes.

A few critics have pointed out how Ocampo utilizes marginalized characters, particularly servants, children and women, in her stories because such people offer an objective point of view which then makes more shocking the fantastic and grotesque images of her work (Klingenberg "Mad" 29; Pezzoni 20–22; Araújo 32). Although we do not consider any point of view to be "objective," our thesis does admit that servants and children in particular, given their places outside the upper realms of the public and domestic middle-class hierarchies, are used by Ocampo and other authors to give the reader a critical inside view of those hierarchies. Blas Matamoro, as well, notes a certain complicity between marginalized sectors in Silvina Ocampo's stories, although he does not consider there to exist true solidarity between them (200). Enrique Pezzoni also groups together children, the ill, servants, animals and those on their deathbed as people who reject any form of a pact with the reigning social order. Such sectors are the only ones to have what he calls a "visión radiante" (18) of the old order, for which their masters nostalgically yearn, but these marginalized people subvert attempts to recoup that order.

In the title story of the collection, there appears to be a kind of cooperation between a child, Cintito, and his nanny, Winifred. That cooperation is tied to a resistance by both to the demands or desires of a young university student, the narrator of the story. Their cooperation, if we are to believe the events as the student tells them, leads to his arrest for the murder of the child. The student describes tender and apparently loving interactions between Winifred and Cintito. The child's presence, and Winifred's responsibility for him, are her spoken reasons for not seeking the privacy of a hotel room, for not leaving aside her narrative in order to satisfy the young man's insistent requests. During the regular trysts between the student and the nanny, which take place in a park, the child, in spite of the pleas of the young man, constantly plays his drum, which contributes to the sense of frustration of the student as he attempts to woo Winifred. It is a source of irritation later, as well, when the man and the child are left alone together in a hotel room after Winifred has abandoned them. During this scene, late in the story, Cintito displays a resistance based on evasiveness, refusing to give a straight answer to the young man's inquiries regarding Winifred's name and other identifying characteristics:

> –Te doy bombones, si me decís cómo se llama tu niñera.
> –Dame bombones.
> –Después. Cómo se llama?
> Cintito siguió jugando con la colcha, con la alfombra, con la silla, con los palillos del tambor. (120)

The child's drumming, besides being a constant reminder of his presence, is an accompaniment to Winifred's testimonial monologues, an incessant beating not unlike that which is intended to establish a trance-like state during the storytelling by *El Hablador* (*The Storyteller*) in the Vargas Llosa novel of the same name. Such a state permits Winifred to attempt to gain, to capture in a sense, the young man's comprehension of her personal plight with stories of her own childhood in the Philippines.

Octavio Paz writes in *El Laberinto de la Soledad* (1950) (*The Labyrinth of Solitude*) that any attempt by a woman to gain the understanding of a male will end in frustration because of the image that the "conqueror" has of her, an image of herself that she may share: "Entre la mujer y nosotros se interpone un fantasma: el de su imagen, el de la imagen que nosotros nos hacemos de ella y con la que ella se reviste.... Su feminidad jamás se expresa, porque se manifiesta a través de formas inventadas por el hombre" (177).

In these tales of her childhood, Winifred focuses on her relationship with Lavinia, a fair-skinned girl who is the ideal female in her homeland: Blonde, devout, well mannered, fearful of nature. It is through the retelling of these stories that we see the child's growing awareness of her marginalization due, primarily, to her race. It is possible to interpret the antipodal images of the two girls as a psychological doubling (Araújo; Klingenberg "Mad") and as a literary mechanism which adds to the shock value of the grotesque and fantastic in Ocampo's work (Klingenberg "Twisted"; Meehan, cited in Klingenberg *Infiel* 16). Klingenberg has noted such doubling in other works by Ocampo where there is an emphasis on the difference in social class between two girls. With regard to *La Furia*, she has stated that socioeconomic disparities remain in the background and are not the central theme of the stories (*Infiel* 41, 65). In "La Furia," however, the two girls are from the same socioeconomic class. Additionally, while the social pressures, especially those of the church, to conform to the image of the perfect, chaste *señorita* are present in the story, they do not appear to lead to the sexual confusion or to feelings of shame or guilt after some sexual act as occurs in other Ocampo stories. We are left in "La Furia" with society's racial preferences as the primary source of the nanny's frustrations.

In the Philippines, Winifred worked to correct her friend Lavinia's "defects," a clear sign of the resistance and frustration that Winifred felt in the face of the racism of the islands. Lavinia's major defect, according to Winifred, was her pride, and the source of that pride was the fact that Lavinia was blonde and had very white skin (116). Winifred, like the protagonist from the autobiographical novel of Capécia (Fanon 45), attacks the signs of Lavinia's white race, attempting to blacken her. First, she cuts one of Lavinia's blonde locks, which leads to a drastic cutting of the girl's hair. Later,

Winifred stains Lavinia's skin with perfume. The epitome of these acts results in Lavinia's death, as she is *carbonizada* ("burned to death") when the candle that Winifred is carrying during a religious procession sets fire to the artificial wings worn by Lavinia. The two were dressed as angels for the event, and Winifred notes that she, as the blue angel, was more important than Lavinia, the pink angel (115–16). There exists for Winifred, then, a value system based on the color of the skin, and it is that system which she became aware of and resisted in childhood. Winifred should not be seen, therefore, as some evil double of Lavinia, rather her acts of "cruelty" should be seen as a child's expression of frustration with an unjust, racially-based value system.

Winifred's recounting of those childhood memories, which are interpreted by the young man as proof of her evilness, is an attempt to find common ground with the student: Childhood is supposedly something which we all have in common, its qualities are supposedly universal, so it is reasonable that she would use tales of childhood to attempt a deeper communication with the young man. The children in this story (Winifred, Cintito and Lavinia) are not the relatively passive representatives of a nation's suffering or a people's marginalization that we have seen in the works by Salarrué and Juan Bosch. They are, instead, actively resisting the powers that be: Winifred does so through her acts of cruelty toward Lavinia and her testimonial monologue with the student; while Cintito displays his resistance through his accompaniment of Winifred, as well as through his evasiveness in his final dialogues and play with the student. While Winifred's tales of childhood reflect the child's knowledge of the dichotomous image of the child held by society, the young man, whose letter is the story we read, must also be mining that ambiguousness in his depiction of Winifred. The ambiguity of childhood is at once exploited by Winifred, the woman of color, and by the young man of letters. While the child, Cintito, collaborates, although unknowingly perhaps, with Winifred in the performance of her testimony, childhood itself is also the central concern of that testimony. Childhood is the site of her recovery of memories which formed her rejection of society's limitations on her, and it is also the student's site of construction of the evil image of Winifred which he needs for his own defense.[12] Cintito's murder is the reason for which the young man is in jail, but that act has been subsumed in the narrative by Winifred's childhood. The narrator ignores the "innocent" child victim as he constructs the image of the "evil" child Winifred. The result of this juxtaposition is that he blames the destruction of the innocent Argentine male child on the evil Philippine female. He has utilized the very good versus evil dichotomy so prevalent in the criticism of Ocampo's work to defend his own murderous act.

The final story in *La Furia*, "La Raza Inextinguible," presents another sort of testimonial in which the speaker emphasizes the scapegoat quality of being a child, as well as the child-like treatment afforded marginalized sectors of society: The child "race" in the tale obviously is a metaphor for the working classes of Argentina. The story begins with a brief introduction by a narrator who has discovered a city in which everything is "perfect and small."

A child with bags under his eyes explains the situation. The children are the workers, the ones who construct the city, and they find themselves in that situation thanks to the "egoísmo" of the parents: "Somos los que trabajamos: nuestros padres, un poco por egoísmo, otro poco por darnos el gusto, implantaron esta manera de vivir económica y agradable" (227). At times the children work and sweat, but at other times they throw fits which last only a brief moment, probably an allusion to labor strikes. A comparison is made between this life of toil and the "inconveniences" with which the parents must live: The things that the children construct are too small for the parents, thus the adults do not fit well in their houses or their furniture, even their blankets are too small for them. The adults accuse the children of being the cause of the adults' unhappiness, and of the lack of growth among some adults; it seems that many people are not achieving their full stature. These lines appear to underscore the "adults'" materialism, their unhappiness with the status quo and their use of the workers/children as scapegoats.

The adults also indulge their appetites. They spend their time playing cards, reading and talking, playing music, loving and hating, "pues, son apasionados," while the children work, build, clean and harvest (227). This is an inversion of the usual hierarchy of qualities assigned to adults and children, and, analogously, to the social classes. Here it is the children who are diligent and hardworking, while the adults whine like spoiled children and are unable to control their desires. The adults complain that everything is too small for them, even the amount of food they receive, though the narrator accuses them of being gluttons: "La palabra *diminuta* [Ocampo's emphasis] está siempre en sus labios. La cantidad de alimentos que consiguen, según las quejas de mis tías, que son glotonas, es reducidísima" (228). We note the child's irreverence in this line, as well as at other points in the story. The narrator also notes the "parents'" delicacy, as they are unwilling to sit on the ground, for example, and complain of the cold. The narrator says that it is the "children" who put on ceremonies and theatrical and film productions, perhaps tying the idea of childhood to the artist, as we will do in the next chapter.

Another aspect of social class consciousness that appears in the story is the narrator's description of certain "mediocre" people who try to "infiltrate" the world of the child race. They look like children, he says, and these "personas de estatura mediocre, inescrupulosas (cada día hay más), ocupa nuestros lugares, sin que lo advirtamos.... Hemos tardado mucho en descubrir a los impostores" (228). These "impostors" would appear to be foreigners, perhaps referring to immigrants to Argentina. The infiltrators speak in a vague manner and mix various languages (228); and, they seem to take the places of the child race, meaning their jobs. (The narrator indicates that society does not treat these impostors well as he was once mistaken for one and does not want to remember the day it happened.) The narrator is adamant that such impostors, who may include the child-race's parents, will not take over the race's place in society. Before that happens, he says, the children will break their machinery, the potable water system, etc.; that is, they will not let the "adults" wipe out the race and then still enjoy the fruits of the "children's" labor. This class-based interpretation coincides with the earlier analyses which link children or childhood to marginalized sectors of society. In this case, the narrator offers a tongue-in-cheek metaphor of the working class as a child living under the capricious elites who know little of the "child's" world, but who occasionally "infiltrate" that world, trying to gain the "child's" confidence. The narrator notes that only the members of the "inextinguishable" race may successfully become smaller and still maintain their identity, and they can do so without trying to fool anyone (229).

Another interpretation, however, could be more psychologically based. If one's childhood experiences determine one's success and "stature" as an adult, then the "construction" work of the child-race could refer to those experiences. Thus, when the narrator notes that children are being blamed for the adults' inability to reach their normal, excessive proportions (228–29), we might interpret this as a recognition of the importance of childhood experience in the formation of the mature person. From this point of view, the "impostors" might be adults seeking to return to a child-like state in some effort to make more comfortable a world that does not fit properly, a world based on the expectations of childhood. The "impostors" might also be a reference to the child-like state of the elderly, as the description of the intruders, who look like tired children and are wrinkled, have swollen eyes and speak in a vague way, mixing various languages (228), could be seen as that of an old person. The narrator himself, we recall, has bags under his eyes, calling into question his identity. This child-narrator, under this interpretation, would appear to be caught, in a sense between the adult and child-race worlds. The narrator notes that he and others of his race are getting smaller, but just the opposite may be meant: As he and other children age, they are no longer doing—nor are they able to do—the "construction" of childhood. Thus when he says that he and his brother and another friend are finding it difficult to lift and use their tools, he may be indicating their emergence into adulthood. Such an inversion of order as that embodied in these child-laborers and aged children also is a narrative strategy meant to better demonstrate the state of Argentine society.

In any case, both interpretations of this story implicate a linking of class and childhood. On the one hand, the working class is presented as a population infantilized by the ruling classes; but, by utilizing a "child's" point of view in the person of the narrator, that dichotomy is subverted to a certain extent as the narrator derides the "childishness" of the ruling classes, as well as emphasizing the important and massive works of the laboring classes. In the second interpretation, the class metaphor is used to emphasize the interrelatedness of the stages of the life cycle in which an adult's expectations and personality are formed during childhood, much as a society's well-being or standard of living (potable water, electrical services, etc.) are actually constructed by the working class.

In our analysis of "La Furia," as well, we have seen a linking of marginalized sectors whose status is based on judgments of race and gender. This linking has involved an exploration of the qualities of childhood, as these sectors are infantilized, and has also underscored the importance of the experiences of childhood, where society's limitations become progressively clearer to the youth. The rebelliousness of the child and that of the lower classes are directly related, as both try to throw off the effects of infantilization. "La Furia's" narrator, in the end, casts himself as a child who has been driven to commit a violent act by the evil child Winifred. In a sense, the student, Cintito and Winifred all share, according to our reading, this rebellious nature as children; it is their "common ground." In the case of the narrator, however, it is a young adult, the holder of superior physical strength and the one who is integrated into the canons of the legal and literary spheres, who "childishly" lays blame on another. His appropriation of that child's discourse, combined with his social power, is deadly, and leads to an unjust condemnation of the Philippine woman.

We have seen in this chapter what we have been calling the exploitation and the exploration of childhood by Latin American authors during times of social upheaval. In the Salarrué stories, the author explores the plight of the Izalco Indians, and by extension the nation, as the government is oppressing the indigenous culture. Juan Bosch, in a more blatantly political way, utilizes child characters to demonstrate the suffering caused the nation by imperialism, war, urbanization and economic distress. He thus utilizes the reader's romantic image of the innocent, uncorrupted child to advocate for a less corrupt, we might say nostalgic image of, society. He also at times equates the condition of childhood with that of the working classes. And this last point, as noted above, is one of the major issues of our analysis of Ocampo's stories, as is the inverse: That the working class, and other sectors of society, are infantilized by the rest of society. In a sense, Ocampo's use of childhood experience and qualities, especially as seen in "La Raza Inextinguible," reflect the ambiguity in society's characterization of children, as her stories leave themselves open repeatedly to dual interpretations. We will see in the next chapter how authors expose that ambiguity as they explore the importance to the Latin American artist of the romantic image of childhood.

NOTES

[1]See Rothstein for a more detailed description of the types of tasks performed by children of particular ages in a Mexican village, and how the tasks have changed with the availability of industrial jobs and public education (40–43).

[2]For a more general treatment of this theme in Hispanic American literature see Aponte.

[3]The connection between the writer and childhood, and how they both represent a threat to that national discourse, will be explored further in Chapter Four.

[4]This exclusion will be related to exile in our examination of the work of Cristina Peri Rossi.

[5]Much of the following analysis appears in my article: "El niño excluido: Relaciones Familiares en *Cuentos de Barro* de Salarrué," *Journal of Interdisciplinary Literary Studies* 4.1–2 (1992): 71–88.

[6]This mystical connection to nature is similar to the female's supposed knowledge of witchcraft, and her use of natural elements to perform "magic." Women have often been described as possessing inherent powers of witchcraft, needing only some stimulus to be awaken them and put them to use. Particularly "uncanny power" was ascribed in New Spain to women of marginalized ethnic groups (Behar 178–81). Woman, then, may be both the moral superior of the male, and a witch who performs evil deeds.

[7]This contrasts with, for example, the tendency to blame children for their mother's death, or for the difficulties of a family's situation, as we see

in some of the stories of *El Llano en Llamas* (1952) (*The Burning Plains*) by Mexico's Juan Rulfo.

[8]Roger Sawyer takes this a step further, going beyond the construct of the patriarchal family to implicate all human beings of all cultures in a basic desire to control others: "It has always been, and presumably always will be, a characteristic of the dark side of the human being that in some way he will try to possess another; by doing so he can indulge his inherent lust for power" (20–21).

[9]The narrator hints here at the connection between author and child: The child's deformity, which is the reason for her family's mistreatment of her, is compared to a story. Both would appear to be natural burdens that one must carry, and both may incite the ire, resentment or fear of others.

[10]The story "El Difunto Estaba Vivo" ("The Deceased Was Alive"), from *Cuentos*, besides its implications for the study of politics and family, has a similar message as the distant, driven father, a pioneering landowner, and his sons all die out in the end, leaving no living human legacy in the land they have colonized.

[11]See, for example, the studies by Nancy Folbre and Martha Roldan, as well as the editors' introduction, in Dwyer and Bruce. Claudia Fonseca has explored the child-mother bond in families of a Brazilian slum. Lola Romanucci-Ross's study of a Mexican village frequently notes ties between mothers and children in the face of changing economic and political circumstances.

[12]This process is not unlike that used by the narrator of "Los Amigos" (217–24). In this story a narrator looks back on his childhood relationship with another boy who was seen as saintly by their families and the neighborhood's women until it is discovered that the boy had a pact with evil spiritual forces. The narrator recounts how the previously saintly friend was responsible for the natural disasters and epidemics that had plagued the community. In the end, the narrator throws a bird into the water and the friend drowns trying to retrieve it. Much like the student narrator in "La Furia," the narrator of "Los Amigos" has likely recreated this evil image of the friend in order to ameliorate the narrator's own sense of guilt over the drowning.

CHAPTER FOUR

The Dangers of Ambiguity, the Requirements of Creativity:
The Artist and the Child in Cristina Peri Rossi,
Reinaldo Arenas, Julio Cortázar and Alfredo Bryce Echenique

> Si pudiera volverme por los años y ser de nuevo niño, cami-
> nante, descansar a mis pulmones en la mano y cantar con todo
> el pecho y el tamaño. Pero ahora estoy totalmente en el ex-
> ilio, he perdido la memoria y el sentido . . .
>
> —Nicasio Urbina

González Echevarría notes that exile is a "founding literary myth, as it is a founding Latin American cultural construct, a strategic form of self-definition" (134). As such, exile is a topic which allows modern Latin American authors to distance themselves from and critique inherited literary platitudes: "One of the topics most commonly used to engage in such an analysis of the modern tradition is exile, for it contains both a longing for a lost motherland as source and a sense of its irrevocable loss. If the land endows people with a special knowledge, exile would be a heightening of that knowledge through the ordeal of separation and return" (González Echevarría 126). The intellectual youth of Latin America must participate in a voluntary exile, making the pilgrimage to Europe, as we see in the first two works discussed in this chapter; they must go through an apprenticeship there which, in a sense, is the exile component of their literary cannon. However, while there, they pretend to engage in revolutionary struggles against canonical art forms and modes of thought. What they do not realize, what Oliveira, the protagonist of *Rayuela* does not seem to realize, for example, is that this struggle and exile have become part of the cannon. The fact that he lauds childhood as the place in which to seek out originality is also a canonical, romantic act; but, even more to the point, childhood is a handy, accessible—both for the artist and the reader—manifestation of exile (as Twain says, we have all been children). The writer resorts to childhood for its relevance to potential readers, and for the very qualities (inherited from the culture) of childhood which it shares with the condition of the artist. Childhood should pull readers in and also should help the reader see the link between the exile of the author and that of the child, as well as that of every human being who has been a child.

One quality of childhood is the spontaneous creativity of child's play, and this is an envied aspect of that time of life. Literature, certainly the language and structure of *Rayuela* or *El Palacio de las Blanquísimas Mofetas*, or the games found in *La Rebelión de los Niños*, for example, may be seen as toys as they remind us of, and challenge our ideas of, what is acceptable or conventional. As González Echevarría says:

> There is a knowledge to be gained from literature, as there is from toys, a knowledge that has to do with people's creation of palpable models as access both to beauty and to wisdom. Some may outgrow toys, but literature, art, replace these as forms of representation that give substance to our ideas and desires. Literature's own peculiar game, however, is constantly to remind us of its conventionality, to afford once and again the pleasure of its own form of self-denial. (135)

Thus, the protagonists examined in this chapter are playing in worlds of toys and texts, the world of children and artists. This is not, we would say, a place of refuge, but rather a dangerous place. It is not so physically life-threatening in Cortázar and Bryce as we will show it to be in Peri Rossi and Arenas, however. What makes it dangerous is the ambiguity assigned to childhood, and its mythic qualities as a time of pure spirituality; the child was seen by the romantics to be connected to God and nature, and uncorrupted by knowledge and the rational; the child was also a scientific laboratory of sorts for those studying the development of human beings, of the species, indeed of life itself (see our Introduction and Chapter One). Both perspectives are dehumanizing, and that is the danger delineated in these works, and also the challenge offered to the children and to society. For being dehumanized—even if it is in an effort to exult one above other humans—is in the end the ultimate form of exile.

The first section of this chapter discusses how childhood is mythologized and, at the same time, is part of the myth of the Latin American artist or writer in search of his or her Latin American identity. Cortázar's attempt to write, or to describe how to write, original material, is dependent upon this myth of the child, of the uncorrupted, objectified body and mind which will be filled by the sum of Oliveira's knowledge, but which in the end signals its own failure. Bryce Echenique's project, on the other hand, is to valorize some of those same characteristics of childhood, and then to maintain contact with them within the protagonist's own artistic life, equating them with the desired qualities of the artist, and then showing how one suffers as child and as artist due to society's inability to accept those qualities. The theme of exile permeates these works, and is below related to childhood as it is a state from which all adults have separated, and which is, or was, also separated from the adult world. Both protagonists end up in a sort of exile, one completely out of touch with reality, and the other still engaged, but suffering and misunderstood.

Julio Cortázar and Alfredo Bryce Echenique have demonstrated a great fascination with the various periods of childhood, and in particular have explored the process of maturation of the young Latin American intellectual. Cortázar has also examined adults' attempts to infiltrate the child's world, efforts which always fail, and has delved into the stereotypical, dichotomous, angel-devil image of the child. Both authors have displayed the relations between adults and children in the bourgeois world and how this class's families can restrict and thwart individual creativity (see our Chapter Two). Cortázar has dedicated himself to showing how, when childhood's games end, the oppression of bourgeois life begins.[1] The two authors' ideas surrounding childhood diverge, however, upon examination of the principal characters in two of their novels which treat the lives of young Latin American intellectuals in París: Oliveira from Cortázar's *Rayuela* (*Hopscotch*) (1963) and Martín Romaña from Bryce Echenique's *La Vida Exagerada de Martín Romaña* (1985) (*The Exaggerated Life of Martín Romaña*. Both authors seem to operate under the influence of romantic ideas about the child and the artist, which drag the respective young-adult protagonists through distinct paradoxes, but which carry them in the end to a vulnerable child-like position. The following quotation from *Martín Romaña* perhaps best describes this paradoxical position of the child, and, most importantly, of the artist or author who struggles to maintain the viability of his or her child-like qualities. While everything is possible for a child, and while one may spend one's life trying to find that realm of possibility, if one attempts to be a child, even for just five minutes, society will "flatten you like a pancake." The statements are made by a minor character in the novel, an author named Bryce Echenique:

> . . . prácticamente todo es posible tratándose de un niño. Y de ahí, Martín Romaña, agregó, lo triste que es dejar de serlo. Se pasa uno la vida buscando la fórmula para seguir siéndolo, pero eso es lo único que no es posible tratándose de un niño. Y todo lo demás son cuentos, viejo, cuentos geniales pero cuentos al fin y al cabo. Haz la prueba de portarte como un niño cinco minutos seguidos y vas a ver lo que te pasa, viejo. Te chanca una aplanadora. (257–58)

This character-author alludes to the possibility that it is only through literature (the "*cuentos*") that one can explore childhood, but that the result or final destination of that exploration, is not some mythical childhood itself, but only "stories," literature itself.

The romantics, beginning in the last third of the eighteenth century, were fascinated by the transformation of one's being, by the desire to perfect oneself or "totalize" oneself. A human being found himself, however, frequently restricted by the pressure to conform to society's models of behavior and thought, and by an educational system that squelched creativity in favor of conformity. What the romantics sought, in their reaction against the enlightenment's rationalism, was a being who could transcend those limits and reach a state of unlimited, constant growth and potential. "In their search for normative figures who could elude fixity in the interests of totalization of potentiality, the romantics frequently turned to two sorts of beings: to artists and to children" (Plotz 64). The ideal artist, indeed the ideal human, would maintain the sense of playfulness, the spontaneity and the creativity present in the child (Plotz 68). These two beings, who exist at the margins of society, share a degree of freedom from fixed social roles. The child, in particular, is capable of existing simultaneously within and outside of such roles. His or her "innocence" does not lie so much with "natural goodness (though that usually is included in the term) as that it implies an utter translucency of behavior—a totally *lived* application of all concepts that are mastered" (Plotz 73–74). Thus, innocence required the space and circumstances in which to live out freely those concepts; restrictions on that freedom would constitute corruption of the innocent, just as restrictions on expression constitute censorship for the artist.

We shall see in the following analysis that Oliveira, influenced as well by leftist, utopian ideals about the family and childhood, considers the latter to be the free zone of the imagination, a poetic heaven where one's essential being lives on (Hass 260). Oliveira is incapable, however, of fusing his intellectual or educated side with his supposedly more spontaneous, artistic, "pure" child side; this character is searching for the revelation of certain existential truths, the inspiration, the affectiveness and the freedom that are lacking in his mundane life, and he hopes that "a clairvoyant bind man" (*Rayuela* 125) will serve as his bridge in that search. Oliveira, who has lost contact with childhood, travels back in time to find that bridge, as he returns to a child-like state at the end of the novel; however, upon achieving that mythic state, he finds himself trapped behind a self-created web of insanity which leaves him isolated, incommunicado, incapable of taking advantage of that long sought-after space. Martín Romaña, on the other hand, follows to the letter the romantic prescription noted above, by maintaining intact the creative, spontaneous qualities of childhood throughout his long education; thus, he becomes the ideal artist in the romantic sense: "'wholeness' is the property of those only who are able to remain alive to their past lives in their present" (Plotz 80). In *La Vida Exagerada* we see the demythification of the grand search (as well as other aspects of the life of the Latin American intellectual in Paris) undertaken by Oliveira in *Rayuela*, and at the same time the successful, though painful, struggle by Martín Romaña to retain the prized capacities of childhood, which in the end convert him into an 'adult' artist.

All adults are, in a sense, exiled from childhood, and most become as rational as Oliveira. He, like the romantics reacting against the Enlightenment's rationalism, seeks out some entity which might possess a clearer and more spiritual vision, which might serve as a bridge, as noted above, and this entity (or state) is the child (or childhood). In order to avail himself of the child's clairvoyance, the intellectual must first mythify the child, strip him of his humanity and in its place create the perfect "bridge" to that sought-after utopia of translucent comprehension.[2] This child-bridge, however, is not capable of communicating to the intellectual his or her perfect vision. The intellectual, therefore, needs a child-prodigy who possesses the vision and innocence of the mythified child, as well as the ability to communicate; however, in the process of learning to communicate, this child is corrupted by society. One of the projects of *Rayuela* is to reveal the corruption from which all literary efforts suffer, since no one can unwrite—i.e., launch a literary revolution—from within the models of extant writings. This paradox is endemic in romanticism:

> . . . a belief in the absolutism, the perfect completion of the child, is united to a belief in the desirability of development into a more spacious and fulfilled adulthood. . . . To the venerator of childhood sanctity, the educational proc-

ess must seem ironic, a forced exchange of a lower for a higher form of wisdom. (Plotz 68)

The romantics, like Oliveira, disdained the collecting of data so dominant in the formation of Western "knowledge," but at the same time the manipulation and improvement of that data is desirable. In a sense, the whole of Western knowledge stands between the adult and childhood, as the Atlantic Ocean separates the young Latin American intellectual studying in Europe from Latin America. One cannot disregard that knowledge upon returning, however, just as one cannot pretend that the ocean-crossing voyage never happened.

We discuss two major points regarding childhood in *Rayuela*. First, that Cortázar kills the innocent-child, in the person of Rocamadour, and then attempts to create that child anew through the novel, which might be considered here to be the collection of letters to Rocamadour which Oliveira mentions in chapter thirty-three (339). This mythification and recreation of the perfect reader-accomplice converts *Rayuela* into an advice book, in a sense, into a pedantic novel in which the "father" Oliveira teaches his "son" how to live, to read and to write (see also our Chapter Two). This process reflects as well the ultimate possession of the subaltern in Cortázar. Lanin Gyurko notes that children in Cortázar's stories cannot be co-opted by the adults (38); in *Rayuela*, the author completely appropriates the child before he can mount a resistance, or be corrupted. Second, we propose that the paradox of the child prodigy and the effort to create the perfect reader convert this novel into a paternalistic text; *Rayuela*'s project, or at least as we identify it here, is analogous to the attempt to raise a child who will turn out exactly as the parent would wish. Cortázar, apparently following the precepts of Morelli, attempts to sacrifice the "passive reader" and create a "reader-accomplice"; and, in that reader-accomplice, whatever is achieved by the author is repeated and magnified (561). In order to create this reader, it is necessary to transport him or her to the author's own time or age, and contribute to his "mutation," and to his education as an accomplice (*Rayuela* 559–61; and see Merrim 54). However, as Ronald says in his interpretation of Morelli, killing that which one is attempting to save—the child-reader, in our interpretation—is a viable alternative, even a necessity: "En ese mundo tecnológico de que hablas, Morelli quiere salvar algo que se está muriendo, pero para salvarlo hay que matarlo antes o por lo menos hacerle tal transfusión de sangre que sea como una resurrección" (616–17). The reader Rocamadour is likely killed, therefore, and resuscitated outside of the text through the work that creates, or re-educates the child in the reader. Utilizing the terminology of Eco, we could say that this ideal reader created by Cortázar through the letters to Rocamadour will serve only as the "intertextual frames" provided in the letters; since he has died, he would not have other such references, and, obviously, he would not have the "common frameworks" gained through mundane experience and which "are mainly rules for practical life" (Eco 21). We have here, as noted in our introduction's discussion of Steedman's work, another association of childhood with death: The end of childhood marks the end of a period of supposedly free exploration and growth; and in the above quote by Ronald, that "death" is desirable as a new starting point, a moment at which a "transfusion" or "resurrection" could take place. We see in the end of the novel, however, that a return to a child-like state not only means the death of the adult, educated man, it also means exile from one's peers, from society and from the ability to express oneself. Ironically, in that moment of "resurrection," however, Oliveira's isolation from his cohorts makes impossible the bridging of the two worlds so sought after throughout the novel. The myth of childhood has driven the protagonist's investigation of Western knowledge, but in the end, it has trapped him in an internal exile.

In *La Vida Exagerada* meanwhile, we see implicated, as Gutiérrez notes in some of Bryce's stories, the presence of a non-represented reader, which behaves in such a way that it becomes the programmed producer of the text (Gutiérrez 111). This reader will make use of both intertextual and common frameworks as he/she produces the text; this contrasts with the presence of the child-reader-accomplice created by the author of *Rayuela*. If we consider for a moment the two protagonists in their roles as readers, we see that Oliveira has practically cut himself off from his "common frameworks," thus becoming a purely literary being, without a past based in reality, without a childhood; he interprets texts only through other written texts or art forms. Martín Romaña utilizes both his "common" and "intertextual" frameworks as he reads and interprets the texts he encounters in Paris; previously read texts and his personal past, meanwhile, influence his current life and his new readings in Paris, and his experiences and readings in Paris alter his earlier experiences and readings. Martín Romaña thus keeps alive his past—he keeps the bridge open—while Oliveira attempts to live only in written texts and cultural production, mythologizing childhood and searching for his "bridge" within that myth. Both end up as exiles, as the cost of returning to childhood for Oliveira is internal isolation, and the cost of keeping childhood alive is exile in Europe for Martín Romaña.

In neither of the two major images of the child in *Rayuela*—the painful situation of the child Rocamadour, and of the child-like Oliveira at the end of the novel—do we find the mythical bridge-child sought by Oliveira, but rather the reality of the physical and intellectual state of a child as helpless, vulnerable and incommunicado. Rocamadour's death, in spite of the efforts of the group to limit their affective relationships (see our Chapter Two), touches those in the apartment. The emotions elicited by the child's very state of exile, his having suffered and died alone, are too much for the group to bear. The child's life, and now its death, are surely reminders of the members' own mortality, and their own exile; exile both from their childhoods, and from their nations and families. The novel begins, then, with the exiled Rocamadour—exiled in his own home—and ends with the exiled Oliveira in a child-like state—exiled within his own country.

These intellectuals, however, though they do not indulge, supposedly, in affective relationships, also have difficulty achieving the desired union of consciences, or locating the assistance they need to travel to some heaven where they would find the truths regarding our existence. These friends have already been contaminated by western knowledge, not unlike children who arrive at an age in which they are finally able to communicate verbally with the rest of the world. After having learned all that western knowledge has to offer, these child prodigies (and it is interesting to note that Amorós, in his introduction and notes to this edition, labels many of the artists and other figures mentioned in the novel as prodigies), they are incapable of breaking completely with that canonical body of knowledge. Efforts to make such a break are the theme of the "des-escritura" ("unwriting") of Morelli and the existencial search of Oliveira.

Just as Rocamadour permeates the thoughts of the members of the Club in *Rayuela*, childhood or Martín's own child-like behavior and status permeate *La Vida Exagerada* and the thoughts of the protagonist himself. He considers himself a child—and others like this aspect of his personality—as well as an adult, and he navigates between the two modes of existence. One of the aspects of childhood most valued by the romantics was his or her freedom of emotional expression. Martín Romaña does not deny his affectivity, indeed he seems to live for those moments when he will experience exaggerated emotions. He finds affectionate or emotional relationships everywhere, with men such as Enrique and with women such as Inés and Sandra. Martín does not seem to be concerned with any mythical union of consciences, but rather with maintaining the current amorous union in his life, first with Inés and later with Sandra. This affectivity, as noted above, is one of the admired traits of the child's personality as sentiment is the underpinning of creative power (Plotz 71). Doctor Llobera helps Martín to see that his affectivity or sensitivity are integral parts of his talent as a writer; that, indeed, his hypersensitivity should not be taken as a

defect, but rather as a virtue, a power, a highly personal strength (516).
Oliveira with his rationalism, and Martín Romaña with his sensitivity, display almost opposite poles of affectivity: Doctor Llobera assures Martín
that he will fall in love again (although he will have to be more aggressive
in order not to suffer terribly in such relationships), whereas Oliveira is
apparently incapable of falling in love.

Neither is capable, of course, of breaking with the western cannon, but
Martín appears more able to put to the test the myths that he has con-
sumed, including that of the qualities of childhood. While Oliveira establishes a relationship with texts which is nearly completely intellectual,
Martín forms a more personal relationship with them: His life and the
texts converge. The young Peruvian goes in search, for example, of the
Paris and Spain that Hemingway had created for him in his work. The
demythification of Hemingway's Europe, and later the creation by Martín
of a new European paradise (Perugia), are derived through the protagonist's personal experiences. What is missing for the intellectual in *Rayuela*
is a reader-accomplice who might comprehend the desired "un-writing,"
while one of the projects of Martín Romaña is to explore the effects of literature on his own life, and also the ways in which his experiences affect
the literature: His literary production as well as his re-reading or reconsideration of the work of others. In *La Vida Exagerada*, as in other
works by Bryce Echenique, the protagonist seeks to make of the reader a
"privileged interlocutor" (Ferreira 37; see also Saldes 120)[3], whereas the
project of *Rayuela* (and other novels of the "boom") is to produce totaliz-
ing narratives which reach that level of totalization at the expense of the
individuality of the protagonist (Ferreira 42). Morelli, and by extension
Oliveira, seek an ideal reader; indeed, Cortázar's prologue brings this
search to the attention of the reader immediately. In Bryce Echenique's
novel, on the other hand, there is no recognition of the existence of such an
ideal reader, instead there is a belief that each reader or reading will establish a relationship with the text and that no one approach to the text is
"ideal" (very much a post-modern as well as a post-Boom perspective).

In Cortázar's novel, there are various notes regarding how to convert
the female-, or passive-reader into a male-, or active-reader; additionally,
Morelli, in chapter seventy-three, describes the characters that his novel of
"un-writing" would have. These characters would be passive, reduced to
mere signs or symbols (Merrim 51–53). Franco has explored the "revolutionary" project of Cortázar, in which vanguardists, operating from a position of privilege based on the stereotype of the passive masses, dictate a
participatory artistic esthetic.[4] For Cortázar, the revolution, an individu-
alist revolution, begins with literature, thus converting the author into a

modern hero who would guide the masses on their journey of self-discovery (Franco, "Crisis" 10–11), but the knowledge that all readers have already been corrupted implies the failure of this revolutionary literary effort. A dead Rocamadour symbolizes the height of passivity and incorruptibility—he was a being who had not yet learned to communicate at more than the elemental level of wails and contented gurgling—and it is to him that all of the revolutionary literary teachings of Morelli and the implicit author of *Rayuela* are directed. Rocamadour is the subaltern possessed by the intellectual, educated by him; he is the absence, so to speak, which is to be filled. In chapter ninety-three, Oliveira makes a connection between literary creation and the engendering of an artistic race, and seems to point to Rocamadour as the first-born of that race:

> Curioso, muy curioso que Puttenham sintiera las palabras como si fueran objetos, y hasta criaturas con vida propia. También a mí, a veces, me parece estar engendrando ríos de hormigas feroces que se comerán el mundo. Ah, si en el silencio empollara el Roc . . . (Cortázar's elipsis). (594)

Although the "Roc" of this quotation probably refers to the bird which transported Sinbad, it is worth noting that the name chosen for the baby in the novel seems to be a combination of "Roc" and "amadour," a form of *amante* (lover), *amado* (loved one) or *amador* (lover). Rocamadour is also a high mountain retreat famous as a site of great inspiration to artists, complete with an altar to the Virgin. He continues, noting the paradox inherent in the desire to create a race that is incorruptible:

> Concebir una raza que se expresara por el dibujo, la danza, el macramé o una mímica abstracta. ¿Evitarían las conotaciones, raíz del engaño? *Honneur des hommes*, etc. Sí, pero un honor que se deshonra a cada frase, como un burdel de vírgenes si la cosa fuera posible. (594–95)

This first-born is highly desired, then, and is the mythical object of a paternal desire on the part of Oliveira. This child is something to be possessed and shaped, and as such is related to the subaltern as seen by the artist.

There exists in the intellectual's and the bourgeoisie's attitudes toward the subaltern a degree of ambivalence. The popular element fascinates the bourgeoisie principally due to the former's "naturaleza corpórea," through which one may establish contact with the other; but, at the same time that physicality, which is denied the bourgeoisie, also scandalizes him (McCard 247, 252–53, 257). In order to satisfy his curiosity and to make contact with the other, the bourgeoisie participate in popular festivities. The intellectuals, for their part, valorize the child and attempt to infiltrate his or her world and fuse with him or her in some way (see Lanin Gyurko for examples of this in Cortázar's stories). This fusion may be intellectual, spiritual or physical. Various characters in *La Vida Exagerada* attempt to penetrate the child-like world of Martín, that childishness which he projects for others, but instead of an internal harmony, they find a person who struggles with his feelings and his bodily fragility. This is one way in which *La Vida Exagerada* serves to demythify the child and return to him a degree of humanity.

Just as the bourgeoisie and intellectuals are fascinated by the physical "lower zone" of the subaltern (McCard), in *Rayuela* we see that Oliveira focuses on the genital and anal areas of Rocamadour's body (e.g., chapter nineteen) and on the screams, coughs and guttural sounds that the baby makes. The odor of "pis" and "caca," and the images of the child suffering the insertion of anal suppositories invade Oliveira's thoughts (253, 257–58, 268). In these images, the child is linked to the elemental functions of the body, and he is seen as a burden which is difficult to support, and as a hindrance to one's self-realization (e.g., 213, 271); such a view concurs with the antagonistic attitude of the intellectual toward the family, which we have noted earlier. This vision of the child also becomes rather monstrous. In chapter twenty-three, for example, Oliveira makes a connection between the images of the animalistic face of Berthe Trépat and the horrifying sight of La Maga trying to control Rocamadour as she administers a suppository; the child twists about, squeezes his buttocks and howls horribly (268). The physique of angels, typically depicted as children in western culture, is grotesque as well (291). These depictions are based on visual descriptions, the key sense with which the West objectifies the other (Kauffmann 322). Once Rocamadour's animalistic traits are established, we would argue, it is that much easier to kill him and recreate him through the novel. In addition, this agrees with the strategy of the creation of myths in which child-gods often possess monstrous aspects (Campbell 316–17).

In *La Vida Exagerada* we see, perhaps, a demythification of the above-mentioned fascination of the intellectual and the bourgeoisie with the "lower zones" of the subaltern, since we are dealing with a character from society's elite who at the same time is treated as—and indeed sees himself as—a subaltern, and who is fascinated by his own "zonas bajas." (It is worth noting that proctologists and psychiatrists are the two most mentioned professions in the novel.) The "adult" version of this fascination, that of Oliveira, transfers the attention onto "the other," onto the child and the homosexual male; but in *La Vida Exagerada* it is the protagonist Martín himself who is found face down accepting the insertion into his anus of needles, surgical instruments and, later, a steel penis. Martín "se vuelve maricón" ("becomes a faggot") temporarily, but due to a physical weakness; and it is his lover, Inés, who inserts the artificial penis. Among other more psychoanalytical interpretations, this is clearly a humorous demythification of the intellectual's serious acceptance of homosexuality. One could say that here it is Martín who allows himself to be "violated," whereas in *Rayuela* it is a woman, La Maga, who was violated in her childhood, and later "used" like an adolescent boy by Oliveira. The "violation" of Martín, however, like that of Rocamadour, is meant to cure: La Maga inserts suppositories into the baby, and Inés a metal penis into Martín, in order to correct ailments. Oliveira's perspective on such insertion, on the other hand, is horrifying, in the case of the baby, or possessive and conquering in the case of La Maga. The writer Martín occupies the more child-like position here, while Oliveira the more adult, omnipotent place of the intellectual establishment.

The intestinal strike that Martín declares, and which leads to his anal difficulties, is carried out for at least two reasons: On the one hand, because he does not want to experience the pain upon defecating caused by an infection he has acquired; and on the other, because he does not want to bother Inés with his suffering caused by that same pain. As his belly swells and his skin changes color, we see his aspect becoming rather monstrous. The descriptions of Martín are visual, like those of Rocamadour, and Martín himself gives not only his view of himself, but also that of the always squinting Inés. In his relation with Inés, Martín characterizes himself not only as a child, but also as an animal, associating thus the child with the animal. One of the variations of Inés's love, he believes, is one in which he takes on the role of the "guinea pig" of all her experiences; thus, it was necessary for her to love him like an animal (257). Before this comment by the narrator, Inés has called Martín a "bestia" for his treatment of his mother.

The fascination for the lower zones in *La Vida Exagerada* is related with childhood as we have also shown was the case in *Rayuela*. Martín's conversations with the proctologist are very similar to those of a father with a child who is going through toilet training. His toilet training and status as a child also, once again, are bound up in his relation with Inés. He becomes a child in her presence, and she is at the same time mother and lover (200). Like a child who fears growing up and losing the security of childhood, Martín does not want to defecate because he knows that Inés will stay with him until he does, that is, until he is cured of his affliction (595–97).[5]

Martín's attempt to control his body is, in a sense, a subaltern's effort to regain some control over his life. The objectification of the subaltern may be achieved through carnal love, which is possessive by nature, writes Planells, and seeks to fuse beings in order to satisfy their attachments, desires and sympathies. While the sexual act may placate physical appetites, however, it can never satiate one's mental voraciousness, which is generated by the emotive and intellectual spheres (Planells 234). In Cortázar's stories the sexual union is seen as a last resort, and as a failed attempt to achieve communication between two beings, to escape from solitude (Planells 233), or to "return home" (González Echevarría 129). It is clear in *Rayuela* that such a union between La Maga and Oliveira does not provide for him that flight from solitude, the contact with "the other side" that he seeks. As Oliveira says, her love torments him as it does not serve as a bridge for him; a bridge, he says, cannot be maintained from just one side (592). If the child is the preferred bridge to that "other side," we might expect to see the protagonist attempt sex with a child figure just as he has with La Maga. In fact, in *Rayuela* there are several references to pederasty, and Oliveira, in perhaps the most erotic scene of the novel, turns La Maga over and uses her as though she were "an adolescent boy" (153–54). However, it is probably in Cortázar's short stories where we would get a better idea of his attitude toward sexual unions between adults and children, whether heterosexual or homosexual in nature.

Puleo, analyzing only the Cortázar works where sexuality is explicit, notes that these sexual relations are actually relations of power, and that they reflect the hierarchies of the society; there is a rejection of the idea of the sexual act as something mystic—it is a political act; it is a union of bodies, but a deep separation of consciences (209–11) (and see also Aronne-Amestoy). In *Rayuela*, for example, Oliveira, when Emmanuele performs oral sex on him, must repeat to himself "coldly" that he is not better than she is (365). Homosexuality and pederasty appear in some of Cortázar's works, and in general receive a pejorative treatment (Puleo 208–9). There are various instances of the violation of girls in his stories, but in *Rayuela* the baby boy dies before there is any desire expressed for him, and before any sexual "threat" is perceived. We do find, however, brief references to homosexuality in general, and to sex with children. "Pederasts" are mentioned in chapters four, twenty, thirty-six and seventy-one. Oliveira makes an emphatic tie between homosexuality and Rocamadour when images of the homosexual Valentín, face down and crying in his bed, accompany those of the baby receiving the suppositories (268). In chapter thirty-six, in addition to the presence of two "pederastas," we see an allusion to the child again during Oliveira's sexual contact with the *clo-*

charde, the tramp who performs oral sex on him, as she murmurs as though talking with a baby: "y con una lengua manchada de tanino le lamiera humildemente la pija, sosteniendo su comprensible abandono con los dedos y murmurando el lenguaje que suscitan los gatos y los niños de pecho" (366).

For Martín Romaña, carnal union also is a matter of hierarchies; however, it is the protagonist who finds himself at the bottom of the ladder, or possessed by another. The woman, whether it is the "mother" Inés or the "gringa ignorante" Sandra, is always in control of the sexual relationship: When Martín becomes impotent due to the effects of a drug, it is Inés who "permits" Martín to receive an injection that will allow him to maintain an erection; Martín manages his behavior according to the messages her perceives in Inés's squints; and, it is Sandra who excludes Martín from a sexual relationship for ideological reasons. Although Martín feels that he is out of control, we see through the narrator, who permits us to enter into the thought processes of the protagonist, just how he circumnavigates (following the mythoid of the voyage with which Martín opens the novel) that control. Although Inés is the mother who controls the situation, it is Martín who works to maintain her in her position as mother so that she will not leave him. He knows, for example, that she will not leave him as long as he is sick, as long as he cannot defecate. He is obsessed by any "maternal" action on Inés's part, such as her efforts to cure his illnesses, and he attempts to prolong those maladies so that she will not leave. Martín also wishes to prolong the writing of his socialist novel on the fishing industry throughout the various stages of his life, in order to keep himself in the good graces of Inés and the rest of the Grupo (147). He actively seeks to maintain his subordinate position.[6]

Martín, like many teenagers, believes that he has to assimilate in order to gain acceptance. In the end, the sexual relationship with Inés is, at least for a while, a relief from solitude in Martín's life, the opposite of what we have seen in *Rayuela*, and perhaps for Martín the relationship is an effort to fit in. Martín's amorous relationships are part of his education, his "modernization," as well. It is under Sandra's influence, for example, that he will assimilate into the group of revolutionaries of 1968, an assimilation that is described as more akin to an adolescent crush than a political transformation: ". . . podía reconciliarme con el presente, modernizarme y reconstruirme para caer de cabeza y feliz y poblado de buenas intenciones entre las celestiales antorchas de las barricadas. Sandra es mi vaso comunicante . . ." (380). The space where he allows himself freedom of expression would not be amongst the revolutionaries, but rather would remain, in a very child-like way, secret; thus, he is the only one who knows the true identities of the characters in the novel he is writing; he is the one who recognizes the power of the depression in his mattress (to which he attributes his and Inés's positive sexual experiences), etc. These secrets are a reflection of what all of these young people are doing in Paris. The narrator shows how many of them violate their revolutionary principles in order to insinuate themselves into the upper reaches of the social and political hierarchies upon their return to their countries. Martín, however, is the one who maintains a type of faith in his secrets as he writes them from his "Voltairean chair." The romantic perception of childhood, as well as that of scientists, held that childhood guarded just such secrets. We return once again, then, to the idea that he who maintains contact with the qualities of childhood, will be able to become an artist and, perhaps, a true revolutionary.

Although the real child in *Rayuela* is seen as a burden due to his excretions, his need to be fed and the other responsibilities brought upon the adults by his presence, there is also talk of paradise and the child in the novel (311-12, 281); and, this child that is found in paradise is not understood by others (at least not by members of the Club, as La Maga says in chapter thirty-two), but is a bridge between the world of reason and the world of innocence and purity (see chapters ninety-eight, ninety-nine and one hundred). The child can perceive the hidden pain of the adult male (346-470), he can dream, and this ability to dream incites fear in the adult male (625); in general, children can reach what Oliveira calls "heaven," but once they find it, childhood ends and they lose the ability to return to it again (367). Oliveira notes that La Maga knew well that one needed "the little stone and the toe of a shoe" in order to reach "heaven"; that is, the tools of the child's game of hopscotch. The name "heaven" was nothing more than a child's name for the "kibbutz" (368) that Oliveira seems so intent upon finding. A return to childhood would appear to point the way to the kibbutz, a way which would not depend upon Zen or any other adult created or mediated means:

> Una piedrita y la punta de un zapato, eso que la Maga había sabido tan bien y
> él mucho menos bien, y el Club más o menos bien y que desde la infancia en
> Burzaco o en los suburbios de Montevideo mostraba la recta vía del Cielo, sin
> necesidad de vedanta o de zen o de escatologías surtidas, sí, llegar al Cielo a
> patadas, llegar con la piedrita. . . . (368)

With the end of childhood, however, one "forgets" the "ingredients" necessary for returning to Heaven and sinks into the adult world of philosophy and art which are meant to show one the way to Heaven, to the utopian kibbutz. Philosophies and novels only lead to the awareness of other "heavens," however, which will trigger other complex games of hopscotch and will lead one further and further from the simplicity of childhood, from its pure, creative pursuits:

> En lo alto está el Cielo, abajo está la Tierra, es muy difícil llegar con la piedrita al Cielo, casi siempre se calcula mal y la piedra sale del dibujo. Poco a poco, sin embargo, se va adquiriendo la habilidad necesaria para salvar las diferentes casillas.
>
> . . . y un día se aprende a salir de la Tierra y remontar la piedrita hasta el Cielo, hasta entrar en el Cielo . . . lo malo es que justamente a esa altura, cuando casi nadie ha aprendido a remontar la piedrita hasta el Cielo, se acaba de golpe la infancia y se cae en las novelas, en la angustia al divino cohete, en la especulación de otro Cielo al que también hay que aprender a llegar. Y porque se ha salido de la infancia . . . se olvida que para llegar al Cielo se necesitan, como ingredientes, una piedrita y la punta de un zapato. (367–68)

Of course, in our interpretation, a major component of the corrupting "novels" and "speculation" is the conception of childhood as some mythical site of transcendence.

The romantics, like Oliveira and other intellectuals of his group, seem to take seriously the biblical warning that "Except ye be converted, and become as children, ye shall not enter the kingdom of heaven." For Martín Romaña, however, one does not have be converted; the idea is to carry childhood with you always (71). One of the manifestations of this puerility is that Martín has the ability to "go crazy" whenever he wants to (e.g., 84). Once again, it is the character Bryce Echenique who clarifies for Martín that this is a natural and fascinating phenomenon, but that it is worrisome and bothersome for the adult world. Children, he says, are, amazingly, capable of perceptions and insights more commonly associated with older and wiser beings, but they may also suddenly return to a younger, more unstable state:

> Me asombró haber captado algo tan profundo en un momento en que me hallaba tan empequeñecido, pero años después, el escritor Bryce Echenique me aclaró este punto, confirmándome así como un niño de seis años podía de pronto comportarse como uno de un año, así también uno de nueve podía de golpe captar algo que otros seres no captan ni a los cien años. (257)

Like the mythical and romantic child of *Rayuela*, Martín Romaña possesses certain clairvoyant powers, and enjoys a degree of intuition. His ability to "become small," to draw out child-like characteristics in himself, is an attribute which gives him special insight and comprehension. There is, however, an aspect of demythification occurring here as quite often his actions or words based on such intuition end in failure (e.g., 84).

In *Rayuela*, Gregorovius seems to recount with irony various scenes from his childhood, and later notes that what the members of the Club appear to be doing in Paris is looking for their "lost childhood" (281, and see chapters twenty-four through twenty-six). The childhood, that lost paradise, which La Maga relates to us, contains scenes of violation and indifference (chapters fifteen and sixteen, and see also chapters four and twelve), while in Gregorovius' tales confusion, sexual repression and abandonment stand out (chapters fifty-six and sixty-five). It is ironic and tragic, however, when one realizes that Rocamadour lies dying while the members of the Club converse, a situation which becomes grave in chapter twenty-eight (although it is not in this chapter when they talk of childhood and paradise). Chapter 117, with its news item about a death sentence handed down in the case of a child who has committed a crime, emphasizes how the end of childhood, the end of its perceived innocence, is dictated by the greater society. According to the tales of their own childhoods related by Gregorovius and La Maga, however, that paradise never really existed, it is simply part of the myth which consumes Oliveira.

Martín does not need to search for a lost paradise since he continues living as a child. As we note above, and as Martín says, he knows how to behave as a man and as a child at the same time, being for Inés both a son and a lover (200). *La Vida Exagerada* seems to demythify that search for paradise lost in several ways. One way is through the failed trips to seek out his family's roots in England and the Basque country (100, 47). In both places, the young Martín finds out that his surnames are quite common; and in addition, he becomes ill and gets into trouble in both places.

We see a similar comment on such searches in the trip that Inés and Martín take to the village from which her family emigrated. Where Inés expects to find the altruism of natural socialism, she finds instead the exact opposite, a severely hierarchical social system. These failed searches call into question the connections with Europe that many Latin Americans have emphasized in the now academically mythic "search for Latin American identity." Childhood is important in this search since many of these seekers go to Europe at a young age in hopes of advancing their education in Paris, the heart and crossroads of world cultures. Although they experience a period of leftist apprenticeship there, in the novel they almost always return to their respective countries where they occupy government posts, as in the case of Mocasines, or they ensconce themselves in very comfortable bourgeois homes, as does Inés. Martín, the one who has been accused so often of being corrupted and rotted by his bourgeois background, is the only one who remains in Paris. While the Paris of leftist intellectuals is demythified, it becomes real—it becomes a home—for Martín, a place where he can put to the test the myths of life and of literature that are part of his being. The others return to their "homes" in Latin America without having done more than exercise for a while on the playground that is Paris, where they have experimented with the latest intellectual fashions.

In conclusion, we have seen in the two novels that childhood is a key state, whether for its creativity or its mystic power, or for its role in the search for origins, but in both works it is also a state which leaves one vulnerable and marginalized. It is obvious that Rocamadour is the most vulnerable character in *Rayuela*. There is a recognition of this vulnerability in the manner in which Oliveira becomes paranoid and constructs traps in his room in the insane asylum as he is returning to a child-like state. In *La Vida Exagerada* we see an example of the exploration of that vulnerability and the ways in which an artist struggles to express himself, by maintaining alive the qualities of childhood and at the same time dealing with the power which others exercise over him due to his child-like status and attitudes. Martín Romaña signals the importance of childhood, of exploring his own childhood, and also of the romantic ideal of not distancing oneself from that time in one's life. The young man expresses the creativity, spontaneity and honesty of the child, but he finds himself in "exaggerated" situations whenever he tries to put those expressions into practice in the adult world. While others go through a "revolutionary" period in Paris, only to return later to the models of behavior of their parents in Latin America, the "modernization" of Martín Romaña is something very "romantically" interminable; he chooses to extend childhood, thereby extending his period of creativity and apprenticeship. Oliveira, on the other hand, has lost his spontaneity, and his attempt to return to childhood is a failure. Although both novels recognize that in childhood all is possible, only in *La Vida Exagerada* does childhood seem to permeate the thoughts of the protagonist. Perhaps this is the lesson of *La Vida Exagerada*, that one should not distance oneself too much from one's child-like qualities, that one should attempt to maintain the child-artist of the romantic duality in spite of the world's hostility to such an ambivalent being because, as *Rayuela* shows us, attempting to return to that state once it is lost will surely end in disaster. *La Vida Exagerada*'s recipe is given a dose of reality as well by the character Bryce Echenique, as he warns, as we have noted above, of the paradox of childhood, as "todo es posible tratándose de un niño" (257–58) ("everything is possible where a child is concerned"), but that this freedom and potential can attract censure and danger.

In *Rayuela* and *La Vida Exagerada*, we have seen intellectuals struggling with their familial pasts and the pressures to conform to intellectual
pressures: Oliveira wishes to define the conditions for originality and sees
a return to a child-like state as the final alternative; Martín Romaña links
his puerile qualities to his creative abilities and suffers in order to keep the
two connected in an adult world. Both suffer a type of exile—Oliveira
from mankind as he sinks into childhood/insanity, and Martín from his nation, family and friends. In the two works to be considered next, Cristina
Peri Rossi's *La Rebelión de los Niños* (1980) (*The Rebellion of the Children*) and Reinaldo Arenas's *El Palacio de las Blanquísimas Mofetas*
(1980)[7] (*The Palace of the Very White Skunks*), exile is still an aspect of the
author's perception of childhood, however the child and artist are linked in
a more violent, life-threatening struggle against outside forces than in the
two previous works considered here.

In the case of Peri Rossi's work, the government's attempts to control
its citizenry are based on the co-optation of the memory and development
of its children. This co-optation seeks to determine the younger generation's use of language and its artistic production, and also to drive a wedge
between children and their families. Just as all art in such a system must
serve the state, the people or the revolution, all of a child's development
and expression must also be ideologically correct. In Arenas's work, the
young protagonist's sensitivity to the pain of his fellow family members is
like that of a young artist or writer. Fortunato takes on the roles of others
in order to better understand their feelings and the personal histories that
have brought them to their current state. He is like the writer who must
understand fully his or her various characters' personalities in order to
write about them effectively. Childhood is important in this attempt at
comprehension in several ways: It is, in a sense, a child-like game of
dress-up, make believe and language play, as is the writing of fiction in
general; this protagonist is in a perpetual state of subordination within the
family, never really maturing; he is in the end a child in search of a strong
and just male figure as he attempts to join the revolution; and, he explores,
in particular, the childhoods of other members of his family, emphasizing
in this way the importance of childhood events and memory on the future
of the person, of society, and of artistic production. In Peri Rossi's and
Arenas's works, we see the effects of political and economic systems on
the characters, rather than the peer pressure among youthful intellectuals to
conform to ideological trends that we have noted in *Rayuela* and *Martín
Romaña*. In all four works, however, the idea of the marginalization of the
artist/author and the child from society is maintained, and that status is tied
to the child-like qualities of the author, which are at once responsible for

artistic production, and seen as a danger within the traditional social system.

Exile is a relatively common theme in the criticism of Peri Rossi's writings, whether due to the explicit content of the texts or to the critics' awareness of the author's own extended stay in exile. In *La Rebelión*, the exile of children and/or their parents is internal, that is, within the country, or psychological rather than geographical. As we have discussed in Chapter Two, families are torn apart in order to "save" those very families; this disintegration produces a form of exile. The child finds himself in a world which he struggles to understand, where he speaks the native language but where the meanings are constantly changing (see Schmidt regarding this in another Peri Rossi work). Like many exiles, this child seeks to recuperate, through memory and artistic production, the lost domestic paradise. The goal of the government's exile of the children and parents is not unlike the result of the self-imposed exile of the protagonists of another Peri Rossi work where "the characters' displacement results in disorientation, humiliation and loss of identity" (Schmidt 223). Recuperation of that identity becomes the goal of life in exile, and often mythification of that identity results from the effort. As we have noted above, González Echevarría calls exile a "founding literary myth," and also an act which allows the exile to heighten his or her knowledge of their cultural constructs "through the ordeal of separation and return" (126, 134). The government's oppressive internal exile of the children in the last story of the collection, "La Rebelión de los Niños" would, and does, result in both the longing for the lost paradise, and the critique of inherited platitudes mentioned by González Echevarría. We examine below just how a regime seeks to control the child, and why, and the ways in which the child reacts.

In Peri Rossi's work there is a special reverence for childhood as the site and time of the creative acquisition and use of language. It is a time of experimentation, which most adults, especially those who support the regime, seek to control. The child must replace his creative, self-generated language with that found in dictionaries and guides, until the child and his/her language are assimilated by the regime. The narrator of "La Rebelión," using his brother as an example, explains:

> En casi todas las actividades—o sea, en casi todos los lenguajes—las cosas se resuelven por imitación o por invención. El niño pequeño—recuerdo a mi hermano—comienza inventando símbolos, hasta que los opresores lo obligan a aceptar un lenguaje ya confeccionado, que viene en todas las guías y diccionarios, como la ropa de los almacenes . . . como todo oprimido, [mi hermano] debió aceptar el lenguaje de los vencedores, y al poco tiempo tuvo que sustituir su 'baal-doa, doa' por 'papá-mamá', que, para ser francos, como inven-

ción—haya sido quien haya sido el inventor—demuestra poca imaginación.
Antes de los tres años, mi hermano ya no ejercitaba más su capacidad crea-
dora, había adquirido una buena cantidad de símbolos verbales al uso de la
comunidad . . . Lo habían integrado. (110-11)

As we pointed out in Chapter Two, in an earlier story of the collection,
"Pico Blanco y Alas Azules," a major focus of the work is the exploration
of how those living under the military regime must re-learn language, and
re-interpret or re-read their surroundings, taking care to recognize the potential "ambiguity" of the meanings of every object or act, just as the soldiers have been re-trained in their searches to identify other potentially
dangerous or subversive meanings in nearly everything (84). This re-
learning takes place at the same time that a young couple's toddler is
learning to speak, thus the parents find themselves infantilized, learning a
new language, that of the regime, along with their son. At the beginning
of the story, the child has lifted his gaze skyward and has seen a bird for
the first time; and it is only at the end of the tale, after his mother has
made a decision to secretly preserve a piece of art that they have found in
their home, that the bird returns to the garden and the child's excitement
and, we suppose, his development, will resume. Thus the child's creativity and growth can only be preserved through an act—saving a work of
art—which the state interprets as subversive.

In "La Rebelión," the military has placed the children of "subversives"
in the homes of families which support the regime, or in institutions where
their re-education and development can be closely monitored. The regime
is particularly vigilant regarding young people's individualized expressions
of all kinds, making it extremely difficult to obtain art and writing supplies:
"Todos aquellos instrumentos que sirven para expresarnos, están riguro-
samente controlados, para evitar que expresemos cosas que no conviene
expresar . . ." (124). This hypercontrol contrasts with the availability of
numerous objects involved in leisure or the gratification of the senses, such
as pornography, chocolates and sports. The availability of the latter set of
objects is meant to distract the children from more creative, and potentially
subversive, activities.

At the close of the story, we see the public display of the young people's re-education as silent, obedient creatures, silence and obedience being
the foundation of their moral, social and civic education; characteristics
such as movement and expression were considered by the regime to be the
keys to subversion and chaos (133-34).[8] In another example, the narrator
and his institutionalized younger brother resort to communicating by way
of postage stamps. This is clearly a subversion of the nationalistic, conservative icons we would expect to find on this regime's stamps, as the

boys re-interpret the stamps' artwork to suit their own communication needs.

Language learning, and the regime's control of the future generations, are dependent not only on the control of the means of expression, but also on the control of memory. As we noted in Chapter One, a nation, in order to unite itself, requires a certain degree of amnesia in conjunction with the creation of a common memory. The contemporary regime must also encourage such absentmindedness if it is to gain the allegiance of the young. In "La Rebelión," the narrator, Rolando, notes that the children are prohibited by their tutors from storing information; their memories, he says, are weak and oppressed: ". . . nuestros tutores nos prohíben archivar información. Confían en el rápido deterioro de la memoria . . . Del presente recordaremos sólo aquello que la memoria quiera conservar, pero ella no es libre, se trata también de una memoria oprimida, de una memoria condicionada, tentada a olvidar, una memoria postrada y adormecida, claudicante" (112–13). As we see in the following, very poetic quotation, Rolando has tried to improve his memory by exercising it and treating it as a living, growing being—a small girl—in need of nurturing and guidance. He leaves behind clues for his memory reminiscent of the crumbs left by Hansel and Gretel as they are led deeper into the forest: ". . . he guiado y ayudado a la memoria de mañana con pistas y señales, porque la memoria es como una niña pequeña, hay que sostenerla y ayudarla a andar, hay que ejercitarla y protegerla" (113). While a work of literature or art has often been referred to as a child, here the memory itself is metaphorized in this way, emphasizing the creative aspects of memory. The need for care, however, emphasizes its fragility, instability and powerlessness; the memory, like the child, is subject to the "guidance" of its elders, but that guidance may be subverted, to a certain extent, by the individual; indeed, that individual agency, along with its resulting artistic production, seems to be the key to surviving the regime's attempts at memory control.

Rolando's interlocutor, Laura, as he decides to call her (she has also named him, the naming act, in both cases, is a typical child's subversion of the traditional parental power to name a human being; it signals as well a new beginning for them), also comments on memory as she wonders about her parents' memories, imagining that her parents would not be able to recognize each other if they were somehow to meet in prison (129–31). There is implied here the girl's concern that they might not remember her either. The fourteen-year-old narrator and his new-found female friend, also fourteen, however, have found ways around the regime's limitations. In their art, created for an exhibition and competition fomented by the regime, they have created works out of the rubble of memory, out of the rubble of violent confrontations with the regime, creations which will, ultimately, serve to subvert that very regime.

The narrator's work of art is an old chair that he has re-upholstered with photos, articles and headlines from newspapers (113–14). The project is an effort to recapture memory: As he works on the piece, he is amazed by how much he has forgotten. He has carefully selected the news items. The first mentioned is that of a child burning with napalm in Viet Nam. Others include two lesbians kissing, the speeches of generals, headlines and photos of Hollywood stars, pieces on the deaths of dissidents and "subversives," accident victims and the failure of the regime to adequately protect children from disease, as well as many other negative indicators of a society's well-being. The generals' words found on the chair are platitudes, vague enough that they inspire conversation; and, the critical message of their juxtaposition with the other news items should cause great concern for the government. Rolando's intent, then, is to inspire communication, or at least that has been the result, and to jog the viewer's memory. This is clearly a dangerous work, from the point of view of the regime, though it has an element of subtlety about it as he is not castigated in any way for the piece within the story, for his art does not seem to be taken seriously by the public or the judges.

Laura's art is similar in that she has rooted through garbage and combed the streets to find broken glass and pieces of metal in order to create out of them a grand fountain (115–16). These pieces of society's rubbish are not unlike the memory clues that Rolando mentions when discussing his effort to retain his memory; the shards of metal and glass are the fractured clues to the nation's past. Laura's fountain contrasts with the old, corroded classical fountain in the plaza where Laura and Rolando meet; the corrosion from this fountain stains her clothing. She uses the workshop supplied by the regime's youth center to meld together the pieces of glass and metal. Both of these artists are attempting to put order into their lives, as the new order which the military and their new "families" have given them does not suffice, does not satisfactorily replace their previous lives. The children have rummaged through the past, picked up the broken pieces of their society and recycled them in order to re-create that which is, however, in reality unrecuperable. This activity is similar to the writer of an autobiography or a historical novel (as with Galván's *Enriquillo*, treated in Chapter One) who reaches back into an individual's past in order to put the present in order and to give society a united memory, or at least a memory around which the public might unite. Her piece too is subtle; it hides its purpose and seems even to be a toy created through the resourcefulness of one of the regime's prized children, a child re-educated after her separation from the supposedly corrupting influence of her parents.

The art exhibit is meant by the government to show off the young people's support of the regime, to display the degree to which the nation's youth has been re-indoctrinated, freed, in the view of the regime, from their past with their own parents. But the two artists have subverted that purpose: Rolando's piece, on its face, criticizes the regime, though Laura declares that it is not much of a protest (117–18); indeed, though the headlines and photos carry obvious messages, many people almost sit in the chair before they realize it is one of the works on display. It is, on the one hand, a mundane object which carries newspaper messages that are familiar, yet subdued in the memories of those who view them. On the other hand, the chair is like a toy to Rolando, and like toys it is not taken seriously by the adults. Laura's piece is also, at its source, a mundane object made of society's refuse. We must wait for the end of the tale to see Laura's artistic protest come to fruition. In the end, she wins the art competition, ironically being awarded a bust of the "máximo general" and a medal for her efforts. She is lauded by the regime's representatives as the future of the nation, the one who will protect and provide warmth for her people: ". . . ella, la reivindicadora, la depositaria del futuro, en cuyo regazo se alimentarían y buscarían calor y protección las generaciones venideras, ella, la iluminada, la vestal a quien se confiaba el porvenir de la ciudad, las llaves del reino. . . " (135). The ironic humor is thick in this passage, as it is in nearly the entire story, and here it serves to present Laura to the reader as the regime sees her: The vestal virgin, the promise of the future.

Laura's artwork, in the end, is converted into a death machine as it sprays with gasoline the congregated people who, on average, are forty years old. She and Rolando have escaped and he throws a flame into the hall to spark the conflagration. In the description of the fountain's spraying of the assembled elites, the narrator uses two images. In one, the sprays are compared to the blood emanating from a decapitated subversive, beheaded by soldiers, thus the elites are metaphorically sprayed with the blood of their victims, and then burned to death by it. At the same time, the people in the hall react like protesters in the street who are being confronted by soldiers; the sprays then are compared to those of the water hoses used to push back crowds. In this image the soldiers' water will burn to death those gathered in the hall, the very people the soldiers were meant to protect (136–37). In both images, interwoven as they are, irony is heavy. It is the fourteen-year-old's irony, of course, bred of the oppression of the military government, and it is an artistic irony in its interlacing images. The young have taken the government's attempt to allow the creation of regime-confirming art and have appropriated it in order to destroy members of that very oligarchy. Laura's capacity as "vestal" is ironic here as well, since the vestal virgins of Roman mythology were charged with tending the sacred flame of Vesta, the goddess of hearth and fire, and Laura destroys members of the regime with her own fire.

At the climax of the tale the two youths flee the scene together, perhaps off on yet another adventure in their prolonged exile. The government has attempted to control the children, yet these beings have exercised the very child-like—and artist-like—prerogative of exploring and surpassing society's limitations. Their exile has caused them to "heighten" their knowledge about their own society, and calculate just how to cross its boundaries. The ambivalence of words and signs is thoroughly exploited by these child-artists (see chapters two and three) in their works of art and in their final violent act. Not unlike the parents and soldiers in "Pico Blanco y Alas Azules" who see a weapon in a razor, a secret communication in a sheet of music (84), in "La Rebelión" what appears to be water is actually gasoline, what appears to be a child's cheerful fountain is actually a deadly weapon. Unlike the works of Salarrué and Juan Bosch treated in Chapter Three, children in this Peri Rossi collection are not only victims of social upheaval, or representative of an oppressed social or ethnic class, they are here used for their ability to transgress the boundaries which families and governments lay down for them—and for their parents. It is the ambivalence of the child which makes the regime attempt to re-educate them in the first place—the adults are apparently beyond hope—but it is that very ambivalence which makes it possible for children to then subvert the regime's efforts. Rolando and Laura are both children, but they are both artists, though not of their own choosing. They are artists because they are children, because the regime told them that as children they may produce art, and because they see in art the possibility of attacking the very system which has ordered them to be artistic. Peri Rossi has utilized children here for the very same reason that the regime has: Because they are ambivalent, boundary-pushing beings. In the next work to be treated, by Cuba's Reinaldo Arenas, we also see internal exile at work, but the protagonist in that novel does not overcome it through art, but rather through death.

The protagonist of *El Palacio de las Blanquísimas Mofetas* attempts to relive the childhoods of various members of his extended family. In doing so he declares himself the "interpreter" and "voice" of their lives (262, 391). In that capacity he was, as the narrator says, a monster, a god, an artist (163), signaling the narrator's acknowledgment of the multivalent, dangerous and powerful perception of such a "voice." Fortunato uses his empathetic power much like an author who must fully understand his characters in order to give them a "voice" in a work. The boy writes obsessively in the novel, though he throws away his writings, and he also occupies the memories of others obsessively. Similar to Laura's collecting and melding together broken glass in "La Rebelión de los Niños," Fortunato sifts through the lives of his fellow family members, piecing together disparate memories of their harsh lives in order to produce a whole work. As we shall see in the following analysis, from a position as an exile within his own family and nation, he explores exile as it is manifested in his family members, producing a sharp criticism of the socio-economic and cultural situation of his fellow Cubans.

Roberto Valero notes that carnival time replaces historical time in *El Palacio* (113). The author engages in a kind of language play similar to that of the "illogical associations," as Valero calls them (131–33), with which the children indulge themselves in their play in the novel. The very narrative structure and style, then, reflect the child-like quality of free association and play, similar to the conversations between parents and children in Peri Rossi's work, or the jazz-like structure of *Rayuela*. This kind of free association can be disconcerting and disorienting to an adult, of course; indeed, this novel tends to inspire such feelings in the reader. Perla Rozencvaig writes that the ludic nature of the child-protagonist's narration in *Celestino antes del alba* (1972) (*Celestino Before the Dawn*) is a strategy for survival, protecting him from the daily trials that assault him: "En suma, las peripecias del protagonista insuflan al texto de un elemento lúdico que impide que el personaje perezca agobiado por las incesantes tribulaciones que le salen al paso" (55) (see also Soto 62). The adult is exiled from that time and place of the artistic use of language and memory, and at times seeks refuge within the infantile world. Childhood, a narrator tells us in *El Palacio*, is a time of great potential and wisdom, a time when a person can be whatever he or she wishes to be, and when everything is permitted. In addition, the child's words, some of them invented, in this case those of the late Esther, have numerous meanings (132–34). However, the narrator notes, Esther was at the height of her wisdom when she died as wisdom ends at the age of seventeen (132). Wisdom and the ability to engage in linguistic play—the writer's work—are joined in this novel then, as we have seen in other works, particularly in our reading of Cortázar's *Rayuela*.

There is in *El Palacio* a lamentation for the brevity of the innocence of childhood, and for the lack of value that the protagonist's society places upon it. Tico, a child, says that "we" will not forgive life for the brevity of innocence; and Anisia adds that "we" will not forgive life for not knowing what childhood is until it has been lost (374). Thus, she recognizes, as a child, that adults have lost sight of childhood's positive qualities; however, once the child has grown, he or she no longer pardons life's oversight since he or she too has lost that knowledge of childhood. It is in childhood that one can see more clearly and go to the heart of the matter, and that only by returning to childhood will we regain that clarity: "Cuando volvamos a ser niños tiraremos con más tino" (374). The child's skills of perception allow for a sharper criticism, for a clearer view, perhaps for a higher degree of truth. The author makes extensive use of the childhoods of his characters in this work as a pointed attempt to "throw with better aim," to criticize more expertly. This is precisely the point that Aponte makes in her discussion of the child as witness in the Latin American short story. They occupy a status as observers and spectators who constantly attempt to comprehend the adult world (11).

Adults in the novel are exiled from their childoods, just as they have been exiled from the countryside to the city, or from one family to another. The countryside, as we have seen in Steedman's description of the nineteenth-century ideal of country life, is at first looked upon nostalgically by the narrator as a natural world well-suited to the rearing of children. Upon closer inspection, as he relives the lives of those family members who have grown up in the countryside, we see the horrors of that life: Girls are violated; children and wives are beaten, deceived and ridiculed; and economically, country life does not sustain the family, thus its members make their way to the city, selling the land to larger interests (the grandfather, Polo, claims that he was cheated in the sale by the sugarcane company that purchased the property; this is a rather deceptive assertion, however, as he originally bought the land with stolen money (54–55, 173–74)). As the narrator revisits the country home, he sees that one cannot go home again. The house does not fit as it should, nothing is really as it is remembered to be, as he dreams it was; he questions whether he could ever have been happy there and whether the memory of childhood is nothing more than a fraud, a myth:

> ¿Acaso allí había sido feliz y ahora que todo había pasado—era irrecuperable—era cuando le estaba permitido saberlo, reconocerlo? Pero la felicidad está en el momento en que se disfruta y no en el que luego se evoca. O, de lo contrario, todo es una estafa, y no existe tal felicidad . . . [ahí] estaban todos los lugares que la infancia había mitificado. (199–200)

As he enters the childhood home, the narrator adds that he feels asphyxiated, that he has been cheated as the house does not seem to be the one he remembers (201-2). The narrator thus places in doubt the very project of the novel of attempting to recuperate, or relive, the childhood memories of the various family members. In a bit of ironic humor he adds that there should be a law against revisiting the scene of one's childhood (204). Less ironic is Onérica's life as a "beast of burden" when she was a child in the countryside (181), and also the fact that Fortunato's killers take him to a beautiful field of jasmines in the country to kill him (388–93). The paradox here is that in the novel's project it is precisely a child-like figure, someone who is occupying the childhoods of others, who must tell us that just such a return to childhood is impossible, full of pitfalls and subject to a memory that tricks us. There does not seem to be any lost paradise to recuperate, except, according to the narrator, the mythical paradise of childhood itself which the culture has produced.

We are warned of this disappointing outcome in the first pages of the novel as death is seen playing children's games in the patio of a house. As we have noted previously, death and childhood are often linked; usually the end of childhood is associated with the death of innocence, or the beginning of the end of life as the being stops growing. This linkage is made in the comments regarding the end of wisdom coming at the age of seventeen, and in Esther's having died at the height of her wisdom. It is when Fortunato decides to stop being a child and to enter the adult world of the revolution, that we see the beginning of his end (117–18, 333). The end of his childhood means his death at the hands of soldiers (see Chapter Two regarding the paternal and fraternal figures of his killers and torturers). This morbid linkage manifests itself as well in Adolfina's comments about children, as when she proclaims, in reference to her sister's children, that it would perhaps be better to kill them now, before they turn into something worse (150). Thus, while the novel delves into the recuperation of childhood, the image of childhood that is presented is more often than not that of misery, neglect and death; the implication in Adolfina's words is that these children will grow into another generation of abusers and that future generations will experience equally painful childhoods. Rather than the limitless potential referred to by Plotz, we see here only abuse, deception and a violent end. Unlike with the children of Gamboa's *Suprema Ley* or Galván's *Enriquillo*, there is no hope for the future in children in this novel, as the above quotation demonstrates, but rather only the repetition of the present; whereas "La Rebelión" ends with a new beginning, with the possibility of change being wrought out of the rubble of the past and the creativity of youth, *El Palacio* sends a message of utter frustration.

Several characters in the novel await or seek a return to a lost paradise: Delfina reminisces about the time when suitors frequented the house; Polo remembers his farm; Celia sees visions of her deceased daughter, Esther.

In addition, many of these characters have experienced a sense of exile: Polo from his land; Fortunato's father and then his mother abandoned him, and he too left the countryside with the family; Digna was put out of her home by her husband. There is also a psychological exile at work, sometimes through silence and at times through derision. The grandfather, Polo, is silent almost throughout the novel. When he does speak, Fortunato runs off jumping for joy (94-95). The silence serves to distance him from the grandfather, and the elder man uses it as a form of self-exile as he silently passes his days in his store. The types of insults hurled at Fortunato and the other children in the novel (at times it is Fortunato reliving the childhood of another) result in a type of exile of the child as well since the epithets reduce the child to something less than human. Fortunato's grandmother, for example, says that he is a beast, a horse, "un pedazo de carne con ojo" (103) ("a piece of meat with an eye"). The adults and children live in exile; they live incomunicado, and all suffer for it.

Fortunato's writing is an attempt to bridge the gap—based on physical distance, or on silence or painful words—between the adult and childhood worlds, and his mother's writing hopes to span the distance between the United States and her native Cuba, between herself and her son. His mother's letters, however, not unlike the mythic childhood inherited by Fortunato and others in his society, are full of empty promises as she never takes him to the United States, as she says she will (102-3). He augments the exile, or perhaps makes it more bearable, by imagining that his mother has died; perhaps because he cannot live without her, and perhaps because he knows that only death can make eternal that which we love. The distance is so great that Fortunato can only ask himself if his mother has any idea how much he loves her (105). Perhaps Fortunato's mother's exile is the most difficult to bear, and the most meaningful for our thesis. His mother has left him in order to go to the United States to care for the also mythical, unseen children of foreigners. Thus, one society's ability to pay for child care pushes the parents of other nations to leave their own children, but with the goal of earning a better living for the progeny they leave behind, not unlike one company's ability to buy the family's farm which results in their displacement to the city.

Besides inventing the death of his mother, Fortunato also invents the perfect child. At times the child, a cousin, is a boy and at times a girl. In either case, this youngster, imbued with all the world's purity and in whom was manifested everything that Fortunato wished to be (107), is violated and/or murdered by Fortunato and his grandfather in the boy's imagination. Fortunato uses society's guidelines to symbolically create and kill off the perfect child, that mythical creature referred to earlier. It is questionable whether this death is like that of Rocamadour in the Cortázar novel treated above. Both novels, if they are leaving a sort of blueprint for the next generation, do so in a negative fashion, leaving behind, in the case of *El Palacio*, a primer on how not to raise children, and in *Rayuela* on how not to educate them. But where Arenas's novel makes clear the emptiness of the culture's perception of childhood, Cortázar's maintains the supremacy of that perception, though it admits the impossibility of recuperating that lost paradise. The narrative structure of Arenas's novel, i.e. the protagonist's occupation of various childhoods, however, would also point to a degree of credibility for the romantics' valorization of the creative, innocent, clairvoyant child, as it is those qualities which allow the narrator to explore the feelings and lives of others.

The link here between childhood and the artist is closer to that found in *Martín Romaña*, where the protagonist and the character Bryce Echenique recognize the creative potentiality of the child, but where they note its extreme vulnerability. The Bryce Echenique novel, however, would seem to send a positive message with regard to the maintenance of the child-like qualities needed for artistic production, whereas *El Palacio* underscores the vulnerable side of the equation and the ultimate frustration inherent in the recuperative exercise. All of the works treated above link such child-like qualities to exile: In the end, Martín Romaña remains in Europe; the children in "La Rebelión de los Niños" continue in their exile, perhaps striking out on their own; Oliveira has practically trapped himself and is seen as insane at the end of *Rayuela*; and Fortunato's exile continues through the moment of his death. The characterization in *El Palacio* of Digna's children and her relationship with them would seem to sum up the dilemma. The children are described as being a combination of angel and beast; and, although she does not know them, they give her life meaning (84). Fortunato adds later that children are punished and suffer by no fault of their own, that parents and other adults are at fault. He considers suicide until he realizes that he is not to blame for the problems of his parents and other family members (100–1).

Perhaps herein lies the value of the artist's exploration of childhood as manifested in Arenas's work: A catharsis of the guilt that has been built up in childhood. Childhood has been assigned as the site of the recuperation of the nation's and the individual's pasts: Failed, broken, exiled individuals will seek to return nostalgically to childhood; and these same people, as well as the regime, will try to correct the wrongs of their own childhoods by re-shaping that of the next generation, though they usually end up by reproducing the same errors, the same abuses and the same exile that they experienced. This is essentially Salarrué's message, as well (see

Chapter Three). The trick is in the writing, to make, through literature, some sort of improvement, to hold out hope that the "interpreter," "voice," "bridge" will truly show the reader, and society, a better way into the future through the work that we are reading. But it is a dangerous proposition. If there is any great truth to be gained from returning to childhood, or from observing and studying childhood, however, it is that there is no great truth to be found there, that such expectations are simply the constructions of adults who have mystified/mythified that time and place. As we have noted regarding the Bryce Echenique novel, childhood can be explored, but that exploration results not in the recuperation of childhood itself, but rather "only" in the creation of stories, literature, which is based on memory and is as unstable and unreliable as childhood. Meaning and word—signified and signifier—are unstable. The word, in the end, is mythologized—and feared, as in Peri Rossi's tales—for that very capacity for duplicitousness that we see mythified into the child.

NOTES

[1]See, among other studies, Lanin A. Gyurko, "Cortázar's Fictional Children," *Neophilologus* 57.1 (January 1973): 24–41; Luis Hass, "Infancia y Cielo en Cortázar," Ed. Pedro Lastra, *Cortázar*, Madrid: Taurus, 1987: 258–67; and Vittoria Borsó, "Americanidad: Des-tierro, Escritura y Des-cubrimiento," *Inti* 22–23 (otoño 1985– primavera 1986): 355–66.

[2]As we note in our introduction, the child is linked to the noble savage in a similar manner; they are both typified, stripped of their individuality in an effort that, paradoxically, is meant to praise them.

[3]Ferreira notes the use of a fragmented identity for the narrator, which places in doubt his authority as an author, a clear recognition of the creative process of the work itself, the presence of colloquial language and experiences more similar to those of the daily life of the typical reader, and the use of humor and popular culture as elements which conspire to make this relationship between reader and protagonist stronger.

[4]For Franco, it is not until *Fantomas Contra los Vampiros Multinacionales* (1980) (*Phantoms Against the Multinational Vampires*) that Cortázar reveals that utopian solidarity cannot be based on a vanguard esthetic, and that a utopia does not require a 'high culture' in order to be

144

transmitted throughout a society, nor do the masses need such authors who would create works specifically for the masses (Franco, "Julio" 115, 117).

[5]There are at least two other situations in which the importance of the lower zones is underscored. One is the moment when the relationship between Martín and Sandra is consecrated, at least in his mind, when she allows him—and no one else—to urinate in her bathroom. Of course, this also pokes fun at and demythifies marriage, as well as being an absurd exaggeration of the bourgeoisie's emphasis on hygiene. The other situation is that of the excursion that Martín and Carlos make to a lower-class neighborhood as they search for adventure. This last situation is not unlike Oliveira's engaging in a sexual act with the *clocharde* in *Rayuela*.

[6]One of the ways in which he attempts to maintain the woman's control is through lying or false representation. The entire matter of his heroism in May of 1968, his participation in the Grupo and the writing by installments of the fishing novel are examples of how Martín is capable of submitting himself to the leftist myths of others in order to stand in good stead with the woman he loves. Martín, in his relation with Inés, transfers the basis of the relationship from the relationship itself to the mattress where they make love. The young man has an obsessive fetish; it is the depression in the mattress that is responsible for his active and satisfying sex life, not the lovers themselves, or their emotions. We could say that this reflects a rather child-like obsession on Martín's part, as indeed his participation in demonstrations and "El Grupo" are really play-acting.

[7]This work was first published in a French translation in 1975.

[8]In two of Salarrué's stories (as we discuss in Chapter Two) there is a significant silence on the part of the two girls who faced sexual violation at the hands of representatives of the oligarchy. That silence is a key factor in the ability of the two father figures to control the girls.

CONCLUSIONS

Historians and literary critics often have difficulty separating the actual conditions for children from the image of children in literature and politics (Steedman 5–6). This difficulty is due precisely to the belief in childhood as a "common ground" for all of the nation's citizens. Ludmila Jordanova writes that scholars of childhood cannot help but implicate themselves in their work as they, without exception, were once children, and because of the complexity of society's perceptions of childhood: "historians are the products of societies that currently hold complex, deeply contradictory, and largely unarticulated views about children. Our capacity to sentimentalise, identify with, project onto, and reify children is almost infinite" (79). This statement brings into question the scholar's capacity for achieving some level of objectivity in the study of childhood. Our intention here has been to reveal certain authors' views on childhood as they appear in the literary works, and how those views are implicated in the writers' re-evaluation of the nation.

Although the qualities of romanticism's child permeate Latin American literature, we see a progression in the exploration of childhood in the works we have studied here. In the colonial period and the nineteenth century, the child was a citizen-in-training, valued not for what they were, but for what they would become. Asunción Lavrin writes that children were "potential adults," and not "vessels of latent wickedness nor glorified sources of joy and purity" ("Mexico" 424). Romanticism's idealism was tempered by the republics' pragmatic need for conformity and order in the adult population. In a late-nineteenth century work such as Federico Gamboa's, then, childhood is not valued so much for its creativity and spontaneity as it is for its perceived "socialism." Children are contrasted with adults in such works in order to demonstrate the degree of degradation of adults and the political, economic and social systems they have created. The plight of the child as victim of such systems comes to the fore in this period as well, and this utilization of children in literature continues today. We have demonstrated how Salarrué, Juan Bosch and Silvina Ocampo have linked the child to other marginalized sectors, with Ocampo making the clearest criticism of the infantilization of those sectors. She begins to call into question the exploitation of the qualities of the romantic child, while at the same time exploring childhood as the site of the revelation of society's arbitrary limitations.

Although children are marginalized beings, they are unlike other marginalized groups in that, no matter their race, class or gender, their status will change as they age. The formation of the child's allegiance to previous generations and their ideals becomes a source of conflict between competing interests in those older generations. In fact, we have argued that *Enriquillo* is an effort to exploit a protagonist's youth in order to convince a people of the merits of an allegiance to its Spanish past, and of a continued subordination to those people, such as the author himself, who are the authorities on that heritage. This competition is explored in its more violent forms in contemporary literature, such as in works by Cristina Peri Rossi and Reinaldo Arenas. In these works the falseness of the "immunity" of children is revealed. Peri Rossi's stories in particular expose the appropriation by the state of the rhetoric of the family—including that of the immunity of children—and how tremendous evil is perpetrated in the name of saving the nation's children from outside forces. That "salvation" is accomplished through a substitution of the state family for the biological family, and by controlling the child's comprehension of language and expressive production of all kinds. Writers recognize their kinship to children for this very reason: They are both pursued by those who would control their growth, their creativity and thus their questioning of society's boundaries. Our examination of *Rayuela* and *La Vida Exagerada de Martín Romaña*, as well as Peri Rossi's stories, makes clear this preoccupation with childhood and artistic production.

Most of the authors considered here could be said to utilize childhood to explore the origins and/or contemporary state of the nation. Isabel Allende's short story, "De Barro Estamos Hechos," brings to bear on the figure of the child a reconsideration of the histories of an ethnic minority, at least two individuals, and the Latin American nation where the story is set. The narrative makes clear connections between the plight of the Jewish people, and that of the children of the fictional Latin American nation. These connections are made as the protagonist recounts, to a girl trapped in mud, events from his own childhood. The nation trains its gaze on the girl for a time, but seems paralyzed, unable or unwilling to help her. Such presentations of childhood invite the reader to re-examine his or her own past, and place it in the context of the nation's present and history. This is, in a sense, a call for testimony from the nation's citizens; a call for a grand, cathartic sharing of childhood experiences. This sort of testimony is attempted by the protagonist in Ocampo's "La Furia," and is most explicit in the above-mentioned Allende story. The child acts as a mirror for the nation, and for the reader. This is part of the child's exile, however, as the child is the other whose identity must serve the superior's need for self-evaluation. Steedman notes this in theatrical productions which use the child's body to bring to life on stage the "deepest springs of the self," a sort of personification of one's interior: People "performed the act of making children's bodies the living emblems of their self and its history" (169–71). In more historical, and less metaphorical terms, Asunción Lavrin notes that Mexico has often turned its attention to children following traumatic periods which have depleted the nation's population ("Mexico" 422). In such terms the child becomes the focus of the adult's concern for personal and national survival.

Lavrin touches on numerous topics related to childhood, including child care, education, gender roles, child abandonment and adoption, health, and definitions of childhood ("Mexico"). If we restrict ourselves to literary sources, there are likewise numerous topics that might be considered. We might include here the role of childhood in various literary movements and/or genres. An area to which our work points is the role of the child in postmodernism. In his 1994 article on the Hispanic postmodern, Mario Valdés notes: "The most recent development in postmodernism has been the subversion of history as the objective presentation of a common past" (461). Childhood is used in the works we have examined as a way of subverting that "objective" mode of historical writing. The child as the boundary-crossing, creative, dangerous being who, at the same time, is considered to be innocent, passive and malleable, would seem to make an ideal subject of a discourse which questions the validity of other discourses, particularly those of national history and the patriarchal family. If the postmodern is to subvert the notion of "history as the presentation of a common past," however, we must question whether that can be done through the utilization of a stereotypical child subject. The child is used precisely because of society's belief in those stereotyped qualities noted above. The belief that all members of a community—perhaps the community of humankind—share a commonality of experience due to our childhoods, should be a part of the "common past" which is subverted in postmodern writing. Indeed, that is our contention regarding the works of such authors as Bryce Echenique, Peri Rossi and Arenas. These writers bring to the fore the question of whether we all share that "common ground" of childhood experience. They ask this question not through the relatively obvious differences of experience due to the child's race, class and gender, however, but rather by probing their societies' acceptance and exploitation of a set of qualities assigned to childhood in general. We have attempted to demonstrate here whether and how writers question the basis for the nation's imagined children.

BIBLIOGRAPHY

Adorno, Rolena. "La «Ciudad Letrada» y los Discursos Coloniales". *Hispamérica* 16.48 (Dec. 1987): 3–24.

Aldridge, Owen. "Literature and the Study of Man." *Literature and Anthropology*. Eds. Philip A. Dennis and Wendell Aycock. Lubbock, Texas: Texas Tech UP, 1989. 41–63.

Allende, Isabel. *Cuentos de Eva Luna*. Buenos Aires: Editorial Sudamericana, 1990.

Anderson, Benedict. *Imagined Communities: Reflections on the Origin and Spread of Nationalism*. 2nd. edition. London: Verso. 1991.

Anderson, Thomas P. *Matanza: El Salvador's Communist Revolt of 1932*. Lincoln and London: U of Nebraska P, 1971.

Aponte Bockus, Barbara. "El Niño Como Testigo: La Visión Infantil en el Cuento Hispanoamericano Contemporáneo." *Explicación de Textos Literarios* 11.1 (1982–83): 11–22.

Araújo, Helena. "Ejemplos de la «Niña Impura» en Silvina Ocampo y Alba Lucía Angel". *Hispamérica* 13.28 (agosto 1984): 27–35.

150

Arenas, Reinaldo. *El Palacio de las Blanquísimas Mofetas*. 1975. Caracas: Monte Avila Editores, 1980.

Aries, Philippe. *Centuries of Childhood. A Social History of Family Life*. 1960. Trans. Robert Baldick. NY: Alfred A. Knopf, 1962.

Aronne-Amestoy, Lida. *Utopía, Paraíso e Historia: Inscripciones del Mito en García Márquez, Rulfo y Cortázar*. Amsterdam/Philadelphia: John Benjamins Publishing Co., 1986.

Arrom, Sylvia. "Changes in Mexican Family Law in the Nineteenth Century: The Civil Codes of 1870 and 1884." *The Journal of Family History* 10 (1985): 305-17.

Arroyo, Anita. *Narrativa Hispanoamericana Actual: América y sus Problemas*. San Juan, Puerto Rico: Editorial Universitaria, 1980.

Balderston, Daniel. "Los Cuentos Crueles de Silvina Ocampo y Juan Rodolfo Wilcock." *Revista Iberoamericana* 49.125 (Oct.–Dec. 1983): 743-52.

Balmori, Diana, Stuart F. Voss, and Miles Wortman. *Notable Family Networks in Latin America*. Chicago: U of Chicago P, 1984.

Barradas, Efrain. "La Seducción de las Máscaras: José Alcántara Almánzar, Juan Bosch y la Joven Narrativa Dominicana." *Revista Iberoamericana* 54.142 (Jan.–Mar. 1988): 11-25.

Behar, Ruth. "Sexual Witchcraft, Colonialism, and Women's Powers: Views from the Mexican Inquisition." In Lavrin *Sexuality*. 178-206.

Bellingham, Bruce. "The History of Childhood Since the 'Invention of Childhood': Some Issues in the Eighties." *Journal of Family History* 13.2 (1988): 347-58.

Bhabha, Homi, ed. "Introduction: Narrating the Nation." *Nation and Narration*. NY: Routledge, 1990. 1-7.

Boling, Becky. "Parricide and Revolution: Fuentes' 'El Día de las Madres' and *Gringo Viejo*." *Hispanófila* 32 (1988): 73-81.

Borsó, Vittoria. "Americanidad: Des-tierro, Escritura y Des-cubrimiento."

Inti 22–23 (Fall 1985–Spring 1986): 355–66.

Bosch, Juan. *Camino Real.* 1933. Santo Domingo: Alfa y Omega, 1983.

___. *Más Cuentos Escritos en el Exilio.* Santo Domingo: Edición Especial, 1976.

___. *Cuentos.* Habana: Casa de las Américas, 1983.

Bravo-Villasante. *Historia y Antología de la Literatura Infantil Iberoamericana.* 2 vols. Madrid: Editorial Everest, 1987.

Britt, Linda. "A Transparent Lens? Narrative Technique in Carmen Naranjo's *Nunca Hubo Alguna Vez.*" *Monographic Review/Revista Monográfica* 4 (1988): 127–35.

Browning, Richard L. "El Niño Excluido: Relaciones Familiares en *Cuentos de Barro* de Salarrué." *Journal of Interdisciplinary Literary Studies* 4.1-2 (1992): 71-88.

Brushwood, John S. *Mexico in its Novel; A Nation's Search for Identity.* Austin and London: U of Texas P, 1966.

___. *Narrative Innovation and Political Change in Mexico.* New York: Peter Lang Publishing Inc., 1989.

___. "La Novela Mexicana Frente al Porfirismo." *Historia Mexicana* 7 (enero–marzo 1958): 368–405.

Bryce Echenique, Alfredo. *La vida Exagerada de Martín Romaña.* 1985. Barcelona: Plaza y Janes Editores, 1988.

Butler Flor, Cornelia. "Roasting Donald Duck: Alternative Comics and Photonovels in Latin America." *Journal of Popular Culture* 18.1 (Summer 1984): 163–83.

Campbell, Joseph. *The Hero With a Thousand Faces.* Princeton: Princeton UP, 1949.

Carrilla, Emilio. *El Romanticismo en la América Hispánica.* 3rd ed. Vol. 2. Madrid: Editorial Gredos, 1975.

Castañeda, Carmen. "La Memoria de las Niñas Violadas." *Segundo Simposio de Historia de las Mentalidades: La Memoria y el Olvido.* No ed. Mexico: Instituto Nacional de Antropología e Historia, 1985. 107–16.

Chanady, Amaryll. "Latin American Discourses of Identity and the Appropriation of the Amerindian Other." *Sociocriticism* 6.1–2 (1990): 33–48.

Chatterjee, Partha. "The Nationalist Resolution of the Women's Question." *Recasting Women: Essays in Colonial History.* Eds. Kumkum Sangari and Sudesh Vaid. New Delhi: Kali for Women, 1989. 233–53.

Cherry, Sherry Young. "Fantasy and Reality in Salarrué." Diss. Northwestern U, 1977.

Cortázar, Julio. *Rayuela.* 1963. Intro. Andrés Amorós. Madrid: Cátedra, 1989.

Cruz Mendizabal, J., ed. *El Niño en las Literaturas Hispánicas.* 2 vols. Indiana, PA: Indiana U of Pennsylvania P, 1978.

Cunningham, Hugh. *The Children of the Poor: Representations of Childhood Since the Seventeenth Century.* Oxford: Basil Blackwell, 1991.

Cunningham, Rodger. "Falling Into Heaven: Pre-Adamism and Paradox in Rayuela." *Inti: Revista de Literatura Hispánica* 34–35 (Fall–Spring 1991–92): 93–106.

Dufault, Roseanna Lewis. *Metaphors of Identity: The Treatment of Childhood in Selected Québécois Novels.* London/Toronto: Farleigh Dickinson UP, 1991.

Dwyer, Daisy, and Judith Bruce, eds. *A Home Divided: Women and Income in the Third World.* Stanford: Stanford UP, 1988.

Eco, Umberto. *The Role of the Reader: Explorations in the Semiotics of Texts.* Bloomington: Indiana UP, 1979.

Elizagaray, Alga Marina. *En Torno a la Literatura Infantil.* Habana: Unión de Escritores y Artistas de Cuba, 1975.

Erickson, Vincent O. "*Buddenbrooks*, Thomas Mann, and North German

Social Class: An Application of Literary Anthropology." *Literary Anthropology: A New Interdisciplinary Approach to People, Signs and Literature.* Ed. Fernando Poyatos. Amsterdam and Philadelphia: John Benjamins Publishing Co., 1988. 97–125.

Fanon, Frantz. *Black Skin, White Masks.* 1952. Trans. Charles Lam Markham. NY: Grove P, 1967.

Fatout, Paul, ed. *Mark Twain Speaking.* Iowa City: U of Iowa P, 1976.

Fernández Olmos, Margarita. *La Cuentística de Juan Bosch: Un Análisis Crítico-Cultural.* Santo Domingo: Editora Alfa y Omega, 1982.

Ferré, Rosario. *Cortázar: El Romántico en su Observatorio.* San Juan, Puerto Rico: Editorial Cultural, 1990.

Ferreira, César Guillermo. "Bryce-Echenique y la Novela del Posboom: Lectura de *La Ultima Mudanza de Felipe Carrillo.*" *Chasqui* 22.2 (Nov. 1993): 34–48.

Folbre, Nancy. "The Black Four of Hearts: Toward a New Paradigm of Household Economics." *A Home Divided: Women and Income in the Third World.* Ed. Daisy Dwyer and Judith Bruce. Stanford: Stanford UP, 1988. 248–62.

Fonseca, Claudia. "Spouses, Siblings and Sex-Linked Bonding: A Look at Kinship Organization in a Brazilian Slum." *Family, Household and Gender Relations in Latin America.* Ed. Elizabeth Jelin. London: Kegan Paul International (UNESCO), 1991. 133–60.

Fowler-Salamini, Heather and Mary Kay Vaughan. *Women of the Mexican Countryside, 1850–1990: Creating Spaces, Shaping Transitions.* Tucson: U of Arizona P, 1994.

Franco, Jean. "Beyond Ethnocentrism: Gender, Power, and the Third-World Intelligentsia." *Marxism and the Interpretation of Culture.* Eds. Cary Nelson and Lawrence Grossberg. Urbana and Chicago: U of Illinois P, 1988. 503–15.

___. "Julio Cortazar: Utopia and Everyday Life." *Inti* 10–11 (otoño 1979–primavera 1980): 108–18.

___. "The Crisis of the Liberal Imagination and the Utopia of Writing." *Ideologies and Literature* 1.1 (Dec. 1976–Jan. 1977): 5–24.

___. "Killing Priests, Nuns, Women, Children." *On Signs*. Ed. Marshall Blonsky. Baltimore: Johns Hopkins UP, 1985. 414–20.

___. *Plotting Women: Gender and Representation in Mexico*. NY: Columbia UP, 1989.

Galván, Manuel de J. *Enriquillo. Leyenda Histórica Dominicana (1503–1533)*. (1882). Intro. de Concha Meléndez. México: Editorial Porrúa, 1986.

Gálvez Acero, Marina. "Sábato y la Libertad." *Anthropos* 55–56 (1985): 89–113.

Gamboa, Federico. *Suprema Ley*. 1896. In *Novelas de Federico Gamboa*. Mexico City: Fondo de Cultura Económica, 1965. 225–463.

___. *Impresiones y Recuerdos*. México: E. Gómez de la Puente, 1922. Quoted in Lay.

Gelpí, Juan. *Literatura y Paternalismo en Puerto Rico*. San Juan, Puerto Rico: Editorial de la Universidad de Puerto Rico, 1993.

Godoy Gallardo, Eduardo. *La Infancia en la Narrativa Española de Posguerra, 1939–1978*. Madrid: Editorial Playor, 1979.

González Echevarría, Roberto. "Literature and Exile: Carpentier's 'Right of Sanctuary'." *The Voice of the Masters: Writing and Authority in Modern Latin American Literature*. Austin: U of Texas P, 1985. 124–36.

Grass, Roland. "Precursors of the Novel of the Mexican Revolution." Diss. Columbia U, 1968.

___. *José López-Portillo y Rojas*. Series in the Humanities, No. 2. Macomb, Ill.: Western Illinois University Bulletin, Vol. 49, No. 4, May 1970.

Gutiérrez Mouat, Ricardo. "Lector y Narratario en Dos Relatos de Bryce Echenique." *Inti* 24–25 (otoño 1986–primavera 1987): 107–26.

155

Gyurko, Lanin A. "Cortázar's Fictional Children: Freedom and its Constraints." *Neophilologus* 57.1 (Jan. 1973): 24–41.

Handelsman, Michael H. *"La Casa de los Espíritus* y la Evolución de la Mujer Moderna." *Letras Femeninas* 14.1–2 (Spring–Fall 1988): 57–63.

Hass, Luis. "Infancia y Cielo en Cortázar." *Julio Cortázar.* Comp. Pedro Lastra. Madrid: Taurus, 1981. 258–67.

Hawes, Joseph M. and N. Ray Hiner, eds. *Children in Historical and Comparative Perspective: An International Handbook and Research Guide.* New York: Greenwood P, 1991.

Helsper, Norma Jane. "Gender and Class Conflict in Contemporary Chilean Prose and Drama." Diss. U of Texas at Austin, 1987.

Henríquez R., Norma. "La Estructura Económica Familiar y el Maltrato Infantil." *Violencia en la Intimidad.* Ed. Casa de la Mujer. Bogotá: Editorial Gente Nueva, 1988. 137–45.

Herskovits, Melville. *Man and His Works.* New York: Alfred A. Knopf, 1970.

Hooker, Alexander C. *La Novela de Federico Gamboa.* Madrid: Editorial Playor, S. A., 1973.

Insanally, Sheik Riyad David. "Parental Neglect and the Displacement of Childhood in *Cien Años de Soledad.*" Diss. Harvard U, 1990.

Iser, Wolfgang. "Toward a Literary Anthropology. *Prospecting: From Reader Response to Literary Anthropology.* Baltimore/London: The Johns Hopkins UP, 1989. 262–84.

Jaksic, Iván. "The Influence of Positivism on Latin American Educational Thought: The Case of Chile and Valentín Letelier." *Latin American Education: A Quest for Identity.* Ed. Nancy J. Nystrom. New Orleans: Roger Thayer Stone Center for Latin American Studies, 1985. 57–72.

Jelin, Elizabeth, ed. *Family, Household and Gender Relations in Latin America.* London: Kegan Paul International (UNESCO), 1991.

Jordanova, Ludmila. "New Worlds for Children in the 18th Century: Problems of Historical Explanation." *History of the Human Sciences* 3.1 (1990): 69-83.

Kason, Nancy M. "El Compromiso Político en 'La Escuela de Noche' de Cortázar." *Literatura Como Intertextualidad. IX Simposio Internacional de Literatura*. Ed. Juana A. Arancibia. Buenos Aires: Instituto Literario y Cultural Hispánico, 1993. 184-92.

Kauffmann, R. Lane. "Julio Cortázar y la Apropiación del Otro: 'Axolotl' Como Fábula Etnográfica." *Inti* 22-23 (Fall 1985-Spring 1986): 317-26.

Klingenberg, Patricia Nisbet. "The Mad Double in the Stories of Silvina Ocampo." *Latin American Literary Review* 16.32 (July-Dec. 1988): 29-40.

___. "The Twisted Mirror: The Fantastic Stories of Silvina Ocampo". *Letras Femeninas* 8.1-2 (primavera-otoño 1987): 67-78.

___. *El Infiel Espejo: The Short Stories of Silvina Ocampo*. Ann Arbor, MI: Universtiy Microfilms International, 1981.

Kuteischikova, Vera N. "El Romanticismo y el Problema de la Conciencia Nacional en la Literatura Latinoamericana en el Siglo XIX." *Contextos: Literatura y Sociedad Latinoamericanas del Siglo XIX*. Eds. Evelyn Picón Garfield and Ivan A. Schulman. Urbana: U of Illinois P, 1991. 1-7.

Kuznesof, Elizabeth A. and Robert Oppenheimer. "The Family and Society in Nineteenth-Century Latin America: An Historiographical Introduction." *Journal of Family History* 10.3 (Autumn 1985): 215-34.

___. "Brazil." In Hiner and Hawes. 147-77.

Lara Martínez, Rafael. *Salarrué o el Mito de la Creación de la Sociedad Mestiza Salvadoreña*. San Salvador: Dirección de Publicaciones e Impresos, 1991.

Lavrin, Asunción. "Mexico." In Hawes and Hiner. 421-45.

___, ed. *Sexuality and Marriage in Colonial Latin America*. Lincoln: U of Nebraska P, 1989.

Lay, Amado. "Visión del Porfiriato en Cuatro Narradores Mexicanos: Rafael Delgado, Federico Gamboa, José López Portillo y Rojas y Emilio Rabasa." Diss. University of Arizona, 1981.

Lenzer, Gertrude, ed. *Auguste Comte and Positivism: The Essential Writings*. New York: Harper and Row, 1975.

Lerner, Victoria. "Historia de la Reforma Educativa, 1933–1945." *Historia Mexicana* 29 (1979): 91–132.

Levinson, David. *Family Violence in Cross-Cultural Perspective*. Newbury Park, CA/London/New Delhi: Sage Publications, 1989.

Lewis, Oscar. "An Anthropological Approach to Family Studies." *Anthropological Essays*. New York: Random House, 1970. 81–89.

Lloyd, Rosemary. *The Land of Lost Content: Children and Childhood in Nineteenth-Century French Literature*. Oxford: Oxford UP, 1992.

Lockert, Lucía Fox. "Silvina Ocampo's Fantastic Short Stories". *Monographic Review/Revista Monográfica* 4 (1988): 221–29.

Lomnitz, Larisa Adler and Marisol Pérez-Lizaur. *A Mexican Elite Family 1820–1980*. Princeton: Princeton UP, 1987.

Loveman, Brian and Thomas M. Davies, Jr. *The Politics of Antipolitics. The Military in Latin America*. Lincoln and London: U of Nebraska P, 1989.

Mallón, Florencia. "Exploring the Origins of Democratic Patriarchy in Mexico: Gender and Popular Resistance in the Puebla Highlands, 1850–1876." *Women of the Mexican Countryside, 1850–1990: Creating Spaces, Shaping Transitions*. Eds. Heather Fowler-Salamini and Mary Kay Vaughan. Tucson: U of Arizona P, 1994. 3–26.

Martin, Biddy. "The Hobo, the Fairy, and the Quarterback." *Profession 94* (1994): 15–20.

Martin, Gerald. *Journeys Through the Labyrinth. Latin American Fiction in the Twentieth Century*. London: Verso, 1989.

Martínez-Tolentino, Jaime. "La Familia Como Fuente de Todo Mal en *El*

158

Obsceno Pájaro de la Noche." Revista de Crítica Literaria Latinoamericana 11.23 (1986): 73-79.

Matamoro, Blas. "La Nena Terrible." *Oligarquía y literatura.* Buenos Aires: Ediciones del Sol, 1975. 193-221.

Matthews, Irene. "Dauthering in War: Two 'Case Studies' from Mexico and Guatemala." *Gendering War Talk.* Eds. Miriam Cooke and Angela Wallacott. Princeton: Princeton UP, 1993. 148-73.

McCard, Victoria L. "El Subalterno en Cortázar." *Revista de Estudios Hispánicos* 17-18 (1990-91): 247-58.

Merrim, Stephanie. "Desire, and the Art of Dehumanization: Macedonio Fernández, Julio Cortázar and Joao Guimaraes Rosa." *Latin American Literary Review* 16.31 (Jan.-June 1988): 45-64.

Meyer, Jean A. "Revolution and Reconstruction in the 1920s." *The Cambridge History of Latin America.* Vol. 5. NY: Cambridge UP, 1986.

Monsiváis, Carlos. "¿Existe una Cultura Iberoamericana?" *Revista Canadiense de Estudios Hispánicos* 18.3 (primavera 1994): 379-92.

Monterde, Francisco. Prólogo. *Novelas de Federico Gamboa.* Mexico City: Fondo de Cultura Económica, 1965. vii-xv.

Mora, Gabriela. "El Mito Degradado de la Familia en *El Libro de mis Primos* de Cristina Peri Rossi." *The Analysis of Literary Texts: Current Trends in Methodology.* Ed. Randolph D. Pope. Ypsilanti, MI: Bilingual Press/Editorial Bilingüe, 1980. 66-77.

___. "El Bidungsroman y la Experiencia Latinoamericana: 'La Pájara Pinta' de Albalucía Angel." *La Sartén por el Mango.* Eds. Patricia Elena González and Eliana Ortega. Santo Domingo: Ediciones Huracán, 1984. 71-81.

___. "Las Novelas de Isabel Allende y el Papel de la Mujer Como Ciudadana." *Ideologies and Literature* 2 (1987): 53-61.

Mount, Ferdinand. *The Subversive Family: An Alternative History of Love and Marriage.* London: Jonathan Cape, 1982.

Muriel de González Mariscal, Josefina. "La Protección al Niño en la Nueva España." *Coloquios I. Reunión Hispano-Mexicana de Historia.* Eds. Emilio Azcárraga Milmo and Valentín Molina Piñeiro. Mexico City: Instituto de Estudios y Documentos Históricos, 1981. 39–63.

Murray, Frederic W. "The Image of Utopia as a Conceptual Determinant in the Structural Development of Spanish American Culture." *Imagination, Emblems and Expressions: Essays on Latin American, Caribbean, and Continental Culture and Identity.* Ed. Helen Ryan-Ranson. Bowling Green, Ohio: Bowling Green State UP, 1993. 29–39.

Myers, Kathleen A. "A Glimpse of Family Life in Colonial Mexico: A Nun's Account." *Latin American Research Review* 28.2 (1993): 63–87.

Navarro, Joaquina. *La Novela Realista Mexicana.* México: Compañía General de Ediciones, 1955.

Niehaus, Thomas. *Children in Latin America: A Preliminary Bibliography.* New Orleans: Roger Thayer Stone Center for Latin American Studies, 1989.

Ocampo, Silvina. *La Furia y Otros Cuentos.* (1959). Intro. Enrique Pezzoni. Madrid: Alianza Editorial, 1982.

Otero, José. "La Historia Como Ficción en *Eva Luna* de Isabel Allende." *Confluencia* 4.1 (Fall 1988): 61–67.

Pasternac, Nora, Ana Rosa Domenella and Luzelena Gutiérrez de Velasco, eds. *Escribir la Infancia. Narradoras Mexicanas Contemporáneas.* México, D.F.: El Colegio de México, 1996.

Paz, Octavio. *El Laberinto de la Soledad.* (1950). Mexico City: Fondo de la Cultura Económica, 1959.

Pena de Matsuchita, Marta E. *El Romanticismo Político Hispanoamericano.* Buenos Aires: Centro de Estudios Filosóficos, 1985.

Peña, Guillermo de la. "Ideology and Practice in Southern Jalisco: Peasants, Rancheros, and Urban Entrepreneurs." *Kinship Ideology and Practice in Latin America.* Ed. Raymond T. Smith. London: U of North Carolina P, 1984. 204–34.

Peri Rossi, Cristina. *La Rebelión de los Niños.* (1980). Barcelona: Editorial Seix Barral, 1992.

Pezzoni, Enrique. "Prologue." *La Furia y Otros Cuentos.* Silvina Ocampo. (1959.) Madrid: Alianza Editorial, 1982. 9–23.

Pfeiffer, Erna. "La Imagen de la Madre en *La Casa de los Espíritus* de Isabel Allende Dentro del Marco del Machismo Latinoamericano." *Beitrage zur Romanischen Philologie* 29.1 (1990): 65–70.

Piña Contreras, Guillermo. *Enriquillo: El Texto y la Historia.* Santo Domingo, Dominican Republic: Editora Alfa y Omega, 1985.

Planells, Antonio. "Represión Sexual, Frigidez y Maternidad Frustrada: 'Verano', de Julio Cortázar." *Bulletin of Hispanic Studies* 56.3 (July 1979): 233–37.

Plotz, Judith. "The Perpetual Messiah: Romanticism, Childhood, and the Paradoxes of Human Development." *Regulated Children/Liberated Children: Education in Psychohistorical Perspective.* Ed. Barbara Finkelstein. New York: Psychohistory P, 1979. 63–95.

Pollock, Linda. *Forgotten Children: Parent-child Relations from 1500 to 1900.* Cambridge: Cambridge UP, 1983.

Poniatowska, Elena. *¡Ay Vida, No Me Mereces!* México: Joaquín Mortiz, 1985.

Poyatos, Fernando, ed. *Literary Anthropology: A New Interdisciplinary Approach to People, Signs and Literature.* Amsterdam and Philadelphia: John Benjamins Publishing, 1988.

Prado González, Manuel. *Trayectoria de la Novela en México.* México: Ediciones Botas, 1951.

Pratt, Mary Louise. "Women, Literature, and National Brotherhood." *Women, Culture, and Politics in Latin America.* Ed. Seminar on Feminism and Culture in Latin America. Berkeley: U of California P, 1990. 48–73.

___. "Las Mujeres y el Imaginario Nacional en el Siglo XIX." *Revista de*

Crítica Literaria Latinoamericana 19.38 (1993): 51–62.

Puleo, Alicia Helda. "La Sexualidad Fantástica." *Coloquio Internacional: lo Lúdico y lo Fantástico en la Obra de Cortázar.* Madrid: Editorial Fundamentos, 1986.

Ramírez, Sergio. Prólogo. *El Angel del Espejo y Otros Relatos.* By Salarrué. Caracas: Biblioteca Ayacucho, 1977. ix–xxv.

Ramos Escandón, Carmen. "The Novel of Porfirian Mexico: A Historian's Source. Problems and Methods." *Ideologies and Literature* 3 (Sept–Nov. 1980): 118–33.

Rebeil Corella, M. Antonieta. "What Mexican Youth Learn from Commercial Television." *Studies in Latin American Popular Culture* 4 (1985): 188–99.

Renan, Ernest. "What is a Nation?" (1882). *Nation and Narration.* Ed. Homi K. Bhabha. New York: Routledge, 1990. 8–22.

Rivera, Julius. *Latin America: A Sociocultural Interpretation.* New York: Irvington Publs., 1978.

Rivero, A. "El Destino de la Mujer." *Revista Científica y Literaria* 1 (1846). *El Album de la Mujer: Antología Ilustrada de las Mexicanas. El Siglo XIX (1821–1880).* Vol. 3. Ed. Julia Tuñón. Mexico: Instituto Nacional de Antropología e Historia, 1991. 57–68.

Rockwell, Elsie. "Rural Schooling and the State in Post-Revolutionary Mexico." Eds. Gilbert M. Joseph and Daniel Nugent. *Everyday Forms of State Formation: Revolution and the Negotiation of Rule in Mexico.* Durham, NC: Duke UP, 1994. 170–208.

Rodríguez Alcalá, Hugo. "Will to Freedom in Argentine Romanticism." Latin American Studies Program Research Lecture Series, #1. Twelfth Meeting of the Interdisciplinary Symposium on Romanticism. U of California-Riverside. 29 Feb. 1972.

Roldan, Martha. "Renegotiating the Marital Contract: Intrahousehold Patterns of Money Allocation and Women's Subordination Among Domestic Outworkers in Mexico City." In Dwyer and Bruce. 229–47.

Romano, James V. "Authorial Identity and National Disintegration in Latin America." *Ideologies and Literature* 4.1 (Spring 1989): 167–98.

Romanucci-Ross, Lola. *Conflict, Violence, and Morality in a Mexican Village*. (1973). Chicago: U of Chicago P, 1986.

Rothstein, Frances. "Caiptalist Insdustrialization and the Increasing Cost of Children." *Women and Change in Latin America*. Eds. June Nash and Helen I. Safa. NY: Bergin and Garvey, 1985. 37–52.

Rozencvaig, Perla. *Reinaldo Arenas: Narrativa de Transgresión*. Oaxaca, Mexico: Editorial Oasis, 1986.

Ruiz Martínez, Cristina. "La Memoria Sobre la Niñez y su Estereotipo del Niño Santo, Siglos XVI, XVII, and XVIII." *La Memoria y el Olvido: Segundo Simposio de Historia de las Mentalidades*. Mexico: Instituto Nacional de Antropología e Historia, 1985. 117–23.

Salarrué. *Cuentos de Barro*. 1933. San José, Costa Rica: EDUCA, 1987.

Saldes Báez, Sergio. "*La Vida Exagerada de Martín Romaña* o 'la Aventura de la Escritura': (Diálogo y Autorreflexividad de un Texto Poético)". *Revista Chilena de Literatura* 25 (nov. 1985): 109–20.

Sawyer, Roger. *Children Enslaved*. London: Routledge, 1988.

Schmidt, Cynthia A. "A Satiric Perspective on the Experience of Exile in the Short Fiction of Cristina Peri Rossi." *The Americas Review* 18.3–4 (Fall–Winter 1990): 218–26.

Sherwood, Joan. *Poverty in Eighteenth-Century Spain. The Women and Children of the Inclusa*. Toronto: U of Toronto P, 1988.

Shields, E. Thomson, Jr. "Ink, Blood, and Kisses: *La Casa de los Espíritus* and the Myth of Disunity." *Hispanófila* 33 (1990): 79–86.

Smart, Patricia. *Writing in the Father's House: The Emergence of the Feminine in the Quebec Literary Tradition*. Toronto: U of Toronto P, 1991.

Solange Albeno. "El Discurso Inquisitorial Sobre los Delitos de Bigamia , Poligamia y Solicitación." (1980). *El Album de la Mujer. Antología*

Ilustrada de las Mexicanas. Epoca Colonial. Vol. 2. Ed. Marcela Tostado Gutiérrez. Mexico City: Instituto Nacional de Antropología e Historia, 1991. 76–77.

Sommer, Doris. "Populism as Rhetoric: The Case of the Dominican Republic." *Boundary 2* 11.1–2 (Fall/Winter 1982/83): 253–70.

___. *Foundational Fictions. The National Romances of Latin America.* Berkeley: U of California P, 1991.

Sommerville, C. John. *The Rise and Fall of Childhood.* Beverly Hills: Sage, 1982.

Soto, Francisco. "*Celestino Antes del Alba, El Palacio de las Blanquísimas Mofetas*, and *Otra Vez el Mar*: The Struggle for Self-Expression." *Hispania* 75.1 (March 1992): 60–68.

Steedman, Carolyn. *Strange Dislocations. Childhood and the Idea of Human Interiority 1780–1930.* Cambridge: Harvard UP, 1995.

Stevens, Evelyn P. "Marianismo: The Other Face of Machismo." *Female and Male in Latin America.* Ed. Ann Pescatello. Pittsburgh: U of Pittsburgh P, 1973. 89–101.

Stewart, John. "The Literary Work as Cultural Document: A Caribbean Case." *Literature and Anthropology.* Eds. Philip A. Dennis and Wendell Aycock. Lubbock, Texas: Texas Tech UP, 1989. 97–112.

Ulloa, Juan. "Infancia y Triunfos de Salarrué." *Cultura: Revista del Ministerio de Educación de El Salvador* 55 (enero–marzo 1970): 90–93.

Uribe, Marta Lucía, and Olga Amparo Sánchez. "Violencia Intrafamiliar: una Mirada Desde lo Cotidiano, lo Político y lo Social." *Violencia en la Intimidad.* Ed. Casa de la Mujer. Bogotá: Editorial Gente Nueva, 1988. 15–79.

Urbina, Nicasio. *Sintaxis de un Signo.* Managua: Decenio, 1995.

Valdés, Mario J. "The Invention of Reality: Hispanic Postmodernism." *Revista Canadiense de Estudios Hispánicos* 18.3 (primavera 1994): 455–68.

Valero, Roberto. *El Desamparado Humor de Reinaldo Arenas*. Miami: North-South Center of the U of Miami, 1991.

Vaughan, Mary Kay. "Rural Women's Literacy and Education During the Mexican Revolution: Subverting a Patriarchal Event?" In Fowler-Salamini and Vaughan. 106–24.

Verani, Hugo J. "Una Experiencia de Límites: La Narrativa de Cristina Peri Rossi." *Revista Iberoamericana* 48.118–19 (Jan.–June 1982): 303–16.

Wachtel, Andrew Baruch. *The Battle for Childhood: Creation of a Russian Myth*. Stanford: Stanford UP, 1990.

Warner, Ralph E. *Historia de la Novela Mexicana en el Siglo XIX*. Mexico City: Antigua Librería Robredo, 1953.

Woolsey, A. W. "Some of the Social Problems Considered by Federico Gamboa." *Modern Language Journal* 34 (1950): 294–297.

Zea, Leopoldo. *El Positivismo en México*. Mexico City: Ediciones Studium, 1953.